FUTURE LANDSCAPES

FUTURE LANDSCAPES

FUTURE LANDSCAPES

Edited by
MALCOLM MacEWEN

With a Foreword by
H.R.H. THE DUKE OF EDINBURGH
and an Introduction by
LORD HENLEY

1976
CHATTO & WINDUS
LONDON

Published by
Chatto & Windus Ltd
42 William IV Street
London WC2N 4DF

*

Clarke, Irwin & Co Ltd
Toronto

ISBN 0 7011 2170 X

© Council for the Protection of Rural England 1976

Filmset in 'Monophoto' Baskerville 11 on 11½ pt by
Richard Clay (The Chaucer Press), Ltd, Bungay, Suffolk
and printed in Great Britain by
Fletcher & Son Ltd, Norwich

CONTENTS

NOTE

The Council for the Protection of Rural England celebrates its 50th anniversary in 1976. To mark the occasion the Council commissioned Mr Malcolm MacEwen to edit this book.

FOREWORD

By H.R.H. The Duke of Edinburgh

RURAL England is not the same today as it was when the Council was founded 50 years ago. Farming practice has developed beyond recognition, the rural population has dwindled and the lives and work of those that are left hardly bear comparison with those of their predecessors. As the standard of living of the rural population has improved it has itself come to expect all the conveniences of urban life. The changing pattern of land ownership, the incidence of various taxes, the ever increasing demands for capital investment in agriculture and forestry and the relatively poor return on capital employed have caused a complete upheaval of the rural scene. Villages have become dormitories for urban workers; large and small country houses by the score have been converted, demolished, evacuated or opened to the public.

So what is the Council trying to protect? In spite of its existence, the rural England of 1926, the year when the Council was established, even the rural environment of 1945, no longer exists. But it can well be claimed that the fact that the English landscape is still relatively unspoilt is very largely due to the efforts of the Council. It played a most important part in leavening the worst excesses of bureaucratic planning and controlling inconsiderate housing and industrial development.

The question for the future is whether the present look of the country can remain unchanged while the life of the country is being so drastically transformed. There are powerful political and social forces which are changing rural life but it might well be asked whether decision by remote committee, and control of the countryside by a bureaucratic process even if it is in the name of faceless society and done with the best will in the world, can either maintain or create a satisfactory rural scene as the intimacy and continuity of family residence and ownership. Traditional rural communities were bound together and to the countryside by more than narrow self-interest. Generations of families lie side by side in the churchyards, their names share places on war memorials and they served together on Parish, District and County Councils. All that is to be seen of man's creative genius was known to have been the consequence of the joint efforts by the ancestors of the living community. 'This other Eden' is not like some great work of art which can be entombed in a museum. It was the continuing creation of a living organism of a particular kind. This organism, the very life of rural England which created the countryside we know and love is going to be radically different in the future and it seems reasonable to suppose that it will give the countryside a different visual pattern.

This book is timely because it both draws attention to these changes and it also reflects the attitudes which have brought these changes about. A different life is developing and the problem for the Council in the next 50 years will be to decide what to protect as the new rural England takes shape.

January 1976   *Buckingham Palace*

INTRODUCTION

by Lord Henley

Chairman of the Council for the Protection of Rural England

E. M. FORSTER was once told by his friends that he must face facts. 'How can I,' he replied, 'when they are all around me.' This is how we stand today, trying to measure up to the many faces of our own crisis in land use. We no sooner attack one problem with some success than we find, as often as not, that we have knocked ourselves off balance and are being assailed from behind by another, itself engendered by our attempt to solve the first.

We are in danger of being overwhelmed by the weight and complexity of these problems. On the one hand, over 100 square miles of rural land goes every year for roads, reservoirs, minerals, houses, schools, universities, factories, out-of-town shopping centres, new towns and so on, an area as big as Berkshire every five years. And on the other hand, we need to produce the optimum amount of food that our temperate climate can produce, having regard to good husbandry and land management.

At the same time, pressure remorselessly builds up for the use of land for recreation, which is as demanding as urban development itself.

However well we use the land, whether for agriculture or recreation, or urban and industrial uses, there is not enough of it now, and there will be less of it as time goes on. Every aspect of this problem is touched on in the present book.

The demand for land, and the need for multiple use of its diminishing area by what is likely to be an increasing number of people wanting a materially richer standard of life, has set up stresses and strains which call in question the very concept of private ownership of that land.

It may be that private ownership of something so inherently public as land is neither so widespread in many societies, nor of such long standing as is often supposed, but in our immediate past it has been that ownership which has wielded responsibility for the shape of the countryside and for its management. Until recently ownership of land has been largely separated from its occupation, that is to say the provision and management of the fixed capital, the land itself and everything on it, were responsibilities of a different kind and in different hands from the working of it. This had certain advantages, for however effectively the rules of good husbandry are followed, land needs the longer-term direction of its fixed capital by some agency other than that immediately concerned with the shorter-term winning of profit from the land.

Not all land can be farmed for maximum food production or maximum profit; if needed it can be agreed what maximum food production is. It is not necessarily the most efficient production. Maximum food production can well be a wasteful siege-economy measure forced on society by circumstance; and maximum profit raises questions of whose profit—the answer may well be not that of the land itself.

Not all rural land can be devoted to agriculture. Agriculture itself must often defer to forestry or mineral extraction, wildlife conservation, recreation, each of which in turn must sometimes defer to another. They all conflict in some degree in their demands on scarce resources, and maximum use for any one must damage another. Where then does the optimum lie, and who will now look to it?

If maximum agricultural production demands the removal of trees and hedges, which consideration shall prevail?

If low-cost housing means using the best agricultural land, who is going to choose?

These, and all the similar decisions of land use, were once taken by owners who, like other human beings, varied widely in their judgement and behaviour, but the result of their decisions was the countryside we seek to protect in all its multifarious beauty, to protect from short-term expediency, from profligate use of the scarce resources and from straight misuse.

But the danger now is that with competing demands on land, and with different patterns of ownership, the proper balance in land use will be lost.

There have been attempts at some sort of co-ordination ever since pressure on land began to make itself felt. We have had some degree of compulsory purchase for 150 years; we have had planning of an increasingly rigorous kind for 69; and now we have before us the latest attempt, in the Community Land Act, to achieve more positive planning and to secure the ensuing benefits for society. Will the Act succeed where other attempts have failed? Or will our planning system break down under the strains at present upon it?

The increased complexity of the ways in which we seek to regulate land use in the interests of conservation in its widest sense has created anomalies, and indeed manifest injustice as between one landowner and another, and this has given a greater impetus from every political angle towards the idea of 'social trusteeship'.

Social trusteeship should not mean the appropriation of what in an imperfect world has been acquired for its financial value, nor the denial to those who own or occupy the land of their just reward from it, any more than it means the denial of similar rights to other creators of wealth, but it does mean a recognition of the fact that land can never entirely be an individual's to do with it as he will—indeed it never has been. It is something of which some part belongs to us all; and it involves an acknowledgement that there is an ultimate public right to decide on the priorities of land use.

There is an ambience which cannot be taken away from land that is in some very real sense public. A man cannot own a wild animal in a state of nature; he cannot own a view—it is there for anyone to enjoy. It is in some degree like the air we breathe and, like the air, must not be polluted by one man to his neighbour's disadvantage.

In our complex society the state is already taking over some of the long-term management of the land which the untrammelled owner once enjoyed, the state exercising the social aspect of trusteeship which owners of land have always felt to be inherent in their responsibility.

I believe that at such a time as this, when the old pattern of trustee-ship is breaking under the pressures this book discusses, and when the concept of social trusteeship is still in its infancy, CPRE has a role to play of the highest importance.

CPRE was founded when, for example, ribbon development, prolifer-ation of advertisements, haphazard development and almost total lack of control over the expanding scene shocked those who witnessed it after the First World War. It became apparent to the founders that this could not just be allowed to happen—a more insidious and more pervasive despoliation than that of the nineteenth-century industrial development.

CPRE reaches its Jubilee at a time when, although we have a better planning system than any other country—and in no small measure over its 50 years CPRE has helped to bring this about—the system is still far from perfect, and at present in danger of collapse from both internal and external pressures.

More than ever do we need to plan our land use with due attention not only to its expendability and its proneness to pollution, some of it irreversible, but also to the long-term trust; and we need to subject planning to the sort of scrutiny which state institutions cannot exercise themselves without help from their citizens through bodies such as CPRE. There is no lack of evidence of the dangers of a state apparatus where nobody can call in question decisions, not necessarily arrived at in secret, or even corruptly, but made by an insensitive majority and mindlessly enforced.

I believe that this is where CPRE comes in. We need to be an organ-isation with membership spread over the whole country, and strong enough at branch level to be able to monitor the changes in land use and development. At the centre we need a tough, professional office which can bring influence to bear in Parliament and in Whitehall. There should be a close relationship between branches and their national office, with an executive committee formed from their mem-bers, and such co-option as they may wish. At the same time, I believe there should be co-operation and consultation with the constituent bodies which form an important part of CPRE structure. The constituent bodies, all of whom have cognate but diverse interests, should not be policy-makers or decision-takers in CPRE affairs. I see them as providing a background of advice and opinion on matters which are of common importance, but not necessarily speaking with the same voice, for it cannot be healthy for one to be seen as merely an arm of another, and indeed there will frequently be occasions when they must agree to differ.

I believe that CPRE must quadruple its membership in the next five years, and greatly strengthen its branch organisation so that every branch has at least a paid officer, a room with a telephone and a committee with members who are themselves professionally skilled in planning and land use. Without such strength in the country, CPRE's national office will be less well equipped to play its part at national level.

We must broaden our base from what was originally a council in London to a movement with a much wider appeal. Rural England cannot be protected from misuse unless many more people, most of them living in towns, understand enough about the problems of land use, and care enough about them, to prevent wrong decisions from being taken.

There is a need for a public voice, and CPRE can help to make it effective.

1

The Unknown Future

MALCOLM MacEWEN

IT is notoriously difficult for people to judge the historical significance of contemporary events. Even so, most of the contributors to this book would probably subscribe to Tristram Beresford's view (Chapter 6) that 1973 was a turning point. He is writing about farming, but it was so for everything else. It was one of the rare moments of truth, when a mountain of false expectations and illusions collapsed and we crossed the watershed into an unknown future. In losing some of our illusions about the inevitable progress into a richer future, and by questioning false assumptions, we regain an initiative we had lost. We recover the chance to find a surer basis for beliefs and for policies, and so to regain some control over events. We face far greater difficulties than we had realised, but we can also perceive new opportunities if we are prepared to question the established wisdom.

The very idea that there is something new in the concept of an 'unknown future' tells us a lot about the recent past. It was only in the 1950s and 1960s, the days of the 'affluent', 'never had it so good' society, that the future seemed to be knowable, plannable and increasingly controllable. But in the 1950s and 1960s we were in fact being swept along by events that were largely outside our control, and governed by ideas that were rapidly losing touch with reality. The foundation of our prosperity was access to unlimited quantities of the oil, food and raw materials that are now dear, scarce or both. The future was predictable, because it was assumed that there would be more of everything, year after year, world without end, Amen. These were the years of the exponential curve, when the most important thing to know was the doubling time. Would car production, or electricity or anything, double every 10 years (good), every 15 (poor) or every 20 (disaster)? All you had to do to know the future was to plot the figures for the last few years on graph paper, extrapolate the curve into the future, and everything would double every so many years. Since the trend was irresistible, all the planners had to do was to go along with it. And so we got into the businesses of 'realistic' planning (if you can't beat the developers, join them) and the self-fulfilling prophecy (build enough power stations to make the demand figures come right).

If all this required the destruction of fine buildings, beautiful landscapes or good farmland, it was regrettable, and largely inevitable—

although some exceptions had to be made, the word *exception* being underlined.

A classic example of the irresistible trend of demand has been the forecasting of the growth of road traffic. Official forecasts have never paid the slightest attention to the ultimate, inevitable decline in the supply of oil, whether from the North Sea or anywhere else. The figures have been arrived at by extrapolating past trends of income and of growth. For a time, as the economy grew, the forecasts were not only fulfilled but exceeded. But, because the figures derive from the past and are largely unrelated to future realities, an upheaval like the Arab–Israeli war of 1973, that rocked the world economy, quadrupled oil prices at a stroke, and changed many calculations about the future, hardly affected the vehicle forecasts. In 1973 the Transport and Road Research Laboratory (TRRL) published a forecast that by the year 2000 the number of cars on British roads would have grown from 13 million in 1973 to 25·9 million (note the precision — not 26·0 million). In 1974, after the Middle East War, the forecast was revised to show a 'middle' figure of 25 million, or a 'low' of 23 million by the year 2000. The TRRL had the wisdom to preface the later estimate with the warning that little or no reliance could be placed on it, but Mr Mulley, the Transport Minister, announced that the 'low' forecast would form the basis for planning and design in his department. Such is the 'scientific' basis on which proposals like the M67 Sheffield–Manchester Motorway through the Peak National Park rest, a motorway costing £80 million whose traffic could be more economically carried by rail or by routes that do not penetrate the Park. Like chickens with their heads cut off, politicians and their civil servants continue to take the trend as law, even when the basis for it has been undermined. For the year 2000, by an interesting coincidence, should see oil supplies falling rapidly below the 'demand' generated by the expanded vehicle fleet.

If the M67 is built, limestone from the Peak National Park will no doubt be used, as it was for the M6, as hardcore — a use that throws away one of our most valuable raw materials. The extraction of minerals and aggregates forms one of the most horrendous examples of trend planning. Aggregates production (currently being studied by the Advisory Committee an Aggregates, chaired by Sir Ralph Verney) rose from 61 million tons in 1948 to 265 million tons in 1973. Our richest sources of rocks and minerals lie in the uplands, largely in national parks and areas of outstanding natural beauty. The Peak National Park Planning Board has estimated that if limestone continues to be extracted from the park at the present rate the hills from which it is extracted will be reduced in height on average by 100 feet during the next century. A similar forecast could, I daresay, be made of part of the Mendips.

Yet, sooner or later, all such trends are brought to an end by the exhaustion of the resource. Some landscapes are expendable, some can be restored, but others must be protected. We have no right to destroy some of our most beautiful countryside for the sake of a short-lived moment of self-indulgence, particularly when some alternative solution has to be found in the end. If Rio Tinto Zinc ever revives its proposal to mine copper ore at Coed-y-brenin in the Snowdonia National Park, the landscape as we know it would be totally destroyed for the sake of a small addition to our copper supplies for a period of 20–25 years. A change in national priorities that would safeguard the landscape by altering the trend would simply advance the day for another solution by 25 years.

Electricity generation, so acutely analysed by Nigel Lucas and Robin Grove-White (Chapter 10), provides a classic example of trend planning and self-fulfilling prophecy. The 'need' of the Central Electricity Board (CEGB) for ever vaster sites in beautiful and remote areas for conventional and nuclear power stations, for ever bigger transmission lines and for pump storage schemes, all derive from its interpretation of its statutory obligation to supply cheap electricity to meet an ever-rising 'demand'. In fact the CEGB decided as a matter of policy not to recover and sell the waste heat it now uses to warm the air, the rivers and the seas. Its critics call it the Central Waste Heat Generating Board, because it produces more than twice as much waste heat as electricity. Having installed excess capacity too, it has consistently stimulated demand by advertising and offering low tariffs. Its entire policy is the product of narrow thinking and restricted terms of reference. Within these constraints it is prepared to make some concessions to the environment. But the real threat comes from the policies themselves and the legislative constraints, which impose unnecessary demands on the environment. The considerable scientific and engineering skills of the electricity and nuclear industries, often allied to a spirit of dedicated service, are concentrated almost entirely on increasing the electricity supply. No comparable effort has gone into energy conservation or the limitation of demand, although to save a kilowatt costs but a fraction of the cost of installing a kilowatt of new capacity.

Water supply too, as Judith Rees explains with equally telling effect (Chapter 11), has based its voracious demands for land for reservoirs on highly skilled but very narrow professional thinking. Water is regarded as a free resource, to be literally 'on tap' in abundance, to the highest standards of purity even for flushing toilets or for industrial processes, and even in the kind of drought to be expected only once in a hundred years. 'Turning the tap' is a metaphor for uncontrolled expenditure or waste. Water is only metered for industrial use, so that leaks go undetected, the householder has no incentive to economise and the manufacturers no incentive to design more economical appliances. As in electricity, all the effort has gone into increasing the supply, little or none into the control of demand. When it is proposed to build a new reservoir at Swincombe, in the Dartmoor National Park, it is rarely understood that an alternative and cheaper solution would be to stop the leaks in the distribution system and provide some incentives for economies and recycling. Plymouth's mains are said to be in such poor condition that half the water entering the system never reaches the taps. In such conditions, new reservoirs are often required mainly to supply an underground irrigation system and to encourage wastefulness.

The continued strength of narrow, compartmentalised thinking, of which water, electricity and highways provide striking examples, is reinforced by specialisation, professionalisation and the growth of large departmentalised institutions. The specialists defend their private territories, and are cut off from other specialists. The establishment of separate boards for coal, gas and electricity seemed to make sense in the 1940s, as did the decision to exclude the local authorities from the supply of gas and electricity. But these decisions have led to the creation of vast, highly centralised monopolies, which are locked into an absurd competitive struggle, and by their very nature inhibit the development of more localised total energy supply systems that could double the efficiency achieved by the CEGB. The establishment of a Department of Energy will not of itself lead to a coherent energy policy until the legislation defining the roles of the nationalised corporations has been rewritten. The formation of the Department of the Environment (DOE) was similarly an attempt to unify policy, by co-ordinating the conflicting policies of different ministries concerned mainly with the built environment. Adrian Phillips (Chapter 8) argues persuasively that, with all its defects, the DOE is better than what went before. But, as he also points out, the principal activities that form the rural landscape — farming and forestry — are to a great extent outside the planning system for which the Department and the local planning authorities are responsible. The basic conflict between the two major rural industries and amenity or conservation remains unresolved. This is yet another case of compartmentalised policy-making.

The Scott report on the utilisation of rural land in 1942, and the Dower report on National Parks in 1945, were two of the series of reports that laid the basis for the post-war planning system. Both assumed that if landscape was to be conserved, the best thing to do was to farm it or afforest it. Farming and forestry were then seen to be conserving uses. As Britain was still suffering after the war the full effects of food shortages and rationing, it is hardly surprising that agriculture and forestry were both largely exempted from the planning controls introduced by the 1947 Town and Country Planning Act. Even in the national park legislation of 1949 no special measures of control were thought to be necessary. The siting of farm buildings was brought under a form of control in parts of Snowdonia, the Peak and the Lake Districts, but hardly anywhere else. The national parks were handed over to the local authorities, in which the interests of local farmers and landowners often weighed more heavily in the scales than the interest in conservation that is the primary purpose of the parks. The elaborate system of safeguards for the landscape of protected areas is largely illusory because, to the extent that farming and forestry have become commercial, industrial operations, they have ceased to be conserving uses of land.

Many members of national park boards and committees do not even understand that their first statutory responsibility is to conserve and enhance the natural beauty of the national park. The second is to provide opportunities for its enjoyment by the public, but since there is nothing to enjoy if the landscape is destroyed, conservation clearly comes first, as Lord Sandford's National Park Policies Review Committee has emphasised.[1] The Act also requires the national park authorities to have due regard to the needs of agriculture and of forestry, and to the social and economic interests of the local communities. These are wise provisions, for unless farming, forestry and the local community are prosperous, neither the goodwill nor the resources required to maintain the landscape are available.

Where, as in the uplands, modern trends in farming have reduced the population almost to vanishing point, the landscape is in peril. But the remedy need not be more intensive farming. It may well be the provision of new incentives to increase the working population and to restore some of the traditional farming techniques that sustain the landscape. In the countryside generally, as Victor Bonham-Carter shows in his chapter on the changing rural community (Chapter 2), the most urgent need is not for negative controls but for positive planning, to encourage productive enterprises that will keep an active population on the land. Better some light engineering than a population of park-keepers.

Such, however, is the pressure to revive the ailing rural economy, and such is the resistance of the farmers' and landowners' organisations to control, that there is now a subtle (and disastrous) tendency to reverse the statutory obligations of the national park authorities. Too many people now speak and act as if the first responsibility of these authorities is to the local economy, to the farmer and the forester—a responsibility to be discharged 'with due regard' to the needs of landscape and of public enjoyment. This attitude, which is frequently expressed by members of national park authorities, was reflected in a lecture[2] on national parks given by Sir Ralph Verney, a Forestry Commissioner and a leading member of the Country Landowners' Association. He laid so much stress on the priority to be given to the production of food, the needs of the hill farmer, the production of timber and the extraction of minerals, that I was left wondering whether the national parks enjoyed, in his eyes, any special protection at all. He was opposed to any form of additional control over farming or forestry, echoing the Scott Committee in saying that 'the farmer seeks not to destroy the landscape but to enhance it'. While Sir Ralph insisted that farmers and landowners can only be won round by persuasion, his recipe for the visitor was the strictest discipline and control.

1. Report of the National Park Policies Review Committee, HMSO 1974
2. 'National Parks'; lecture by Sir Ralph Verney, Royal Society of Arts, 9 April 1975

Yet the plain, and undeniable, truth, expressed by Professor Gerald Wibberley in his speech to the Jubilee Conference of the Royal Town Planning Institute in 1974,[3] is that farmers and landowners are largely free to ravage the landscape unchecked. This does not mean that they all do so. Far from it. But there is a minority of farmers and landowners, and particularly the new institutional landlords such as pension funds, that bitterly oppose any interference, are indifferent to landscape or wildlife and are governed only by the narrowest calculations of profit or of loss. Without some powers of control, such as are universally accepted despite their imperfections in towns and cities, the greedy or the indifferent will remain free to spoil or to ruin some of our most precious landscapes.

Farmers themselves have become increasingly disturbed by the pressures to which they are subjected and the techniques they have to use. The leader of the National Farmers' Union has said that farmers are 'the custodians of the landscape'. There are signs that an increasing number of farmers no longer regard concern for landscape or wildlife as the prerogative of cranks. Similarly, conservationists understand far better than they did that landscape can only be nurtured by a prosperous farming community. Unfortunately the converse is not true: a prosperous farming community can, and does, destroy landscape to achieve prosperity. A new relationship between farmers and conservationists calls for an acceptance on both sides—and not only on the conservationists' side—that the other has a legitimate point of view. If conservationists now accept, as they do, that farmers cannot be expected to maintain the landscape entirely out of their own pockets, it does not follow that the only solution is to pay the farmer, as the Ministry of Agriculture often does, to destroy fine landscapes. Ways can be found to harmonise conservation with both farming and forestry, so that it pays equally well to manage farms or woodlands in ways that conserve or enhance the landscape.

These aims will not be achieved by asserting, as the Ministry of Agriculture blandly does in its white paper[4] on agriculture that 'the continuing improvement of grazing and of hill land can contribute to a better-looking as well as to a more productive countryside'. As a general proposition there is nothing wrong with this statement. There are many upland areas where well-farmed green fields enclosing well-fed cattle and sheep can indeed contribute to a better-looking and a more productive countryside. But the white paper makes no exceptions to this general proposition. It ignores the fact that there are many key areas, particularly in the Exmoor, Dartmoor and North Yorkshire Moors National Parks, where moorland provides landscapes of unsurpassed quality, to which the public flock in large numbers for their enjoyment. Enclosure not only destroys the landscape, but deprives the

3. 'The Proper Use of Britain's Rural Land', by Professor Gerald Wibberley, *The Planner*, July/August 1974
4. 'Food from Our Own Resources', HMSO 1975

public of access to areas of open country that are essential to their physical recreation and spiritual refreshment.

Before writing this chapter I drove with Geoffrey Sinclair over large parts of Exmoor. We took with us the maps on which, since 1965, he has been recording for the Exmoor Society the steady loss of moorland by ploughing, conversion by other techniques and by sward management. Since no records were kept by the former national park committees, the precise area that has been lost since the national park was designated in 1954 cannot be exactly stated. Sinclair believes, however, that designation did nothing to check the loss of moorland, and that at least a fifth of what was already a fairly small area of some 60,000 acres has been lost in the 21 years since designation. The tragedy is that the loss is almost wholly attributable to the Ministry of Agriculture which, through its capital improvement schemes, has paid half the cost of ploughing and fencing, and has then paid the headage subsidies without which few farmers would have been prepared to stock the new fields. To make matters worse, over considerable areas the 'improved' land is now infested with rushes, providing neither the beauty of the moor nor the beauty of good pasture. A shocking instance of this destruction-for-nothing is to be seen on Fyldon Common where, in the foreground of the superb view from the Exmoor ridge towards Dartmoor, the once glorious, open, heather moor is now an ugly, unproductive, rush-infested, fenced-off agricultural slum that does little credit to the farmer and is a living condemnation of the failure of national park legislation to 'conserve or enhance the landscape'.

Why does the Ministry of Agriculture pay these subsidies, as of right, regardless, it seems, of the landscape quality, the agricultural potential or the farmers' capabilities? The answer is to be found in the Ministry's subservience to the farming lobby, and to its inability to escape from the fetters of its own compartmentalised thinking. Conservation is not the responsibility of the Ministry of Agriculture. Although it began to take some interest in conservation under Cledwyn Hughes, this was killed off by James Prior in 1970, and the courses in conservation for its advisory officers were stopped by Fred Peart as an economy measure in 1974. The Ministry pays little or no regard to Section 11 of the Countryside Act (which requires all Government departments to have due regard to the desirability of conserving natural beauty). Yet there would be no real difficulty, if the political will were present, in devising a system by which capital grants were paid in national parks only where this was consistent with conservation or enhancement of landscape, where the agricultural potential is good and where the farmer can be relied upon to do the job properly. Means would have to be found to support in other ways farmers who did not qualify for these grants. This, too, could easily be devised, and would simply represent the cost to the farmer of managing the landscape in ways that fell short of exploiting its full agricultural potential. Nobody suggests that we should plough up all our golf courses, our public parks and the great parks around our stately homes. So why should we plough up equally precious landscapes in the hills? The Sandford Committee put the cost, in 1973, of compensating farmers for managing their land in this way at no more than £1 million a year.

The problem is essentially political. Landscape conservation does not come very high in the priorities of the Department of the Environment, which carries such enormous burdens as housing, planning, local government and transport. But the Ministry of Agriculture gives the highest priorities to keeping the farmers and landowners happy, and maintaining food production. In any conflict, the contest is hopelessly unequal. By raising the emotive cry of food production (farmers who want more money always say the nation needs more food) the Ministry and the farm lobby have successfully resisted every effort to bring farming under planning control, even within the national parks and ASONB. The resources of the Countryside Commission, the agency of the DOE in these matters, are tiny by comparison with the sums that the Ministry of Agriculture can put in the farmers' pockets. It is not surprising that the arguments of the Countryside Commission for the integration of farming and conservation policies have fallen on deaf ears in Whitehall.

The subordinate position of the Commission seems to inhibit its freedom to speak freely. But it is no excuse for the weak and compromising response it has made to the massive changes being made in the landscape by modern farming techniques. The Commission accepts modern farming without reservation.[5] It say that over much of lowland Britain the landscape created by the enclosures has disappeared or will soon do so. It advises the retention of existing landscape features only where they have particular value—which means, according to its Director that only a tiny proportion of the existing lowland landscape should be protected. The terms of reference it gave to consultants in 1972 for a study of the impact of modern farming on lowland landscape excluded any consideration of means by which the impact could be diminished or existing landscapes conserved. They were asked 'to find out how agricultural improvements can be carried out efficiently in such a way as to create new landscapes no less interesting than those destroyed in the process'.

The consultants' report, published in 1974 with a statement from the Commission, both called 'New Agricultural Landscapes',[5] concluded that without a change in the policy of maximising food production regardless of its side effects, landscape quality would continue to decline. It found, perhaps inevitably, that new landscapes 'no less interesting than the old' could indeed be created. The Commission endorsed the consultants' view that new landscapes could be created by landowners on land surplus to agricultural production, and by the public

5. 'New Agricultural Landscapes', Countryside Commission, 1974: (a) consultants' report, CCP 76; (b) Commission's discussion statement, CCP 76a

authorities on publicly owned land. By putting these two together, and strengthening farm, parish and other boundary hedges, a new landscape network could be created. These ideas would have had some merit if they had been put forward as proposals for improving rather than for replacing landscapes. Similarly, the Commission's suggestions that public authorities should plant more trees, enter into management agreements with farmers to encourage planting, and that the Government could attach landscape conditions to agricultural grants or offer tax incentives for landscape conservation all have some value. But the positive elements in these reports are vitiated by the acceptance, in advance, of the whole bundle of techniques, good and bad, known as modern agriculture, regardless of the good or the harm they do. It requires an act of faith, that the sketches by the consultants do not encourage, to believe that the new landscapes will be 'no less interesting' (not, mark you, no less beautiful) than the old. It would also be a remarkable coincidence if the bits of land the farmers don't want, and the bits of land the public authorities happen to own, were to knit together to form a landscape pattern in any way as fine as that created by the enclosures. The Commission seems to be making the mistake that the urban planners made in the 1960s. The latter were so convinced of the need to plan for the trend that they permitted, or encouraged, the destruction of some of the most interesting parts of our towns and cities, in the belief that the new townscapes would be 'no less interesting than those destroyed'. They were often disastrously wrong.

But the Commission's suggestion that landscape conditions should be attached to Ministry of Agriculture grants does open the door to the radical change that is needed. Comparable ministries in Europe already have some responsibility for landscape conservation, wildlife protection and the rural economy, in addition to food production. These interests are not necessarily incompatible, and can in practice be harmonised. Two papers at the *New Scientist* conference on self-sufficiency[6] showed that self-sufficiency in food production actually requires the most drastic changes in the techniques of modern farming which the Countryside Commission so weakly accepts. Professor David Hughes and Clive Jones of Cardiff University calculated that Britain's organic refuse and effluents (from domestic garbage, sewage sludge and farm waste) form a food resource equal in potential size to half our present cereal production. Dr Kenneth Baxter FRS, of the Rowett Research Institute, Aberdeen, argued that 'the UK could so crop its land that it becomes self-sufficient in providing the energy and protein requirements of its people, provided that waste is eliminated in the entire process from farm gate to consumer's plate' — and provided, too, that we would reduce our consumption of sugar, fat and meat. This suggests that some trends in modern farming may themselves be the product of the compartmentalised thinking that is to be seen in other

6. 'Waste Not Want Not', by Prof. David Hughes and Clive Jones; 'Can Britain Feed Herself?' by Dr Kenneth Baxter, FRS; *New Scientist*, 20 March 1975

fields. Economic conditions seem likely to modify farming policies and technologies, but the transition would be easier if the Ministry of Agriculture were to have a far broader responsibility, that would oblige it to see the interests of farmers and food production in a different context. Efforts to increase food production can aggravate the conflict between farming and recreation, which is also in conflict with wild life. These conflicts are not concealed in this book. Bruce Campbell, who is moderately optimistic about the prospects for wildlife, clearly believes that nothing would be better for wildlife than the complete cessation of countryside recreation, although I need hardly say that he does not advocate this. At the opposite extreme, Marion Shoard (Chapter 4) makes a passionate plea on behalf of the urban population for the countryside to be opened up as their playground. In my view she underestimates the severity of the conflict, and the difficulties that her approach would create for farmers and landowners. But is is far too easy to dismiss her plea as unrealistic. The townspeople's ignorance of the natural processes that support life is terrifying; I wonder, too, how many farmers really understand the relationship between their own operations and the fauna and flora that they affect. Opening the countryside to townspeople as a playground may not be the right way to close the gap between town and country. But to place large areas of the countryside virtually 'out of bounds' to townspeople, as many farmers and conservationists would like, is to ensure that the townspeople who elect our governments will remain ignorant of the most elementary truths about nature, and heedless or unsympathetic to the needs of the rural community. It will also deprive them of a basic human experience, direct contact with the countryside.

The Countryside Commission has for some time been urging the need for a review of countryside policies. It may well be right in thinking that only an impartial inquiry, before which all the bodies concerned would have to justify their attitudes and their policies, will create the political climate in which serious institutional reforms would become possible. The inter-departmental committee of officials from the Ministry of Agriculture and the Department of the Environment that has been looking at their mutual problems lacks the status and the impartiality to resolve them. The present depression in farming, by slowing down the process of change, has created an opportunity, which may be short-lived, to set up a high-powered committee of inquiry, with instructions to report quickly, on the integration of farming and conservation policies.

Bringing farming under control does not mean, as farming and landowning interests suggest, that farmers would have to apply for permission to undertake the normal operations of husbandry. Industrialists are completely free to manage their factories, introduce new models and re-arrange the internal layout. It is only when they want to develop land that they have to get planning permission. Similarly, control of farming operations need only extend to operations that make significant changes in the landscape. Such a system could be introduced gradually, beginning with a notification procedure in the most sensitive areas. There are precedents both for a step-by-step procedure and for notification of landscape changes. Brucellosis control and structure planning have both been introduced area by area. Section 14 of the Countryside Act 1968 already authorises the Secretary of State for the Environment to make orders requiring occupiers of land to give six months' notice of their intention to plough or otherwise convert moor or heath in national parks to agricultural use. The fact that Section 14 is virtually a dead letter is attributable more to the resistance of the NFU and the CLA, and to the feebleness of the follow-up procedures for compensation and management, than to any inherent defect in the notification procedure. But, just as a map of the critical amenity moorland in Exmoor had to be prepared before Section 14 could be applied, so a survey of hedges would be necessary before a procedure for notifying hedge removal could be introduced. This would provide a record against which notifications could be judged without difficulty. This survey would also open the way to the introduction of reasonable machinery for control, such as the management agreement that the Countryside Commission and the Sandford Committee have both recommended. The farmer or land-owner would agree, in return for suitable compensation to manage land in ways that would conserve or enhance the landscape.

There would also have to be powers of compulsory purchase to deal with the Philistines, the bloody-minded and those who resist all reasonable persuasion. There is no need for the phrase 'compulsory purchase' to send a rush of blood to the heads of landowners. The irony of the situation is that they have accepted it for well over a century, provided the price is right, and provided that the land is taken *out* of agriculture for roads, railways and a host of other mainly urban uses. It is illogical to object to its use to protect the most beautiful landscapes, in exceptional cases, against those whose greed or indifference threaten its destruction.

If Professor Miles (Chapter 5) is right, our landscape is not going to survive without an increasing measure of positive public intervention. His argument is that taxation and the changing pattern of landowner-ship are making it impossible for the shrinking number of traditional landowners to make long-term investments to conserve landscape and buildings. Farming, as Tristram Beresford says (Chapter 6), is a business, and the farmer is essentially an entrepreneur, who is unlikely to take kindly to policies that curtail his independence. He differs from other businessmen in that farming is often his way of life; he does not, as a rule, sell out when prices are high, and he hangs on when commercial sense might tell him to get out. But his very character as an entrepreneur means, in present conditions, that somebody else will have to invest in landscape if farm economics discourage the entrepreneur from doing so. That somebody is less and less likely to be the traditional landlord, whose responsibilities for long-term conservation can only be transferred to some public body. The farmers' fears of state interference and of bureaucratic forms of socialism are understandable. But the problem is not solved by leaving the owner–occupier or the tenant to their own devices: a solution requires the encouragement of forms of public intervention and public ownership that retain the small-scale, intimate and personal relationship that existed between the better landlords and their tenants in the past, while injecting both money and a measure of control in the wider interest of the non-farming population. The fact stands out a mile, whether farming is seen from Beresford's, Miles' or Sinclair's viewpoint, that unless there is a substantial investment by the public authorities, standing in the shoes of the old landowners, the landscape is going to suffer. This, too, was one of the messages of 'New Agricultural Landscapes' and of the Countryside Commission's discussion document. And the message remains true, whatever the state of the national economy. A nation that values its heritage may invest more in it in good times. In hard times its willingness to protect it is the real test of its civilised qualities.

But we are in danger of assuming that the impact of economic difficulties is always negative. Some of the effects undoubtedly are, as when central and local governments reduce their budgets for environmental protection and improvement. For example, the progress being made in creating smokeless zones under the Clean Air Act has been virtually stopped. The new river authorities' programmes for cleaning up the rivers have been cut almost before they have started. Perhaps the most dangerous aspect of this trend will be the temptation to let farming rip in any way it pleases, in the belief that food production should stop at nothing.

The pressures that have caused so many problems in the recent past have often been the result of affluence and extravagance combined with the ready availability of cheap energy. The new economic pressures could also diminish the impact of farming on the landscape. Shortage of money, the high cost of energy and shrinking 'demand' have already led to cuts in the capital programmes, and will lead to further reductions in their planned expansion. The enormous capital cost of investment in road, water and electricity are bound, in the end, to compel both managements and their political paymasters to seek more economical and probably less damaging ways of meeting our real, but not our artificial, needs. Although cuts have been made in environmental protection, public concern about the environment is at a higher level than it has ever been, and the demand for effective public participation seems likely to become greater in the future. As the cruder forms of cost/benefit analysis become discredited, and greater importance is attached to the unquantifiable benefits associated with the quality of life rather than *per capita* consumption, the benefits to be derived from a safe, beautiful and satisfying environment will become more apparent, and the costs of achieving it will be more easy to justify.

On balance, I am inclined to think that the positive pressures may prove stronger than the negative. Whether they do or not will depend very largely on the shifts in public opinion. If our people were literally driven to the brink of bankruptcy and starvation the voices of amenity and conservation would probably be drowned completely by the panic-stricken cries of people struggling for survival. But today we have an opportunity to correct some of the mistakes into which our pre-occupation with the production of consumer durables has led us. The timetable of the depletion of the world's fossil fuels does not give us a very long time in which to make quite radical changes in the way we live. The sooner a fundamental re-assessment begins, the more time we shall have, and the less likely that the cause of conservation will be lost in a fit of panic. The job of the voluntary bodies in the next decade is, above all, to bring about a real shift in the public mind, by a continu-ous process of information, education and exposure, and to do so quickly. Roy Gregory's study (Chapter 13) of the whole voluntary movement for amenity confirms the potential that these bodies have for effective action. But the realisation of this potential is going to call for a very large expansion in their membership and their resources. The shift that has already begun, away from an exclusive concern with the local issues to concern with national, regional and local policies, will con-tinue. Until now objectors have usually asked the Inspector at an inquiry to shift objectionable development somewhere else, or to press for the modification of its scale or design. There will always be cases where the development itself is acceptable and the only issue to be decided is the precise siting and design of the works. But contributors to this book have shown (to my mind conclusively) that the main area of conflict has shifted from the details to the merits of the policies them-selves.

2

The Changing Rural Community

VICTOR BONHAM-CARTER

THE title gives the game away at once. Rural Community? Why not Village? The solution is simple; we no longer know what the word means. If you were to conduct a house-to-house inquiry on the subject, or a sample survey in the best modern manner, you would certainly fill your files full of answers, many of them contradictory. Yet there would be a certain pattern. From townspeople—whether you caught them at home in the town, or on holiday in the country or in retirement in no-man's-land—you would probably secure two general impressions: one physical, what they thought a village looked like or ought to look like; in effect any nice-looking place from Cornwall to Cumberland, with cottages of thatch, brick or stone, an inn, an Early English church, Elizabethan almshouses and a Jacobean manor house now run by the National Trust: in other words, an idealised postcard view. The other impression would concern village society as culled from books and films, tinged possibly with youthful memories of cricket on the green, or tea taken at the rectory against a background of immemorial elms (now of course decimated by Dutch elm disease); but essentially a stylised concept with squire and parson at the top, farmers and tradesmen in the middle, and labourers at the bottom: in other words, a stage view. From countrypeople—by which I mean people who have lived and worked in villages or on farms for several generations—you would receive different impressions, although with superficial links. They would talk to you of severely practical things—the older people of raising a family in the 1920s on thirty bob a week, the cost of coal, chapel outings, the workhouse, pubs, clubs, friends, families and feuds. Such memories would be a mixture of 'good riddance' to the poverty, bad housing and the ailments and injustices they had had to put up with; of nostalgia for the simple enjoyments now being suffocated by sophistication; and even of affection for the eccentricities of some of their former employers. The younger people would of course dwell far less on the past, and take the material urbanised improvements—TV, a car, the free health service—all for granted.

So at first sight the inquiry would not tell you very much: merely that the 'village', whatever it was, had changed a great deal in the last fifty years and was still changing. To find a definition that makes sense today, you would have to do what I propose to do now, namely glance back very briefly into history.

Originally the village was simply a community of farmers. Once husbandry had progressed beyond the nomadic stage and been stabilised by settlement, the physical village evolved as a group of cottages and barns (often combined into single buildings), closely sited for defence, near water and surrounded by the land it lived off. The men — and many of the women — went out to work by day and returned in a body at night. They supplied their own craftsmen (many of them part-time farmers as well) and formed a virtually self-sufficient community, socially self-reliant through kinship and common interest, usually under the protection of an overlord to whom they rendered obligations of labour and other services instead of rent. A similar pattern applied to villages dependent on fishing or mining. The primitive village was thus a survival unit — in all senses — and this was the basis of feudalism which lasted, in England at least, until the early sixteenth century. By that time wool production was changing the face of farming. Feudalism capitulated to commerce, and while a number of villages actually disappeared under the spreading sheep-runs, others (especially in the Cotswolds and East Anglia) throve through the development of cottage industries which processed the raw wool into yarn and cloth. A new and prosperous class arose of yeomen or middle-class farmers, either freeholders or tenants; and when wool gave ground to corn in the seventeenth century, most of these farmers held tight to their place of power. Some became large landowners and helped create a new aristocracy in place of the old and largely defunct feudal families.

Progress in cropping and stock breeding, the enclosure of open fields and commons, price protection and the rising demand for food, made farming increasingly commercial in character, a business rather than a way-of-life: although the change did not become urgent and obvious until the great enclosures *c.* 1760–1820, when the whole momentum was accelerated by the population explosion associated with the Industrial Revolution and the emergencies of the Napoleonic Wars. Even then hardly anyone — except Arthur Young, William Cobbett and a few others — tried to explain what was happening to rural society. The metamorphosis in the attitude to country life — from a tradition of mutual support, when every cottager had a patch of arable and rights of grazing, to a free-for-all system underpinned by a race of landless labourers, who survived on starvation wages plus parish assistance — was brought about by economics, which made everything seem inevitable and therefore right. Anyway there were far too many influential people who welcomed and profited from the change. Perhaps the most brutal event was the passage of the Poor Law Amendment Act 1834, which replaced out-relief by the workhouse, and so made life for the poor as hellish as possible *by law.*

But the poor remained, and the village survived as a viable community for a very long time. Its persistence was remarkable, partly because no system of settlement, as old and successful as the English village, disappears overnight. Half the population of England and Wales lived and worked in the countryside as late as 1851; and for the next 25 years, despite the repeal of protection by Parliament, home farming was to enjoy a period of prosperity, largely because overseas countries had not yet become mass exporters of food. Farming however was not, and never had been, the sole employer of rural labour. Primary jobs — farming, forestry, quarrying and the like — were always balanced by a profusion of crafts and small industries, serving the land or producing consumer goods; and it was these two elements of employment, primary land work and secondary rural industry, that gave the village — and the countryside as a whole — its economic base and balance. Owing to the technical development and growth of urban industry in the midlands and the north, the industrial element in rural life was the first to suffer, flickering out like the flame of a dying candle all through the nineteenth century. County directories (White's *Devon*, for example) told the tale. The amazing thing was that so many bakers, basketmakers, potters, smiths and wrights, held on as long as they did; indeed individual craftsmen lasted much longer than, say, small engineering works making farm implements or repairing steam engines. But the end result was the loss of jobs *alternative* to work on the land, creating a gap that has never been adequately filled since, and causing a heavy imbalance in rural employment. On the other hand mechanisation did not undermine farming in the same manner or on the same scale. On the contrary it created a number of new jobs that absorbed many of the countrymen (or their descendants) who had lost their holdings under enclosure and who would otherwise have left the land altogether. What started the great agricultural depression in the mid-1870s (lasting virtually until the late 1930s) was the breaking of the prairies in the New World, the dominance of the doctrine of free trade as preached by the manufacturing interests, who welcomed the import of cheap food from North and South America and Australasia — all at the expense of home farming which was deliberately abandoned to sink or swim. It nearly sank. By 1914, at the latest, the heart had gone out of the village as an economic unit.

Remunerative work is the foundation upon which a vigorous society is built. That being so, social decay in the countryside was inevitable. Folk life was already on the wane by the 1850s, and the fact that folk speech, songs, dances and customs had to be collected and recorded by a devoted band of scholars, was a sure sign that they were on the way out. But the most significant sign was the decline of the rural hierarchy. Resident landowners, who lived off their farm rents, quickly diminished; while even those who survived depended increasingly on their industrial investments, or were replaced by urban intruders who came to the country for sport and prestige. The parson had more staying power; but gradually his functions as teacher, preacher and welfare officer were whittled away by changes in education and local govern-

The village of Welton, Staffordshire, in the early 1930s. Mobility and the growth of social services have swept such sights away, as villagers have acquired urban standards and amenities. *(Photo: CPRE)*

ment; and even where the country town superseded the large village as the centre of local trade and administration, the harsh winds of centralisation began before long to blow from Whitehall or its provincial counterpart.

And that was not the end of the story. The weakening of the countryside invited active exploitation by the town. Whereas railways had facilitated urban and suburban development, introduced commuting and rendered many rural places (especially on the coast) accessible to crowds at the weekends and for holidays, their effect was still limited: because outside the railway station the horse and bicycle still barred 'progress'. Not so the internal combustion engine, which overcame all obstacles and burst the countryside wide open. Before planning control, mobility by motor was usually disastrous in its impact on rural life: at its worst between the two world wars, when land was treated purely as a commercial commodity—a period of free-for-all that produced, for example, the hill-and-dale devastation of iron ore mining in Northamptonshire, by-pass villadom, the horror of Peacehaven on the Sussex downs and ribbon building (wedded to tasteless design) on the outskirts of even the smallest village. Moreover the vestiges of commun-

29

ity life in the countryside were threatened with total extinction by the growth of dormitory estates and the multiplying of holiday homes, unoccupied for half the year. Such was the pattern already evident before the last war.

The 1930s however did yield indications of new attitudes and the promise of future action. For reasons of economic necessity and defence, the Government began to assist agriculture, notably by establishing Milk and other Marketing Boards, by crop and fertiliser subsidies and later by a massive ploughing campaign. The Forestry Commission, a state enterprise started in 1919, had planted over a million acres of softwoods by 1939. Land settlement too was stimulated in a small way, while farm wages inched their way upwards: so that, despite a steadily contracting labour force, the prospects for primary employment on the land began to revive. Revival was piecemeal however and snail slow, and it lacked the most elementary foundation in that land was being lost to indiscriminate development at the rate of 100,000 acres a year. Without control of land use, the future made no sense. But Parliament gave little help at first, beyond two toothless Planning Acts in 1932 and 1935. It was left to voluntary effort and a handful of far-seeing individuals to rouse public opinion: notably the Council for the Protection of Rural England (founded in 1926) to prod the nation into an awareness of amenity, plead for national parks and make people see the necessity for planning in order to conserve land; likewise it fell to the Land Utilisation Survey carried out 1931–3 under the direction of Sir Dudley Stamp to provide the basic statistics on which planning might build. Out of such efforts and the emergency of the war, came a vast surge of private enthusiasm and a spate of historic Government reports, which in turn yielded the post-war legislation designed to safeguard the land for optimum use—whether for agriculture, amenity, nature conservation or necessary urban development.

By 1950—with the passage of the New Towns Act 1946, the Town and Country Planning Act 1947, the Agriculture Act 1947, the National Parks and Access to the Countryside Act 1949 and the setting-up of the Nature Conservancy also in 1949—many people, I for one, hoped that a minor millennium had arrived; and that the way was now open for a resurgence of country life suited to contemporary conditions. I was farming at the time, close to a village on the edge of Exmoor, and well placed to observe what actually happened. In fact of course our hopes were not realised, although the tale was not all one of woe. What then has been happening in the 25 years that have since elapsed?

Let us consider land first, since it is literally the raw material of our existence. As we need it both to live on and live off, it must be the prime concern of any community, rural or otherwise. The time when Britain was able to grow all its own food was left behind at least 150 years ago. Even so, owing to the intensification of husbandry and the support of the State, we are still managing to produce more than half our overall requirements. None the less two deterrents to the revival of farming as a source of employment have been at work. At the end of the war, we knew that re-housing and re-development were necessary on a massive scale and demanded the highest priority. At first the emphasis on urban renewal helped in a back-handed way to stem the demand for fresh rural land, reinforced by the fact that food was still short and rationing had to be prolonged. But the restrictions did not last. In the event no one anticipated the scale and pace of the post-war demand for land, its multiplicity and intensity, and the ways in which the various uses reacted upon one another, each one posing a fresh set of problems. Moreover expansion was accelerated by the sharp rise in population (from 50 to 56 millions between 1951 and 1971), and by the salient fact that Britain cannot escape the legacy of the Industrial Revolution. In other words having become a heavily industrialised country, it is compelled to devote space and resources to towns, factories and communications, at the expense of the countryside. Land lost to urban demand, though less than pre-war, has been running at a minimum of 50,000 acres a year, much of it flat and fertile in the neighbourhood of centres of population; and that, according to the simplest mathematics, diminishes both the raw material of food and the number of jobs available in agriculture.

The second deterrent also concerns the impact of farming on the rural community. As the total acreage diminishes and the demand for

The car has changed everything. Many village railway stations, like this one at Leadenham, Lincolnshire, are now private homes. Work is more likely to be found now in a neighbouring town accessible by car than in the village itself.

(Photo: Simon Warner)

food rises, production per man and per acre has to be increased. This is an inescapable fact, not negatived by temporary surpluses in western Europe of beef, butter or any other agricultural product, for these are essentially problems of distribution and finance. Intensification of husbandry means *inter alia* more mechanisation and other expensive short-cuts to output. It means that, if things go on as now, there is no prospect of increasing employment in agriculture, which already supports less than five per cent of the population. The alternative—a return to labour-intensive farming—involves a major revolution in social attitudes, economics and techniques, and for that reason appears unlikely in the short term. It may however be forced upon us one day, either owing to the sheer need to survive in a world running out of food, or—as the organic school of thought contends—because current intensive methods are destroying the inherent fertility of the soil, which will bring about the same result. My reading of human nature is that no such revolution will take place until demonstrably we reach the very edge of catastrophe. Meanwhile we cannot expect the rural communities of Britain to find work in farming, forestry or other primary industries, for more than about a quarter of their labour force.

No rural community can thrive without a minimum of local employment. If work is not available or not wanted on the land, the majority of breadwinners in the countryside must perforce rely on secondary sources—on manufacturing and service industries, shops, the professions and local government administration. In short we are confronted with the historical problem originating in the loss of rural industry and crafts, and the general reduction of village trade, at one time an integral part of village economic life. The situation is of course different to what it was, due to mobility, sophistication and the broader distribution of wealth. Cars, road improvements and now motorways have provided the many with what, even as recently as the 1930s, was enjoyed only by the relatively few. Today a man may live in a village and drive daily 20 or 30 miles to his job without a backward thought; others may travel further or work the week away and return home at the weekend. Conversely many families living in towns pour out of them on Friday night, or keep a country cottage for the summer and other holidays, leaving it unoccupied for the rest of the year. Some villages are literally half-empty for months at a time; many others exist simply as satellites to larger centres—mere dormitories, maintaining a handful of shops and institutions and a skeleton population during the day. The pattern is so familiar as to be no longer remarkable, but its effect is to shrivel the very roots of country life. Many families—especially where the husband is the chief or sole earner—having no economic stake in a place, apart from the house in which they live, find it hard to identify themselves permanently or profoundly with it; and that in turn detracts from any sense of identity inherent in the place itself. Interaction between man and place is mysterious, but all communities—especially rural ones which are small and therefore vulnerable—depend for their

The health of a village can often be measured by the social amenities it retains. Alwalton, Cambridgeshire, has kept its thriving C of E school (*above*), but many smaller communities have not been so fortunate. The old school at Staverton, Devon (*below*), for example is now a private home. (*Photos: Simon Warner*)

social character upon the vitality they generate; however neither vitality, nor ultimately existence itself, can continue without an economic *raison d'être*. That is why so many villages have deteriorated into dormitories or havens for the retired, without positive identity, and without anything rural about them, other than the landscape around.

It amounts to this. What kind of work can be introduced into the countryside to give it new life? The term 'rural industry' can be misleading in that it conveys the sense that such industry has to be *rural* in character. But what does *rural* mean? Use of local raw materials? Handicrafts? A minimum of machinery and repetitive processes? Is a country garage servicing tractors and cars less rural than a sawyard? The Dartington Hall estate in Devon has demonstrated over the past 50 years—and there is plenty of evidence from enterprises in almost every county now—that size, not 'ruralness', is the critical factor, in association with location and the character of the business. This is confirmed by the experience of the Council for Small Industries in Rural Areas (COSIRA), successor since 1968 to the Rural Industries Bureau (RIB). This organisation was originally founded to salve and reanimate the traditional crafts of the countryside; and there is no doubt that, but for the technical, financial and other services provided, some occupations (such as thatching) might have died out. In aggregate however their number is small, and so the final answer does not rest with them. None the less, although restricted to helping firms employ-

Traditional rural employments such as thatching (as here, in Great Abington, Cambridgeshire) have been nourished in recent years by the Council for Small Industries in Rural Areas (COSIRA). But COSIRA has also given extensive support to technologically more sophisticated trades and enterprises in rural areas—concentrating principally on small units employing less than 20 workers.

(*Photo: John Topham*)

ing not more than 20 or so skilled operatives and ancillary staff, COSIRA now offers assistance to a remarkably wide range of enterprises, including engineering, boat building, textiles, plastics, construction and a multitude of repair shops. The volume and variety of its work show that a surprising number of trades are viable in small units, whether for technical or managerial reasons. Quality goods, not amenable to mass production, offer obvious scope. I am personally familiar with many successful examples; glass-making at Torrington, die-casting in Northamptonshire, toy-making in Lynmouth, farm machinery in Porlock, furniture-making in the North Riding and sail-making at Bideford, to name a few. In addition a number of country firms are under contract manufacturing small parts and components which large factories do not wish to bother with, and find it better business to farm out. In such instances mobility is an essential. Good communications by road offset distance from markets and sources of supply, while location in a village offers two-way attractions—jobs for locals (especially part-time work for women), and homes close by in pleasant surroundings.

A number of larger firms, outside the scope of COSIRA, have also survived or sprung up in the countryside. Some have been subsidised by the Government to settle in rural areas, such as mid-Wales, in an effort to halt depopulation. Others have been persuaded to go to selected country towns, where labour and housing are available and facilities for expansion exist. This is sound policy: namely to develop centres for local employment and administration, each serving a radius of, say, a dozen miles. But the pattern is uneven and has to be carefully controlled, otherwise the surrounding countryside may be devitalised still further. Moreover, technical objections apart, not every entrepreneur finds the country attractive for work, nor out of conservatism do all countrymen want light industry, although in the same breath they may complain of the lack of opportunities. Yet, for reasons of scale and diversity, a range of small industries offers the best prospects, since they are more certain of providing that core of permanent employment upon which other trades, shops and services depend. The focus can often be a large or key-sited village, rather than a small town; or a collection of smaller places within a rural area, each one housing one or more elements that, in sum, compose a balanced rural community—be it a factory, a market, a co-operative, a comprehensive school or perhaps a community college serving that part of the county.

There is yet another source of rural employment—tourism—now a major industry, and a major factor in our national life. Economically it affects such diverse interests as the production of cars, caravans, camping and boating equipment, expenditure on travel, the patronage of hotels and cafés, indeed the consumer trade of whole regions from groceries to gimmicks. In general it is a seasonal phenomenon, which means that many places thrive for four or five months, and then survive on their profits for the rest of the year. The pattern is familiar in seaside and other places where holidays are the tradition; and it is fast becoming so in the less fashionable national parks and other parts of the country, scenically attractive, but not long favoured by visitors. This surge for leisure is of course presenting the planners with multifarious problems of traffic, access to open country, rights-of-way, conservation and physical erosion due to over-popularity—subjects outside the immediate concern of this chapter. It suffices to say that many rural communities, not used to tourism, are now discovering the pros and cons at their own level: busy in the summer with letting and catering and the sudden expansion of everyday trade, but at other times left to their own devices. Tourism only presents difficulties in such places, if they allow themselves to become over-dependent on it. Farmers who take in visitors know better how to cope. Money for summer accommodation is regarded as a useful cash crop, but the farm will survive without it; although in moorland and hill country, tourism can and may in future play a more decisive part. Upland farmers are coming to realise that it pays to keep the land clean and in good heart, otherwise the countryside may fail to attract that 'summer crop'.

Abroad the seasonal character of tourism is fully recognised and provided for. Many countrypeople in south Germany, for instance, living outside the mountain areas and unable to profit from winter skiiing work, sustain several permanent jobs. In the winter they are busy in small workshops (some of them producing goods for the tourist trade). In the summer they work in hotels, restaurants and shops; while throughout the year all will help with the farm and forest work as may be necessary. Multi-employment could be taken much further in this country; and it emphasises yet again the need to sustain a certain minimum of jobs of an industrial and trading character which, together with land work, would ensure a living on the spot for *at least half* the breadwinners of a rural community.

From the foregoing it is clear that the countryside has to carry a minimum population, if rural communities are to survive, not as relics but as viable units of society. In other words there have to be enough people living and working there to provide, as I have said, labour for local economic enterprises, a market for goods and services, and staffing for local administration, in order to maintain a standard of living comparable with that in the towns. If the countryside is depressed, people will leave it, as they have done in the past; or they will exploit it and kill it that way. Moreover opportunities for a vigorous social life require the presence of people, not only in sufficient numbers but of differing status, incomes and interests. You cannot have clubs and pubs, expeditions and evening classes, sport or any broad range of recreation, without a corresponding variety among those who participate and make such things possible. And it is fruitless to argue—as some still do—that the civilisation of the countryside must remain inviolate and be perpetuated in past forms. Merrie England lost its meaning long ago, the forms have largely vanished and Giles is no longer with us. Of course where—as in field sports—tradition is simply a continuation, as opposed to mere survival, then the past does not deter the present. Izaak Walton would no doubt be delighted at the proliferation of 'compleat anglers'; and, despite the opposition of those who oppose it on moral grounds, hunting is as popular as ever and, if anything, more democratic. Rural society still has some ghosts, more an aura than a reality, embedded in the idea that the cricket club or the old people's outing can depend on a spectral class known as 'they' to meet the annual deficit. This is a hangover from the days of the 'big house', as out-of-date as it is bad finance.

Society does not thrive that way now. Nor are rural amusements limited to a Saturday afternoon jumble sale or a hop in the village hall, with prizes blackmailed out of the local traders. That is not to say that local activities are not popular, because indeed they are. They reflect an essential aspect of local life anywhere—the need for neighbourliness and the ability to create your own amusements, which means enjoying the effort as much as the event itself; but, unlike the old days, that is no longer the limit of the horizon. It is true that for some people the old era of simplicity and self-help has been virtually extinguished. A television set can inhibit a whole family from doing anything in the evenings except sit and stare at the box. But that need not be, and happily is not often the case, for simplicity is compatible with sophistication and—whether we admit or not—that is how we live.

Everyone today, townsman or countryman, is in varying degree a sophisticated person and lives simultaneously at two levels. At one level we depend upon and enjoy many of the material and other advantages of our age—electricity, cars, television, the printed word, piped water, packed foods, any amount of ready-made goods and services. The list is endless, and our ability to profit from these things is largely determined by choice and purchasing power. That is the level common to all, whether we live in a block of flats and sell insurance, or in a tied cottage and milk cows. The real differences occur at the personal level, where we are indeed beings apart, each with his or her intimate interests and relationships; and we need these differences in order both to alleviate the collective pressures and make best use of common advantages. In the countryside even those who live relatively remote lives are distinguished far less than formerly by the idiosyncrasies of their calling, or by ignorance of affairs. A visit to the nearest town is no longer a seven-day wonder, nor is a trip to London or Glasgow the unique experience of a lifetime. To live in isolation is already an anachronism. The everyday world is becoming a wide and open place. This is to the good, for we shall need all our reserves of knowledge and understanding in order to control our destinies; and so the sooner we recognise the dualism of our existence the better. The man of tomorrow will consciously have to combine his collective life with his individual life, and accept the fact that he is a hybrid: which means, in this tight little

37

island of ours, being part-townsman, part-countryman, the balance swinging up or down according to circumstances.

The way forward then lies with the integration of townside and countryside: not the imposition of one civilisation upon the other, nor progressive suburbanisation which passes for both but is neither. The rural community will remain a reality, or become one afresh, if it satisfies certain requirements. It must contain (within itself or within a limited radius) a minimum population, sufficient to sustain a variety of interests and activities, resulting in a lively and balanced society. But the whole social structure cannot survive *in vacuo*; it must rest upon an economic foundation that generates wealth in that area; in other words a mixture of local employments, suited to small-scale operation, and giving work to at least half the resident labour force. A pattern of this kind will help generate that sense of identity which residence alone cannot provide. Without it, villages—as I prefer to call them—will either disintegrate into physical and spiritual emptiness, or become characterless appendages to the nearest town.

3

Transport in the Countryside

IAN HARRIS

'I love to be in such places where there is no rattling with coaches, nor rumbling with wheels.' JOHN BUNYAN, 1628–88.

MANY things have combined to effect a quiet revolution in the countryside in this century. Changes in farming technology have drastically reduced the farming population. Piped water, light and power at the drop of a switch, TV and, above all, the internal combustion engine have transformed the lives of those who remain, and of the new car-borne country dwellers. Travel is easier and faster than ever before; barriers between communities have broken down, horizons have been widened. A whole way of life has developed on the basis of the new mobility.

In looking to the future, most of us think of further dramatic and revolutionary changes, in which new forms of transport will displace the familiar motor car, bus and lorry. But the truth is more mundane. Transport requires such massive investments, and established systems or policies acquire such enormous momentum, that change is a gradual process. Fifty years ago the motor car, the lorry, the bus, the train and even the aeroplane were all in use, although in less developed forms than today.

The roads of Telford, and even of the Romans, the railways of Brunel and Stephenson, will probably remain in use for hundreds of years. Major road or rail projects take ten or more years to come into being, and construction programmes once authorised acquire a momentum of their own. Most of the buildings that will stand in the year 2000 exist today. Our reasons for travelling remain much the same, and better telecommunications such as the videophone are unlikely to prove a substitute for human contact. Rising costs, shortage of capital and increasing environmental awareness have dimmed the prospects of such radically new modes of travel as the hovertrain or the vertical take-off aircraft. Expensive new transport technologies now seem less likely either to 'solve' our transport problems, or to pose new threats to the countryside.

Technical progress seems more likely to take the form of refining the transport we already have, making it safer, more economical in energy and money, quieter, more environmentally acceptable and more responsive to the needs of a public that may have to adjust itself to less mobility than we used to take for granted. But the fact that technical change may be gradual does not change the need for a radical reassessment of the transport policies we have inherited from the past, or, in the longer term, for modes of transport related to the energy supply systems of the future.

The uncertain future

Past certainties have been dissolved by the energy crisis and the related threat to the world economy. The immediate problem is the higher price of oil demanded by the oil-producing nations, whose ranks we have just entered. Beyond that lies the problem of the depletion of world oil reserves, on which transport is almost totally dependent. The era of cheap and plentiful oil is over, though the North Sea gives this country some time to adapt to the new situation. Domestic transport accounts for less than one-quarter of UK oil consumption, but it is far more difficult to substitute other fuels for oil in transport than it is in, say, electricity generation.

In retrospect we even may come to welcome the rise in oil prices of the 1970s as giving an incentive to develop alternative sources of power and better public transport. It seems much more likely that we will succeed in developing road vehicles powered by batteries or fuel cells than that we will be forced to abandon individual mechanised transport and develop radically different forms of settlement or life-style in the next 25 years.

Faced with the new uncertainties (not to mention the higher costs), we must be far less profligate in the use of fuel. We must be wary of locational trends (such as the replacement of village stores by cash-and-carry warehouses or hypermarkets) or transport changes (such as the building of motorways) that encourage or necessitate an excessive amount of travel. We must discriminate between different forms of transport according to their energy efficiency, encouraging walking, cycling and the use of public transport rather than cars occupied by only one or two people. The emphasis in vehicle design must be switched from performance and styling to economy of fuel and resources.

The role of the car

It would be easy to turn an examination of transport in the countryside into a polemic against the car and the 'juggernaut' lorry. The catalogue of problems created by road transport is long, but it would be fatal to ignore the benefits of the car (or the lorry), or to underestimate the strength of the desire to own and use personal transport. The car provides door-to-door transport in one vehicle with complete freedom from time-tables and route-plans, and the ability to transport luggage, shopping, clothing or food. For a family visit to the town or the countryside it is relatively inexpensive even at current fuel prices, yet it can be a warm, private, sheltered indoor environment, a shopping basket and a picnic centre. As Nan Fairbrother put it,[1] 'a motor-car is a way of life, not a way of travel'.

In the countryside the car has eased the isolation and remoteness of generations. In many rural areas, movement demands were never sufficient to support regular bus services, even in the public transport heyday of the 1920s and 1930s. The country-dweller can now obtain the services and facilities of the town, and the town-dweller can gain easy access to the countryside for his leisure. Rural life is no longer so closely centred upon the village and the distinction between town and country has become blurred. Many organisations and social activities — clubs, societies, Women's Institutes, church activities, agricultural shows — draw their members or supporters not from one village but from a wide area. It is scarcely surprising that the highest levels of car ownership are found in rural areas or that many country people regard a car as a necessity.

The decline of rural public transport

However, this new degree of rural mobility has not been available to all. A sizeable proportion of the population remains wholly or partly dependent upon public transport, whose viability and very existence has been undermined by the spread of car ownership. It is no exaggeration to claim that those without cars in rural areas frequently face a transport situation worse than any experienced this century, because of the disappearance of rural buses, trains and earlier horse-drawn vehicles.

Lois Pulling and Colin Speakman, in their study of the impact of declining transport services on rural life, wrote that 'between a quarter and a third of country people suffer an isolation unprecedented since the age of the stage coach'.[2] Branch railways have been closed, many rural bus services have been reduced in frequency or withdrawn altogether, and fares on the remaining services have risen rapidly. Even walking or cycling have been made dangerous and unpleasant by the growth of motor traffic. The ownership of a car has become a virtual necessity for the heads of rural households to get to work, though it frequently places a great strain on the family budget. However, the main impact of declining public transport has been upon other members of the community — particularly mothers, old people, children and teenagers.

Various studies in Devon, West Suffolk, Bedfordshire and elsewhere have shown how people adapt to the withdrawal of public transport. Often other authorities step in. The education authorities provide

1. *New Lives, New Landscapes*: Nan Fairbrother, Penguin Books, 1972 (first published by the Architectural Press, 1970)

2. *Changing Directions*, The Report of the Independent Commission on Transport, Coronet Books, 1974, Appendix 6

school buses, employers organise works bus services, and ambulance and hospital car services have to be augmented. The financial savings from withdrawing a service may be illusory, the burden merely being transferred to other authorities. Moreover, although some of the basic needs of the community may be provided for, many people will suffer hardship and the quality of rural life is profoundly affected. Old people become virtually prisoners in their villages; journeys to shops, doctors or chemists become difficult; children cannot participate in after-school activities; social trips, visiting patients in hospital and participation in social, cultural and adult education activities all become impossible or dependent on the charity of a neighbouring car owner—and why should the provision of a basic necessity like transport be dependent on charity? 'Institutionalised' lift giving, such as the 'social car service' operated by the WRVS in the Bridgnorth area, may be welcome in this situation, but it can provide only a minimal level of mobility in a form that many women are reluctant to accept. In other words, people may adapt to their situation, but not without considerable restrictions on life-style and choice of activities. As people without cars gradually move away and car owners replace them, the social composition of the village changes.

The local bus at Stoke by Nayland, Suffolk—but for how much longer will it call? The run-down of rural bus services since the Beeching report on the railways has made life difficult for many country dwellers. County Councils are allowed to subsidise unremunerative services—but they still allocate only a tiny fraction of their transport budgets for this purpose. (*Photo: Simon Warner*)

The decline of rural public transport has affected not only the country-dweller, but also the townsman. As the Ramblers' Association[3] has pointed out, the decline in rural public transport, which has been particularly marked on Sundays, has deprived the non-car-owning town-dweller and many young people of access to the countryside.

In the absence of substantial financial assistance, a further deterioration in rural public transport can be foreseen. Costs of operation will continue to rise, and the demand for the services may continue to decline, though probably more slowly than in the past.

Most official studies of rural transport seem to have assumed that the cost of providing an adequate standard of public transport services to rural areas would be prohibitively expensive. Very little is known about the social consequences of providing different levels of public transport service, or what level could be regarded as 'adequate'. The Independent Commission on Transport[4] estimated the cost of restoring bus services in Great Britain to their 1956 level at around £31 million per annum in 1972 (some of which would have been recouped in fares).

This does not appear outrageous, yet the attitude that public transport must be profitable dies hard. Is it unreasonable to suggest that citizens in a community should have a right to mobility, and that it might be more socially desirable and just to provide basic mobility for all members of the community than, say, to reduce the travel time from London to Birmingham by 20 minutes? Many rural facilities such as electricity, postal services or water are already heavily subsidised, but few people suggest that they should be withdrawn or that minor rural roads should be closed down because they are not sufficiently used or are too expensive to maintain.

Recent policies have encouraged the concentration of shops, employment, schools and health services in large units, each serving a larger catchment area in order to achieve economies of scale. In consequence, many village facilities have been reduced, thereby increasing the need for travel. All too often the planning authorities approve the location of new facilities without taking account of the travel problems of people without cars. Either the policy should be reconsidered, or financial support for public transport should form part of the plan. But the Transport Policies and Programmes of the new County Councils, which are now free to allocate their resources either to highways or to public transport, show a marked reluctance to subsidise public transport. Few counties have allocated more than five per cent of their transport spending for 1975–6 to support for buses, while Devon and Somerset have earmarked less than one per cent for this purpose. Many county surveyors find it difficult to visualise diverting their precious highway funds to public transport. A stronger lead is needed from central Government in this direction.

3. *Rural Transport in Crisis*, Ramblers' Association, 1973

4. *Changing Directions*, The Report of the Independent Commission for Transport, Coronet Books, 1974

Although scheduled bus and rail services should provide the back-bone of rural public transport, there is much scope for experimentation and innovation, especially in very sparsely populated areas. The rapid increase in fuel prices may curb the growth in car ownership, and we may see the car and public transport moving closer together. The car may become more like public transport, with the spread of car-hire and car-pooling and sharing arrangements, while public transport may move towards providing a more individual service through the use of minibuses owned and operated by rural communities for the benefit of their members and more responsive to passenger demands. More use of school buses by members of the public, the introduction of combined passenger and freight vehicles (including postal buses), and the development of car-hire, minibus and taxi services have all been sug-gested. Unless carefully regulated, developments of this kind can undermine remaining conventional services, and the needs of freight or the mail may receive priority over the needs of passengers. It is essential that the county councils use their new transport powers under the 1972 Local Government Act to ensure that these developments are co-ordinated with conventional scheduled services.

There is also scope for developing conventional services. Many of the large bus operators, based in the towns, have proved unresponsive to the needs of the rural community. Many more services could be based in the rural areas, operated either by independent operators, or by 'out-stationed' vehicles of the large companies. These could perhaps be operated on the 'dial-a-bus' principle, feeding into conventional inter-urban bus and rail services at suitable interchanges. At the same time, inter-urban bus services could be made more attractive since they would no longer need to divert into small villages along minor roads (for which large conventional buses are often unsuitable). As traffic restraints begin to bite in the towns, the potential for 'park-and-ride' facilities at railway stations in rural areas may also be in-creased.

The motorist and the countryside

The decline in public transport services in rural areas has not been visible to the casual observer, but the effects of traffic on amenity and landscape have been all too apparent. Between 1963 and 1973, traffic on the roads of Great Britain increased by 73 per cent. In the urban areas, few people now believe that it is desirable to attempt to accom-modate the full potential growth of traffic by providing more road and parking space, but in the countryside, the balance is not so clear. The relative advantages to the user of the car *vis-à-vis* public transport are much greater in rural areas than in towns. There are fewer problems of congestion or parking, and noise or pollution affect fewer people, whereas public transport services are bound to be comparatively sparse and infrequent.

Nevertheless, traffic is making a serious physical impact on the countryside. Increased leisure time, higher incomes and the spread of car ownership have contributed to a massive increase in 'leisure motoring', which has created acute problems in many of our most beautiful areas. More than 100,000 visitors' cars enter the Peak District National Park on a fine Sunday, the number having doubled between 1963 and 1970. A majority of these visitors to the countryside do not participate in active pursuits—they are touring, picnicking or just relaxing; about 70 per cent of visitors to popular beauty spots such as Box Hill or Windsor Great Park never stray far from their cars.

Visitors' cars congest narrow lanes, block farm gateways and tear up roadside verges. The character of quiet country roads is destroyed as cars penetrate leafy lanes and remote byways and make them unpleasant for walking. The indiscriminate parking of cars detracts from the beauty of any area. Solitude is increasingly difficult to find, and over-visiting of beauty spots can destroy the very amenities that people come to see, threatening their physical characteristics by erosion of vegetation and soil. Although high fuel prices may slow down the future growth of leisure motoring, serious problems are likely to remain.

A broad approach to solving these problems is now emerging. One aspect of it has been the designation of country parks which, it is hoped, will 'siphon-off' some day visitors to national parks and other remote areas. But, even if they are successful, the pressures on national parks and other outstandingly beautiful areas from people seeking exceptional scenery or open countryside are still likely to increase.

A number of authorities, including the Sandford Committee,[5] have suggested a policy of zoning areas within national parks and other outstanding tracts of countryside. Some parts would be suitable for intensive recreational use, absorbing large numbers of visitors, while others would require protection from over-visiting, including limitations on the penetration by motor vehicles. Once such areas have been defined, an appropriate transport system can be developed to serve them. The first step should be the designation of a hierarchy of routes, recognising the different, and frequently conflicting, requirements of different types of road user. Heavy traffic, tourist traffic, walkers, cyclists and horse riders each have different demands and each sees the countryside in a different way and at a different speed. 'The convenience and pleasure of each means of travel is less if all types of traffic are on the same road.'[6]

The tourist, once he has reached an area of natural beauty, wants to drive at a pace that will allow the scenery to be appreciated and frequent stops to be made. The pleasantness of the drive is more important than the directness of the route or the speed of travel. A road with many surprises and changes of view is much more enjoyable than a fast modern road. These requirements of car tourists are quite different

5. Report of the National Parks Policy Review Committee, HMSO 1974

6. *Routes for People*, An Environmental Approach to Rural Highway Planning, Derbyshire County Council and the Peak Park Planning Board, 1972

from those of other drivers. To mix tourist traffic with long-distance car and lorry traffic can be frustrating to both as well as dangerous.

The Peak Park Planning Board have shown how a hierarchy of routes could be created in part of the Peak District;[6] routes have been defined for heavy traffic (including quarry traffic), visiting motorists, cyclists and horse-riders and walkers. A hierarchical road system has also been proposed for the Lake District by Wilson and Womersley.[7]

Once a road hierarchy has been defined, it should be used to plan road improvements in a co-ordinated rather than a piecemeal way; the standards adopted for any improvements should take account of the planned function of the road in the hierarchy. Too many highway authorities are still following the simple objective of providing wider and 'better' roads wherever and whenever they are able. The economics of this are highly questionable, especially in areas in which heavy tourist traffic occurs on only a limited number of weekends and Bank Holidays (generally when there is little commercial traffic on the roads).

The designation of a road hierarchy—in which landscape, planning and environmental considerations would play a major part—would help to determine whether particular roads ought to be improved, and if so, to what standards. It would also help to decide the appropriateness of particular sites for developments which generate traffic, such as hotels, industry, leisure centres or caravan sites, and to decide where restrictions on the weight, size or speed of vehicles are desirable and practicable.

There could be economic as well as environmental benefits from such a policy. The Marshall Committee on Highway Maintenance[8] referred to the damage caused by heavy, wide vehicles using minor roads, and argued that they should be prohibited from using them on the grounds that 'it is uneconomical to maintain all roads in a state suited to all traffic'.

The designation of a road hierarchy implies the creation of 'environmental areas' in which environmental needs would be paramount and where traffic would be discouraged. Country lanes were not meant for modern traffic, and to widen and straighten a lane to handle it quite simply destroys its character, since, to quote Nan Fairbrother, 'A lane is its boundaries—its containing banks and walks and trees and hedges, its windings and unexpected corners.'[1] Once this is recognised, the need to restrict the number, size and speed of motor vehicles becomes obvious.

The most extreme form of restriction is the closure of a road to all traffic (except for access). The road through the Goyt Valley in the Peak National Park is closed to traffic at weekends in the holiday

7. *Traffic Management in the Lake District National Park*, Report prepared for the Friends of the Lake District by Hugh Wilson and Lewis Womersley, 1972

8. Report of the Committee on Highway Maintenance, HMSO 1970

The Goyt Valley, before and after the Countryside Commission's experiment with a
rural traffic-free zone in the Peak National Park.   (*Photos: Peak Park Planning Board*)

season and a free minibus is provided from surrounding car parks. Three-quarters of the visitors have approved of the experiment. They stayed in the valley longer and were willing to rediscover the joys of walking. There have been some snags (particularly the expense of hiring minibuses and marshals, and the variability of demand for the minibus depending on the weather) but schemes of this type do seem to be suitable for self-contained areas with little through traffic. In some places, motorless zones might be introduced without any alternative motorised transport; the opportunity to enjoy a totally vehicle-free area may become highly prized as in some Alpine resorts or in Venice.

Limitations on leisure motorists in some areas should be accompanied by positive provision for their needs elsewhere. Recreational traffic should be guided to selected recreational routes, parts of the existing road system linked into pleasant drives with frequent opportunities for stops to enjoy the countryside. The Forestry Commission has already pioneered the scenic drive.

Harsh and rigid highway design near Penrith, Cumbria, where the A66 meets the A592. Curbs and lamp standards appropriate to a town are an intrusion in a rural area like this one at the gateway to the Lake District.   (*Photo: Geoffrey Berry*)

Highway design

The improvement of roads in rural areas requires the utmost sensitivity, since the roads themselves are frequently an important element in the character and attractiveness of the area. Even minor improvements can be damaging. Some features are more suited to urban areas than to rural—concrete kerbstones, crash-barriers, intrusive street lighting. 'Trees are felled, hedges grubbed up and the age-old feeling of enclosure, of friendliness, is sacrificed to the interests of safety, speed and efficiency; the result is at worst ugliness and at best monotony.'[9]

The 'suburbanisation' of many villages has been exacerbated by the imposition of rigid highway design standards in new developments. The conventional highway standards in housing areas, ruthlessly applied by highway authorities, are unnecessary as a recent manual by Essex County Council[10] has shown. These standards, designed to achieve unimpeded vehicular movement, 'eat up the ground and in doing so take precedence over such social considerations as a decent-sized private garden'. New housing areas all 'tend to look alike with the same road widths, junctions, curves, alignments and surface finishes; the same type of turning heads, the same pavement and kerb details, the same street lights and ubiquitous concrete columns'. Convenient and safe vehicular movement need not be incompatible with higher densities or with design that is sympathetic to landscape or the character of towns and villages.

Motorway standards

Motorways are particularly difficult to fit into attractive landscape on account of their width and their vast intersections. The improvement in the design of more recent motorways is attributable, at least in part, to the work of the Landscape Advisory Committee. But not enough attention is paid by the designers to the visual experience of the road user. Frequently landscaping is on too small a scale to be appreciated by passengers in a moving car, and travel on a motorway is 'a curiously remote experience, cut off from the life of the areas we pass through'.[1] Improved landscaping would make motorway journeys pleasanter and might also make them safer.

But landscaping is still essentially a cosmetic treatment; while it can soften the impact of motorways on the countryside, it cannot eliminate it. Only in a few wild and rugged areas can motorways designed to current standards be fitted into the landscape rather than dominate it. There appears to be a strong case for building new roads to lower standards, particularly in areas of great beauty. The welcome decision of the Department of the Environment in 1974 to increase the design capacities of different types of roads means that highway designs

9. *People and the Countryside*, H. E. Bracey, Routledge & Kegan Paul, 1970
10. 'A Design Guide for Residential Areas', Essex County Council, December 1973

Every mile of modern three-lane dual carriageway motorway occupies upwards of 26 acres. Here, the Plymouth by-pass sweeps past Saltram House in Devon. *(Photo: Robert Chapman)*

need no longer be dictated by brief peak hour traffic demands. The fact remains that roads are still being designed for the traffic flows anticipated in 20 years' time or more, calculated by projecting into the future the trends of the cheap petrol era. These flows may never materialise.

Moreover, the new capacity standards do not anticipate any lowering of design speeds, in spite of the introduction in December 1974 of a speed limit of 50 mph for single carriageway roads. The DOE recommendations still state (in March 1975) that 'design speeds below 60 mph are not recommended for trunk or principal roads in rural areas'.[11]

The interests of fuel conservation and the preservation of landscape go hand in hand in suggesting lower highway design speeds. Design speed is one of the most critical factors determining the landscape implications of road improvements. In its study of the proposal to 'improve' the A66 through the Lake District National Park, the Countryside Commission said: 'The slower the design speed, the more latitude exists in vertical and horizontal alignments, therefore, the more freedom the designer has in fitting the road to the landscape. Further, the narrower the road, the less impact it will have on the scenery, and the more likely it is that existing roads will be able to be utilised.'[12] The study compared an improvement to normal trunk road standards (60 mph design speed) with a more modest improvement of the route to a 40 mph 'tourist route' standard accompanied by a diversion of heavy traffic to West Cumberland on an alternative route outside the Park. The impact of the two routes on the landscape was compared by calculating the length of road in cutting or on embankment.

The results were:

	60 mph standard	40 mph standard
Area of cutting (sq yd)	77,900	18,250
Area of embankment (sq yd)	104,500	40,100
Length of new alignment (yd)	26,050	3,330

Not only would the slower road have blended better into the landscape and have created a lesser 'scar', but it would also have provided a much more pleasant scenic drive for the tourist, with better views of the surrounding countryside. The decision of the Secretary of State for the Environment to approve the upgrading of the A66 to high speed standards, in spite of this evidence, set a most deplorable precedent. Yet the Minister, such is the immobility of departmental thinking, has

11. 'Layout of Roads in Rural Areas', HMSO 1968
12. West Cumberland Trunk Road Study, Countryside Commission/Lake District Planning Board, 1972

LINE OF PROPOSED NEW ROAD. RIVER GRETA NADDLE BECK CROSSING HELVELLYN PRESENT A66

The A66 'improvement' is passing through some of the Lake District's most beautiful
landscapes, including St John's Vale (*above*, seen from Lonscale Fell). It is designed to
provide a high-speed link with West Cumbria. (*Photo: Geoffrey Berry*)

refused to reconsider the design standards, in spite of repeated representations about the environmental intrusion of this road, particularly the
proposed dual carriageway alongside Bassenthwaite Lake.

Inter-urban transport

The countryside is affected not only by its own transport needs, but
also by the massive movements of people and goods between urban
areas. Despite the creation of the Department of the Environment,
there is no coherent national transport policy. Decisions on investment
in roads, railways and waterways appear to be taken in isolation from
each other, often using different criteria. A full and rational appraisal
of all transport modes is urgently required, particularly in the light of
current uncertainties about the energy situation. A clear national
policy framework is also necessary to ensure that the Transport Policies
and Programmes of the counties are set in a meaningful context and
are co-ordinated with each other. Whether such a framework will
result from the integrated transport policy promised by DOE during the
first part of 1976 remains—at the time this book goes to press—to be
seen.

A re-appraisal of national transport policy would not necessarily result in a major transfer of passengers or freight from the roads to the railways (or waterways). No other mode can offer the same flexibility and door-to-door convenience as road transport. But the price of this convenience is often high and, in the past, the balance has swung too far in favour of movement at the expense of the environment. But environment is not 'priceless' and a true balance must be sought. We must avoid measures that would impose an intolerably high price on the movement of people or goods in relation to the environmental benefits they would yield.

Freight

The heavy lorry has become the target of strong public criticism in recent years, because it inflicts so much environmental damage. But there are many misconceptions about the nature of the problem and possible solutions. The replacement of large lorries by smaller ones would probably worsen rather than improve the environment, would increase fuel consumption and would create more congestion.

The designation of lorry routes to which the largest and heaviest of lorries would be confined is attractive in principle and is now official policy.

The Heavy Commercial Vehicles (Controls and Regulations) Act, 1973 (the Dykes Act) requires local authorities to prepare plans for local lorry routes by 1977, and the DOE issued a consultation paper in 1974 setting out a national system of lorry routes. But the practical difficulties are immense, because most of the existing roads are unsuitable for heavy lorries to a greater or lesser extent. The dispersed nature of the activities which generate many lorry trips (shops, farms, homes, factories), and the short length of the typical journey all make it exceptionally difficult to introduce and enforce compulsory lorry routes. They relieve some places by aggravating the situation in others. In farming areas, milk tankers, livestock trucks and certain types of agricultural machinery are among the largest vehicles, but it would be almost impossible to confine them to lorry routes.

In spite of these difficulties, a system of lorry routes seems likely to emerge eventually. It should be associated with strict control over the location of all new developments that generate heavy traffic, and with a system of transhipment depots at which goods could be transferred from large to smaller lorries. Recent experiments in Britain and Holland[13] have suggested that transhipment centres when properly organised would not increase costs, as British road haulage interests fear, but can reduce them by facilitating the consolidation of deliveries and the faster turnround of vehicles. The transhipment depots could also fulfil the roles of lorry parks and warehousing and distribution centres, and be linked wherever possible to rail.

13. 'Lorries and the World we Live In', A report to the Minister for Transport Industries, Department of the Environment 1973

Crash, bang, wallop! as heavy lorries in Haddenham, Buckinghamshire (*above*), and Wargrave, Berkshire (*below*), make their way along unsuitable roads. Between 1962 and 1972, there was a trebling in the number of motor vehicles in the UK of over 5 tons unladen weight. The Department of the Environment began consultations in 1974 with a view to restricting heavy lorries to certain routes throughout the country; but this too has problems. (*Photos: Civic Trust*)

The transfer of freight traffic to rail is a popular solution to the heavy lorry problem, but most road freight consists of small consignments travelling relatively short distances, and is therefore unsuitable for rail. The average haul of lorries over three tons is only 30 miles. The limited number of access points to the rail system means that most goods have to be transhipped *en route*, thereby incurring additional costs and causing delays.

Nevertheless, some longer-distance freight could be transferred to rail, and more could be done to encourage the provision of private railway sidings. One estimate, made by the Independent Commission on Transport, suggests that up to one quarter of the ton-miles currently performed by lorries could be transferred to rail. But even if all these approaches were vigorously pursued, a large volume of lorry traffic must inevitably remain, inflicting great physical and environmental damage, and bitterly resented by the public. The only way out is to provide some additional roads to take extraneous lorry (and other) traffic out of towns and villages. They need not be built to motorway or high-speed standards. Lower standards and design speeds would make it possible to relieve more small towns and villages within a given budget and time scale.

Passenger transport

National policy on inter-urban passenger transport seems to be based on the assumption that road traffic demands must be accommodated, and cannot be seriously reduced by investment in rail. But this approach takes little account of the social costs of accommodating more and more traffic, or of the obvious dangers of relying too much on the car at a time of energy uncertainties. There has been a phenomenal growth in personal transport, from 130,000 million passenger miles in 1953 to 271,000 million passenger miles in 1971, of which the car accounts for 77 per cent.

The 1970 White Paper 'Roads for the Future', which still forms the basis of current plans, envisaged a continuous 'primary' inter-urban road network of about 3,500 miles (2,000 miles of them motorway). The Department of the Environment attempts to justify this programme with arguments which imply that the main users of the new roads will be goods and 'essential' traffic. In fact, goods traffic accounts typically for only about one-quarter of the economic benefits attributable to new roads, and the National Travel Survey shows that most long distance car journeys are for recreation, social and holiday purposes.

The full impact of motorways has not been understood. Building a motorway produces a change of such a degree that it is bound in time to weaken the competitive position of rail (and thus lead to additional road traffic), to generate extra journeys (particularly leisure trips) and to increase the average length of journeys. Little is known of the magnitude of these effects, but if they are as great as is sometimes alleged, then motorways do not even represent a solution to road traffic problems. The cuts in Government expenditure made since 1973 are seen by the DOE as merely deferring the date of completion of the inter-urban road network, but the ultimate aim is unchanged. Such a massive reduction in expenditure should lead to a radical re-appraisal of the whole roads programme. The present policy of building completely new high-standard inter-urban roads should be compared with a policy of building new roads (or upgrading existing ones) to lower standards.

The policy of closing railways has recently been halted, more because of fears of the political implications and redundancy problems of rail closures than because of any real conviction that rail investment can obviate the need for road construction. It is argued that there is little evidence of substitutability between rail and road. Motorway building and train service improvements have each been found to generate extra traffic, but to divert few users from the other mode. Such conclusions are, however, drawn from a fairly limited range of circumstances, and more radical policies of restraint on car use and rising fuel prices seem bound to cause some drivers to consider alternative modes.

Railway plans, conceived in isolation from road plans, envisage heavy investment in the Inter-City passenger services to provide higher standards of speed and comfort. This investment in the main radial routes from London is highly profitable to the railways, but is it the best use of scarce investment funds? Is there a need for higher speeds on these main routes, most of which already enjoy good services, and on which rail already has a large share of the market? The 125 mph train does not merit a high social priority, nor is it necessary to compete with road or air which are becoming less competitive. While it may generate profitable rail traffic, it is bound to create operating problems, which may restrict the ability of British Rail to handle freight traffic diverted from the roads.

The guidelines given to British Rail since the early 1960s have ensured that, while good Inter-City services are made better, the other services are starved of investment. Most of the cross-country and medium distance services (such as Liverpool–Manchester–Leeds–Hull, Manchester–North Wales and Birmingham–Leicester–East Anglia) are served by elderly diesel multiple-units which were noisy, uncomfortable and rough-riding even when new. Today they are barely acceptable, yet current plans envisage their retention for about ten more years. No real improvements can be expected until British Rail is free to give greater weight to social and environmental considerations. If the railways can be freed from the constraints of their existing remit, a host of improvements could result, including a rolling programme of electrification, integration of rail services with bus feeder lines, improved car-hire and parking facilities, and reduced charges for bicycles, whether parked or in transit.

Conclusion

Like almost all industrialised nations, Britain has been rushing head-long towards almost total dependence on the oil-powered motor car and lorry. In recent years, however, more and more people have begun to question whether the price of increased mobility is worth paying. The increased costs of oil and the threat of oil shortages in the longer term make the re-appraisal and integration of transport policy all the more pressing.

A re-appraisal might well conclude that we have little choice but to rely on the motor vehicle to satisfy most of our transport needs until the end of the century at least. If so, we must make far more intelligent use of it in the future than we have in the past. Restrictions on the use of cars are increasingly being accepted in the towns, and they will become more widespread in the countryside. But restrictions will not be accept-able socially or politically unless public transport is lifted right out of the depressed state into which it has been allowed to decline. If the use of cars becomes much more difficult or expensive, while public tran-sport is left to rot (and that is what is happening now), the country dwellers will be the worst sufferers. The rural communities will be threatened and further depopulation of the countryside could follow. From this, it would be a short step to the deterioration of a landscape that has its roots in a thriving rural economy.

4

Recreation: the Key to the
Survival of England's Countryside

MARION SHOARD

'Yeh, I love the country. I've just come back from it. Cranbrook. I was at D C (detention centre) there. Fantastic. The peace and quiet, the wilderness like. I lost 23 lbs and an inch off my chest. I go anywhere in the country. To different places. Where it's peaceful and beautiful. I like to see the unusualness, the branches on the floor. I'd like to go and live in the country all the time. In a way these are fantasies: I wanna get away from here—it really breaks you up.' Views on the countryside of a 19-year-old unemployed man interviewed by the author in Deptford, South East London.

CPRE has laboured long and hard—and not without success—to preserve the countryside. It has worked consistently within the planning system and exploited the system to the full; but if when CPRE comes to celebrate its centenary, there is to be anything significant left of the countryside, it will only be because in the meantime conservationists have widened their political base.

Ever since the industrial revolution, the political power of those sections of the community based on the land and interested in its protection has been waning. Not surprisingly the battle for the countryside has been a series of defensive actions: occasional safeguards won, the occasional bill amended, the occasional planning appeal won.

But the small section of the community which conservationists comprise has failed to fire the people's minds with their cause. New housing means homes. New industry means jobs. These are the things for which politicians win votes and on which public opinion will be against the conservationists more often than not.

Seventy-five per cent of the English live in towns or cities. Unless these urban dwellers come to see the countryside as something significant in their lives, their approval of conservation will remain an empty principle and the countryside a pleasant extra to be dispensed with whenever the contrary pressures mount.

And to the existing pressures—power stations, mineral quarrying, reservoirs and so on—will now be added immense pressure for housing development.

Since April 1974 the housing authorities have been district councils formed by merger of the old rural districts and town councils. Townspeople tend to be in a majority on the new councils and it is they—rather than country people as before—who are now deciding which parts of the countryside should be developed. And it is often these very councillors who for years past have coveted the broad acres of the old rural districts for housing.

The risk that the countryside will be developed faster than ever before—so far only averted by economic recession—now stands to be heightened by the Government's proposal that councils should buy up land to be developed for housing and lease it to private developers (the Community Land Act 1975). The Government proposes that the increase in land values arising from the development shall be subject to a tax which will be divided between the Exchequer and the local council.

Thus local authorities will have a direct financial incentive to encourage development, especially on farm land which can be bought at current use value and then leased to developers at the market rate for residential land.

Against such pressures what argument can the conservationist pray in aid? He can point to the need for producing more food at home, but even if this were conceded *in toto* it would not serve to maintain the landscape we know—the pattern of hedge and spinney, wood and downland—the kaleidoscope that makes rural England what it is.

For the farmers themselves are destroying this very pattern. In Dorset alone, 11,000 acres of downland—a quarter of the County's total—went under the plough between 1957 and 1972. Hedge removal is currently proceeding at the rate of about 2,500 miles a year, shows no signs of levelling off and as a recent report has shown,[1] this trend is now hitting the stock-rearing and dairy-farming country of the west as well as the arable land of the east.

If these pressures are to be countered effectively, then the townsman must be convinced that the countryside as it is holds something for him, that it is more than space for houses and more than a food factory. The only way this can happen is for the countryside to fulfil a new role as the people's playground in addition to its present functions. Instead of trying to protect the countryside against our fellow men we must turn it over to them, so that their recreation becomes one of its major roles. But this will need no less than a revolution in countryside and urban recreation planning.

The current orthodoxy in recreation assumes three unspoken premises which will need to be overturned. These assumptions are:

(1) that recreation is an optional extra, not a need. This means that equality of access to a range of recreation facilities is not at the moment seen as an aim worthy of the same level of pursuit by local authorities as are, for instance, educational or medical goals;

(2) that the main issue in countryside recreation is protecting the countryside *from* people rather than opening it up for their enjoyment;

(3) that virtually all opportunities for townspeople's informal recreation should be provided in towns.

1. 'New Agricultural Landscapes', by R. Westmacott and T. Worthington for the Countryside Commission, CCP 76, 1974

I shall take each of these assumptions in turn, describing the ways in which they are translated into policy, the implications each will have for the countryside if it continues to hold sway, and the set of assumptions and policies that should replace them.

(1) Recreation — an optional extra rather than a need

Although man's need to escape from the turmoil of cities into the peace of the countryside has been expressed in one way or another ever since cities have existed, very little cash is currently spent on rural recreation by either local or central government. Whereas approximately £3,000,000 were ear-marked by the Government to aid spending on countryside recreation in 1974-5, £3,356,000,000 were allocated to education. As far as local authorities are concerned, recreation falls within non-key sector finance; it tends to be considered last in budget discussions, taking whatever non-key finance is left after other demands have been met. This is borne out by the spending of Nottinghamshire County Council — a not atypical authority — on recreation. In 1974-5 it spent approximately £3,264,000 on leisure services (including the arts, sport and libraries), only about £350,000, or approximately 10 per cent, of which went to providing facilities for informal countryside recreation.

But the 1973 Select Committee of the House of Lords on Sport and Leisure were particularly forthright on the need for recreation to be recognised as a human need. They said: 'The needs of leisure have been seriously underestimated in this country, and the significance of recreational provision has not been appreciated. Too often recreational facilities are treated as an optional extra. The Committee reject this idea and consider that the greatest impediment of all to the development of recreational facilities in this country is the belief that those facilities are not essential. . . . The provision of facilities for the enjoyment of leisure is part of the general fabric of the social services. . . . Society ought to regard sport and leisure not as a slightly eccentric form of indulgence but as one of the community's everyday needs.'[2]

One of the main measures the Select Committee put forward to alter this state of affairs was the imposition of a statutory duty on local authorities 'to secure, in conjunction with other suppliers, that adequate facilities for recreation are provided in their area'. But it is a revolution in local authorities' attitudes — not just a new duty — that is needed to spark off real action in this field, sufficient to change men's attitudes to the countryside. Townspeople must come to see town and country as a dynamic, organic, interdependent whole, the town unable to operate effectively without the countryside from which its people draw their spiritual refreshment.

2. Second Report from the Select Committee of the House of Lords on Sport and Leisure, HMSO 1973

Britain is uniquely well-endowed with rural public footpaths, a historical legacy to be cherished. Many farmers respect the law which requires them to ensure that rights of way on their land are usable—as at Timberton Bottom, Kent (*above*). But where the law is flouted (as *below* where a footpath has been ploughed up), walkers may find their passage barred by anything from shoulder-high wheat to Friesian bulls.

(*Photos: John Topham*)

If local authorities are to recognise countryside recreation as a need, one particular strategy would play a crucial role. This is a drive to secure access to beautiful countryside for all members of the community.

At present about half the population do not have the chance of re-invigorating their spirits in beautiful countryside. On Tyneside, for instance, 61 per cent of the people have no car—according to the 1971 census. Public transport services to the surrounding countryside are very poor, and most of those services that do exist are geared solely to the country population's need to get to towns. It is hardly surprising then that when CPRE asked the team charged with preparing a plan for the Northern region (which will form a framework for the region's structure plans) to look into how the landscape of the North could best be conserved and what plan for countryside recreation would be most appropriate, the team replied that these were not matters that would concern them except in so far as they might relate to the region's economy. The team's steering group is dominated by representatives of the metropolitan councils (Tyne and Wear and Cleveland) as opposed to the rural councils of Northumberland, Durham and Cumbria.

To illustrate the vagaries of access to the countryside I want to look at one particular case: access from the Luton–Dunstable conurbation to an adjacent 52-square-mile tract of the Chilterns Area of Outstanding Natural Beauty (AONB)—a case I believe to be not atypical.

On one summer Sunday in 1969, 98 per cent of the visitors to Dunstable Downs arrived in motor cars. Only 0·5 per cent of the 1,509 groups interviewed by Bedfordshire County Council came by bus. It is easy to see why. There are, at the time of writing, no Sunday bus services crossing this area at all, save one from Dunstable to Whipsnade Zoo; and there is one Sunday service skirting the area along the Icknield Way (see Map on p. 64). It is theoretically possible for someone without a car to get into the area on a Sunday, but the inconvenience, particularly for an elderly person or a young family, of getting to the most attractive part, the Ashridge Estate, is incomparable to the ease of access others enjoy in their motor cars. Like access to countryside at weekends from London as revealed by Law and Perry,[3] you can reach some sort of countryside by public transport if you are prepared to spend several hours getting there and several more getting back, but it is unlikely to be the best, and your choice of destination will be limited.

A Government survey by K. K. Sillitoe in 1966 illustrated the prob-lem at national scale. It showed that approximately three times as many trips to the country were made by car-owning households as by households without a motor vehicle of any kind.[4] Yet at present 48 per cent of households in England and Wales do not have a car. Nor is the problem disappearing. Political and Economic Planning, the research

3. 'Countryside Recreation for Londoners: a Preliminary Technical Study', by S. Law and N. H. Perry, G.L.C. Research Memorandum 267, 1970
4. 'Planning for Leisure: Government Social Survey', by K. K. Sillitoe, HMSO 1969

institute, have estimated that even in the year 2001, on optimistic assumptions about growth, 60 per cent of the population will not own a car and 18 per cent of people will be in non-car-owning households.[5]

The Select Committee on Sport and Leisure came up with a luke-warm response. [We] 'urge strongly that some form of public transport should be provided to take people from urban areas to country parks. This would help the young and old to get into the country parks, which otherwise they might be unable to do.' While an admirable suggestion in itself, this does not go nearly far enough. How many towns have country parks close at hand? And country parks tend to be created in second-rate countryside, certainly not normally in areas designated for their great beauty—national parks and AONB. The Select Committee seem to assume it is only the young and the old who are deprived in this way. Admittedly approximately 90 per cent of the households of elderly people do not have a car, and Sillitoe's work showed the effect of car ownership on the number of recreation trips was especially marked in the case of elderly people; but the non-car-owning popula-tion comprises all sorts of sections of the population—low-income groups, the unemployed, the partially disabled, one-parent families, as well as the more obvious groups. Are we to deprive all these people of easy access to attractive countryside, or at best lay on buses to ferry them to their nearby unprepossessing country park?

Taking the study area—part of an AONB—as an example, what could be done? The solution for the study area might centre around two bus routes, running on Sundays all the year round. One (A on the map) would run from Luton station to Tring station, looping through Luton and Dunstable and then going along the Icknield Way. The other (B) bus would travel through the study area dropping people and picking them up at places where there was access to attractive country-side. It would link with A at C and D.

This would provide the essence of the provision for non-car-owners in the South Bedfordshire conurbation. But it could be supplemented by an attempt to reduce the unattractive traffic congestion car owners create in their pursuit of country pleasures.

I would propose that on summer Sundays and bank holidays only, the two bus systems should be accompanied by a park-and-ride scheme. Motorists would be encouraged to leave their cars in a car park at the foot of Dunstable Downs and to ride round in bus (B). Parking would be heavily restricted elsewhere in the study area, and a heavy advertising campaign would spell out the advantages of park-and-ride. On these summer Sundays, motor vehicles would be banned from the length of road indicated on the map: the road involved, which is heavily congested in summer, goes through very attractive country-side without providing access to settlements.

The whole scheme would ease pressure on the beautiful but

5. 'Personal Mobility and Transport Policy', by Mayer Hillman with Irwin Henderson and Anne Whalley, PEP Broadsheet 542, 1973

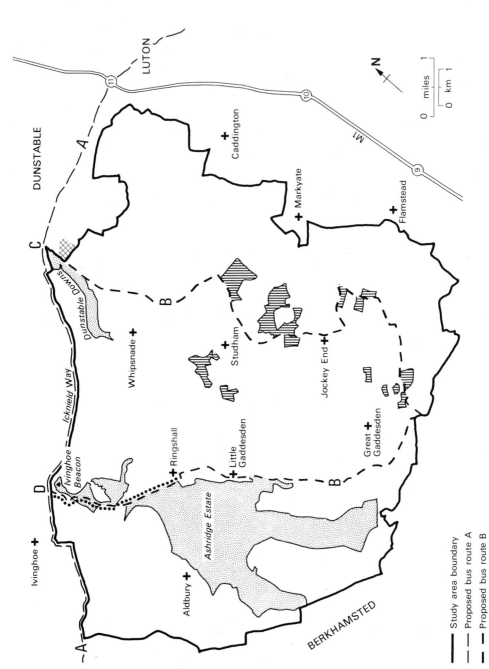

Making the countryside available: the study area.

In summer this quiet country road between Ivinghoe Beacon and Ringshall in Buckinghamshire is choked by visitors' cars. The creation of a motorless zone at holiday time could protect the area's charm and peace for all visitors. *(Photo: Tony Mardell)*

beleaguered Ashridge Estate and Ivinghoe Beacon, while maximising the advantages of an area in which access to open country is already generally very good, though not so good that the judicious securing of access over certain woods would not increase the chances of success of the scheme.

Refinements could include specially designed buses for the very old and the disabled which could pick people up from their homes and put them down at places where there were appropriate facilities.

The cost of a scheme such as this would not be outrageous. A single-decker 55-seater bus would probably be more economical than a mini-bus. If about 27 per cent of the costs were recovered from fares as in the Goyt Valley scheme, eight buses running every Sunday throughout the year giving a 20 minute service would cost about £12,000 a year. The Goyt Valley minibus costs about £2,000 a year, though this is a much less sophisticated scheme than the one I am suggesting.

If townsfolk are to come to know and love the countryside we must break down the barriers which exist for many of them. Contrary to popular belief—according to which all townspeople are monsters out to destroy all they see in the country—many urban citizens are extremely timid about venturing into the countryside and are completely

65

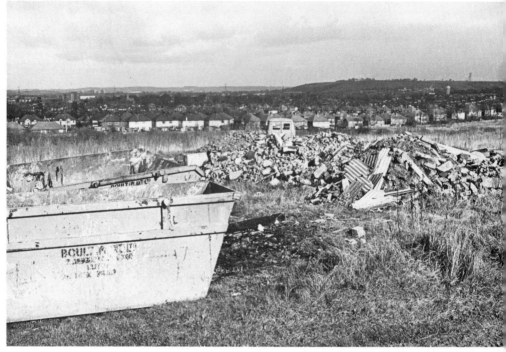

This, believe it or not, is a corner of the Chilterns Area of Outstanding Natural Beauty adjoining Dunstable, Bedfordshire. If used as a car park, this tract of land could play a vital role in a park-and-ride scheme of the kind described in Chapter 4.

(*Photo: Tony Mardell*)

baffled by some of its mysteries. I recently asked some 16-year-olds outside Kidbrooke School in south east London if they would go into a wood in the country in which was pinned a notice 'Keep Out: Trespassers will be Prosecuted'. The reasons they gave for keeping clear highlight this baffled confusion: ''cos something might bite my head off', 'might get electrocuted—things on the ground and that', 'get mangalised', 'never know what's in there—might be a killer'.

Education and interpretation are needed to break down these terrifying Grünewaldian attitudes to forests and to nature.

In ways such as the two I have just described, the vision behind the National Parks and Access to the Countryside Act of 1949 that 'access and facilities for holiday-making and open-air recreation should be . . . available for the public at large, not just for some privileged section or sections of the community'[6] might at last be realised, and the countryside opened to millions of townspeople to whom it might otherwise remain a closed book.

(2) Protecting the countryside from people

The second major assumption underlying current recreation plan-

6. 'National Parks in England and Wales', by John Dower, Cmnd. 6628, HMSO 1945

ning orthodoxy I want to look at is that the main issue is how to protect the countryside *from* people rather than open it up *to* them. This assumption has been translated into policy in the majority of county structure plans published so far.

There are two major ways open to councils of opening up tracts of countryside to the people.

The 1949 National Parks and Access to the Countryside Act empowered local planning authorities to make 'open country' available for public access by making an access agreement, an access order or by acquiring the land. 'Open country' was defined in the Act as land consisting wholly or predominantly of mountain, moor, heath, down, cliff or foreshore. Access orders are rarely used. An access agreement consists of an agreement drawn up between a local planning authority and the 'grantor' (usually the landowner) whereby the grantor agrees to allow the public to wander over the land in question without treating them as trespassers; and the authority usually agrees to make the grantor an annual payment in return and to make bye-laws to prevent damage and provide a warden service to enforce them. Other activities may take place on the land covered by the agreement such as rough grazing, growing trees and shooting since access can, under the terms of an agreement, be temporarily restricted and also because the access is usually of low intensity.

Parliament enacted these access provisions in order to open up to the people large tracts of the most beautiful countryside in England and Wales. As Lewis Silkin, the then Minister of Town and Country Planning, put it during the debate on the 1949 Bill: 'Now at last we shall be able to see that the mountains of Snowdonia, the Lakes, and the waters of the Broads, the moors and dales of the Peak, the South Downs and the tors of the West Country belong to the people as a right and not as a concession. This is not just a Bill. It is a people's charter — a people's charter for the open-air.' In 1949 Parliament provided for Exchequer grants to be paid to local authorities in national parks and ASONB alone in order to encourage these councils in particular to realise Silkin's vision. Grants for access were later extended to all countryside.

The 1968 Countryside Act introduced two changes in this field. First, it greatly widened the definition of 'open country' to which the access provisions apply to include woodland, lakeside and river-bank. Second, it introduced the concept of the country park.

Country parks are typically areas bought up by the local authority and devoted exclusively to high intensity recreation. In contrast to the access provisions, the country park provisions, which have been very much used, were designed for protecting the most attractive and vulnerable countryside from people rather than opening it up to them. They do this by decoying townspeople into places where they cannot do much harm. As such they fulfil a valuable function. But they must be complemented by a recreation strategy embracing the countryside as a whole.

The majority of country parks have been established near to the large centres of population, in line with the nature and role of country parks as expressed in the White Paper 'Leisure in the Countryside', (Cmnd. 2928, 1966), which proposed that country parks should:

(a) make it easier for those seeking recreation to enjoy their leisure in the open, without travelling too far and adding to congestion on the roads;

(b) ease the pressure on the more remote and solitary places;

(c) reduce the risk of damage to the countryside.

The countryside recreation policies of most of the structure plans published to date—including those of Warwickshire, Worcestershire, Herefordshire and East Sussex County Councils—contain proposals for establishing country parks to relieve pressure on the most beautiful, vulnerable areas, but fail to propose, as a complement to this, the securing of access for low intensity recreation to the more beautiful areas.

Imbalance of facilities also underlies non-statutory policies like those of Hertfordshire and Buckinghamshire County Councils. These two councils seem to be trying to keep people away from the lovely Chilterns AONB by diverting Londoners before they reach the Chilterns into country parks like the Colne Valley Regional Park. Whereas the provision of country parks is an excellent thing in itself, neither council goes out of its way to inform Londoners that areas more attractive than these country parks exist beyond them, and certainly neither goes out of its way to open up the more beautiful areas for low intensity recreation.

I suggest the spirit of the 1949 National Parks and Access to the Countryside Act is served only when local authorities attempt to open up countryside of the highest quality as well as providing playgrounds in drabber, if more convenient, parts of the landscape. Unless this is done city folk will never come to love and depend on the countryside as they must if their support is to be mobilised behind protecting rural England in its present form.

To this end special action must be taken in areas of outstanding natural beauty. In accordance with current policy on the location of country parks, there are very few country parks in ASONB, which is as it should be. However, in the vast majority of these areas, there have been no major complementary moves to open up appropriate country for low intensity recreation. Although, as we have seen, Parliament in 1949 singled out ASONB for special treatment as far as access to open country is concerned, of the 5,372 square miles of England and Wales that had been designated as ASONB by 1 January 1973, the 1949 Act had been used to secure access over only 14 square miles.

Yet ASONB are situated near to the urban areas of lowland England and their landscape is usually of the pastoral, undramatic type English people seem to prefer.[7] If a predominantly urban nation is to obtain the maximum benefit from the countryside — and thereby ultimately benefit it — this gulf between Parliament's intentions 26 years ago for ASONB and the way they are interpreted today must be bridged. Councils must change their emphasis from protecting ASONB from the people, to opening them up for their enjoyment.

(3) Opportunities for townspeople's informal recreation

The assumption that virtually all opportunities for townspeople's informal recreation should be provided in towns is inextricably bound up with the second. It bears fruit in the majority of town and country recreation plans. The draft structure plan for the metropolitan area of West Cleveland (Tees-side), for instance, proposes that, 'as a general policy, the development of recreational facilities will be concentrated close to or within the urban areas'. Tragically, the Select Committee on Sport and Leisure also based their thinking on this assumption, and so made matters worse. For their solution to the difficulty that 'dense population, high land prices and intensive lowland farming combine to make public access to the countryside difficult in South East England' rests on this very assumption. They say 'where there is a high urban population the policy should no longer be to divert their recreation towards the countryside but to provide day visit facilities close to the towns'.

While there is a need for even more recreation facilities in towns than are currently provided, it is equally essential for local authorities to pay proper attention to the natural playground of the great outdoors which lies beyond the houses, waiting to be exploited.

One final notion that must be swept aside if townspeople are to have a proper choice of countryside they can visit for recreation, particularly in the ASONB of lowland England, is the supposition that different tracts of land must be zoned for different, single uses. And so we have the country park exclusively for recreation, private woodlands for growing trees and maybe shooting too.

In our small and densely populated country, so many different users of land are demanding space in the countryside that we cannot continue this approach for much longer, and certainly not in the lowlands. We must develop a more sophisticated approach and think in terms of multiple rather than single land use planning. The access agreement,

---

7. As D. Lowenthal and H. C. Prime say (*Geographical Review*, vol 55, 1965) in their review of landscape tastes: 'The English like landscapes compartmented into small scenes furnished with belfried church towers, half-timbered thatched cottages, rutted lanes, rookeried elms, lich gates and stiles'; and: 'What is considered "essentially English" is a calm and peaceful deer park, with slow-moving streams and wide expanses of meadow-land studded with fine trees.'

which can combine low intensity recreation on the one hand with landscape and nature conservation, forestry and shooting on the other in the lowlands, and recreation with any of these activities and hill-farming besides in the uplands, is exactly the sort of tool we should be thinking of using.

The experience of Surrey County Council—one of the very few authorities in the lowlands which takes active steps to open up its most beautiful countryside—shows how the access agreement can work in this sphere.

Surrey have entered into agreements with landowners for access over six areas, ranging from 60 to 804 acres, totalling 1,632 acres, and including substantial tracts of woodland. Under these agreements, the land is managed by the County Council, and this involves supervision by wardens, the making of bye-laws, litter collection and the provision and maintenance of car parks.

To return to the study area, I have suggested some ways in which the provision of a bus service for people without cars and for motorists who have abandoned their cars in the park-and-ride scheme could be combined with opening up specific tracts of woodland for recreation.

It is of course true that some of the townspeople attracted into the countryside will uproot the wild flowers, steal the birds' eggs and otherwise damage what they have come to see. They will also leave gates open and in other ways pose real problems for farmers. To some extent this will be a price to be paid for the hearts and minds of the towns-people; and even the farmer stands to gain politically from a wider public understanding of the difficulties. But there are plenty of ways in which the damage done by the new visitors can be minimised. The most obvious solution is of course education. I want to single out two other measures for special mention.

Firstly, the strategic siting of country parks. The map of country parks in England and Wales shows that, although these tend to be near towns, they are not all located in the best positions to serve their blotting paper function of relieving visitor pressure on the more beautiful areas. As the Select Committee say, 'Existing provision owes more to the energy and initiative of particular planning officers than to a conscious allocation of resources on a national scale.' Some areas are particularly deficient: there are for instance only two country parks sited so as to entice the 512,000 car-owning households of Liverpool and Manchester on their way to the Lake District National Park and Forest of Bowland AONB.

Secondly, motorless zones. Visitors' cars mar the beauty of many rural areas in summer. Up till now, motorless zones have usually required sizeable car parks in an attractive area—at each end of the Peak District's Goyt Valley for instance. In future they should be sited wherever possible outside the area in question. I have already de-

THE NATIONAL TRUST
IVINGHOE BEACON
RESTORATION of DOWNLAND

THE BROAD WHITE SCAR WHICH CAN BE SEEN ON THE SIDE OF IVINGHOE BEACON HAS BEEN CAUSED BY THE CONSTANT PRESSURE OF VISITORS' FEET. TO RELIEVE THIS PRESSURE WHILE AN ATTEMPT IS MADE TO RESTORE THE TURF THE BEACON CAR PARK HAS BEEN CLOSED. VISITORS ARE ASKED TO FOLLOW THE SIGNS TO THE TOP OF THE BEACON FROM STEPS HILL. THE NATIONAL TRUST HOPES THAT THE PUBLIC WILL CO-OPERATE BY KEEPING CLEAR OF THE BADLY WORN AREAS OF THE BEACON.

The erosion of heath and downland at popular beauty spots has become a nation-wide problem. Here, at Ivinghoe Beacon in Buckinghamshire, a comprehensive plan for the area, including a motorless zone, could help to control and distribute the pressure of human feet. *(Photo: Tony Mardell)* scribed how this principle could begin to operate in one particular area (see Map).

So the elements I consider a countryside recreation plan for a particular county or region should contain are:

(i) *A plan for the strategic siting of country parks in the area*

Planners should draw up proposals for the creation of country parks skirting conurbations which would relieve pressure on the most beautiful areas.

(ii) *Policies to secure access for low intensity recreation within the more beautiful areas*

The opening up of countryside of the highest quality by means of access agreements, footpaths and land acquisition is an essential complement to the provision of country parks in less spectacular parts of the landscape.

(iii) *Policies for securing public transport access to the area's countryside for townspeople without cars*

Arrangements should be made for providing public transport access to the country by local authorities running services or encouraging bus companies to do so.

(iv) *Traffic management measures to minimise the damage to beautiful areas of visitors' cars*

I am thinking here in particular of motorless zones and the environmental area concept pioneered by the Peak Park Planning Board whereby different types of traffic from cyclists to lorries are channelled to different routes.[8]

(v) *Proposals for implementing the strategy*

In most parts of the country at least eight public bodies or categories of public body have certain responsibilities in the field of countryside recreation which they interpret in their own peculiar ways. In the Northern region for intance there are the Countryside Commission, local planning authorities, national park planning authorities, the Northumbria and English Lakes Tourists Boards, the Northumbrian and North West Water Authorities, the Northern Sports Council and the Forestry Commission.

There is a need for a framework for the integration of the activities of these bodies so that resources are not duplicated nor public money wasted and so that the facilities that are provided are of such a type and located in such a place as to best serve the countryside recreation needs of the people of the area concerned.

8. As described in *Routes for People*, An Environmental Approach to Rural Highway Planning', Derbyshire County Council and the Peak Park Planning Board, 1972

The Government have already announced their intention of replacing the Sports Councils with new 'Regional Councils for Sport and Recreation'. In regions such as the North the new body might be made the forum in which some of the problems thrown up by the present administrative confusion could be resolved — if its membership is made to reflect all the bodies with real sway over the matters at issue, and if its terms of reference are wide enough. Unfortunately, experience suggests that the opportunity provided by this modest reorganisation will be lost, and the new councils may well end up doing no more than proffering advice blandly from the sidelines. If this happens, it is to be hoped that the county planning authorities or the regional planning authorities will summon up the energy to bring the relevant bodies together on an informal basis.

If there is no revolution in countryside recreation planning, the vast majority of townspeople will be cut off from attractive countryside. And the countryside from which the townsman is excluded will be built over. The GLC policy document 'London: The Future and You' (1973) gives a sense of the way the wind is blowing: [the green belt] 'must become more accessible than it is at present or it will be difficult to justify its inviolability in the future'.

Local government reorganisation has put more townspeople into county halls. If they can be given a lead they have the power to implement the proposals I have outlined, and they will be helped greatly in this if the recommendation the Select Committee made for recreation committees, combining the features of urban recreation committees and countryside committees, are implemented.

But will the new county councils be sparked into action or not? Will the representatives of Luton people, for instance, who now sit at County Hall in Bedford, continue to look within the town boundaries to satisfy their voters' recreation needs? Or will they cast their eyes further afield to the incomparably more beautiful private woodlands in the middle of the county, secure access over them and provide public transport access to them?

The opening up of the countryside to thousands of townspeople to whom it might otherwise remain a closed book is of course something to which anyone whose heart is in countryside conservation might well be expected to aspire. Lewis Silkin, when introducing the 1949 National Parks and Access to the Countryside Bill to the House of Commons, said that if his Bill failed the people would be 'fettered, deprived of their powers of access and facilities needed to make holidays enjoyable. With it the countryside is theirs to preserve, to cherish, to enjoy and to make their own.'

But what has changed since 1949 is that if the people as a whole do not make the countryside their own, no one else will be able to. For if they have not taken it to their hearts in the next few decades, it will cease to exist in the form we know and love it.

5

Land Management and Land Use

C. W. N. MILES

DURING this century the pattern of landownership has undergone a steady, if not dramatic, change. Where, before the First World War, most farms were tenanted, by 1976 more than half of them were occupied by their owners. Over the same period, and as a part of the same trend, the number and size of agricultural estates in private ownership declined, and although today there are many still in existence it is not hard to predict the ultimate disappearance of the private large-scale landowner. Who will take his place is not so easy to forecast.

In the past few years agricultural land has been bought by financial institutions of various kinds as a means of diversifying their property investment portfolios and in the anticipation of a continuing increase in its monetary value. Recently however the value of farms has declined and hopeful entrants into the farmland market like these have been fewer; indeed some, who have held their property for a short time only, have sold, even though at a loss. Other large-scale landowners are charitable and educational establishments, local and government authorities and statutory bodies (usually for very specific purposes) and the National Trust.

Over the years many agricultural landowners have held their farm land as owners, not as occupiers, and their woodlands as owner-occupiers. But since the war the individual owner has increasingly taken land in hand to farm himself and has been engaged therefore in enterprise management as well as in land management, and has been a farmer as well as a forester. Institutional and corporate owners on the other hand have shunned land occupation, either as farmers or foresters, and have chosen to remain investors in, and not users of, land: indeed many seem to prefer not to be involved in woodland at all either as owner or occupier. Separate business organisations have grown up, however, which have specifically invested in forestry to take advantage of the taxation concessions offered. The future may bring a large number of corporate owners into the business side of land occupation in the hope of improving the return on their ownership capital, or perhaps because good farming tenants may be more difficult to find than they were.

If land were to be nationalised there would probably be few occasions upon which the state would actually undertake the business of farming, and all individual farmers would be tenants. Currently some occupiers operate as farming syndicates, of one sort or another, having established themselves with the aid of schemes of varying complexity: currently also some owners are in partnership with their erstwhile tenants and others are seeking means of establishing special partnership, co-ownership or co-operative schemes for the future farming of their agricultural land. The ownership pattern and the occupation pattern of farm land in this country is, by these various means, changing; more quickly at some times, more slowly at others. This change is being brought about mainly by taxation, and by the pressure of an altering financial and social climate.

This very brief survey of the kaleidoscopic pattern of landownership is not immaterial to the theme of this chapter, for it is upon the landowner that much of the responsibility for the shape of the countryside depends. He has a responsibility towards the management of his land which cannot be gainsaid; and that responsibility persists whether the owner be a private individual, an institutional investor, a corporation, a company, a public authority, the National Trust or the state itself. How the responsibility is interpreted varies, and the emphasis which each class of owner puts upon certain elements of it varies also. The responsibility is that of ownership. It is exercised by the management of the investment in land. It is not the same as the responsibility of the occupier whose aim, as a land user, may well be different from the aim of the landowner. The occupier, who is using land as a tool of his trade, is managing an enterprise. Enterprise management and investment management are different things whose objectives are not uniform and may at times be in conflict.

Land ownership

While the landowner has a responsibility to manage and maintain his land as a member of the community, his responsibility as an owner, as opposed to an occupier, is for the maintenance of that fixed equipment of the land which is necessary for its efficient use. Maintenance responsibility covers not only the repair of fixed equipment but also its renewal and replacement so that it may conform to the occupational pattern and use of the land. This means continual change. In the past the pace of change in farming practice was slow. The design and layout of farm buildings were therefore reasonably stable. The buildings themselves, depending upon the local materials available for their construction, were not necessarily durable yet gave to the countryside a form and texture natural to it, for they were of the district.

Today this is not so. Many new buildings are made of universally available materials and to a pre-fabricated design: hence the uniformity and lack of design standards so often apparent in widely separated parts of the countryside. It should however be appreciated that the term 'fixed equipment' covers more than buildings; it covers works of a capital nature, such as roads and bridges and water supplies and drains and ditches and fences and hedges, all of which are man-made or man-induced artefacts. The need for fixed equipment and for its continual maintenance, is not a need of farming alone, it attaches to the occupation and use of land. Thus arises the proposition that it is land occupation, not land ownership, which has the most telling effect upon the appearance of the countryside. While, however, the needs of occupation give rise to the need for investment and change, it is the practice of ownership which satisfies those needs. The needs may spring from occupation, their satisfaction tends to rest in ownership.

The distinction between the demands of land-occupation and those of ownership is often a fine one. While it is necessary for clarity of thought to be able to draw a distinction between the functions of the owner and the occupier (even though they may be carried out by the same person), in the domestic sphere ownership and occupation can often not be prized apart. The eighteenth-century landowner laying out his gardens, grounds and park was functioning as both owner and occupier, for this indeed was what he was.

The responsibility of the landowner can only be fulfilled if he has the resources available and, ultimately, these resources should come from the success of the occupational enterprise. The businesses of farming or forestry, for example, should generate the resources necessary for the maintenance of the fixed equipment of the land on which those businesses are run: indeed, in common with any other viable enterprise, they should give rise to sufficient capital formation to provide for improvement as well as for maintenance. In the hands of the owner the resources which he needs for maintenance and improvement should come from the rent of the land upon which the occupational enterprises are being run. In theory this rent ought to be large enough to provide a return on capital and also for repairs and maintenance and for capital formation. That it is usually not enough to do this is in part because capital values have been distorted to a level above agricultural land values, in part a fault of current rental levels and in part because expenditure out of income on improvements and replacements is only relievable from tax over a ten-year period. Thus it is usually necessary for the owner of land bent upon improving and maintaining the fixed equipment to look beyond the immediate land holding to finance this work.

Since the end of the First World War many agricultural estates have found it possible to provide the capital necessary for maintenance and improvement by re-organising holdings and selling the surplus assets thrown up by this process. Some estates have been able to improve land and buildings by borrowing money on favourable terms and repaying the loans thus established by taking advantage of the effect of inflation on values and rentals. In many cases also capital available outside the agricultural portion of the estate has been realised by the sale of valuable building land or of other investments. In whatever way the money has been found the process, which includes the amalgamation of holdings and the realisation of estate assets, has had a continuing effect upon the landscape.

A viable and prosperous countryside over which ownership responsibilities are properly fulfilled is usually devoted to a wide diversity of uses, some more permanent than others, which may range from farming and forestry to manufacturing and extractive industry. Some of these uses will have been brought about by the very need of the landowner to acquire the resources necessary for maintenance and improvement.

Land management

While the landowner has a responsibility towards his property, it is in fulfilling such a responsibility, or trying to, that the art of land management is exercised. In this context it should be realised that the management concerned is that of the ownership enterprise not of the occupational enterprise. Sometimes the owner-occupier, who is himself using his property for commercial purposes, fails to realise the distinction between the management of the ownership enterprise in land and the management of the occupational enterprise in the same land.

Management of the ownership enterprise is concerned, as already detailed, with investment in and the maintenance of the fixed equipment of the land. The extent to which this management function is, or ought to be, exercised is controlled in turn by the size of the unit, the terms of the occupation of that unit and the pressure of demand for the land for alternative uses. Management is therefore concerned with the allocation of resources and, once that has been decided, with their use. The resources being the resources of ownership, not the resources of occupation. Ownership management can, and certainly should, take a longer view than enterprise management. In exercising his functions, the owner of the land, standing apart from the occupier, should find himself able, where necessary, to resist the temptations of the moment; to refuse, for example, an over-risky and short-term investment which, to the occupier, appears essential. Where the two management functions rest in the one person then he must be prepared to recognise this fact.

Farming, like any trade, responds to the immediate market; land management has to take a view over a longer period. Perhaps indeed this is why the enterprise of forestry is usually part of the owner's function.

Enterprise management on the other hand is the day-to-day running of a business which may be using the land in one way or another for the purpose of profit. The management of this enterprise is often one of quick decision making and of an ability to anticipate the market and to switch short-term resources. In this business long-term planning is difficult, even sometimes inappropriate. Enterprise management, particularly in farming, can have a rapid effect on the appearance of the countryside; seasonally by a changing crop rotation; longer term by changing from stock farming to arable or vice versa and even longer term by affecting the fixed equipment of the land, but this latter is really an ownership as opposed to an occupational function. For example, the wholesale removal of hedges to make possible the use of large machines in arable country, and to reduce the increasing cost of hedge maintenance, is essentially an enterprise management decision though it is one which may be restrained by the decisions of ownership management. If the decisions are to be made by separate persons then enterprise management and ownership management may enter a conflict—the resolution of which may depend as much upon the personality of the decision makers as upon the terms and conditions under which the land concerned is let. Where the conflict of decision lies between the ownership and occupational functions of one individual then, unless higher authority intervenes, he must grapple with himself.

It must however be acknowledged that decisions will be influenced by the availability of grant aid and the push and pull of tax policy. Such financial incentives may mis-shape a decision.

In the eyes of the nation ownership is less sacrosanct today than it used to be and the ownership of land is regarded with greater suspicion than the ownership of many another asset, possibly because its functions are misunderstood and because they are exercised by comparatively few people. Little distinction is made by the public between the role of the landowner and that of the land occupier. The farmer or the forester is usually assumed to be the owner and in full charge. Furthermore over the last few years an awareness has spread that the delights of the countryside do in a sense belong to all of us. The owner and the occupier of land are aware that they cannot run their businesses without regard to the public good and to the climate of public opinion. The need to look beyond the immediate elements of ownership and occupation make the exercise of their respective management duties that much more complicated, for their decisions cannot now be solely based upon immediate or future private benefit or cost but must often be taken in relation to probable public benefit or cost. Many a large-scale landowner has so exercised his trust, even if in something of a patriarchal way; others have signally failed to do so. However, as the size on the ownership unit decreases so the responsibilities of the individual owner lessen. He can affect less by his decisions; and the financial sacrifices which he may be prepared to make for the sake of the landscape are not balanced by financial gains elsewhere. This raises two points which are discussed later on, namely the possible need for greater public control of rural land use and development, and for compensation to be available to those whose enterprise management is curtailed by that control.

While large-scale landowners remain it is possible to hope for the maintenance of a wide concern for the countryside generally. But the investor in land, whether he be a private owner or a corporate body, must be expected to allow his concern for the countryside to be, to some extent, subservient to the needs of finance. Unless money is available he cannot fulfil his ownership responsibilities, and is unlikely to place such heavy restrictions upon the enterprise management of his tenants that the rental value of the land in the open market is reduced. Similarly, of course, an occupier is unlikely to place such restrictions upon his own enterprise as will cause his income to fall substantially. It is self-evident that the objects of ownership and the objects of occupation will affect management policies. Particular owners will be prepared to put restrictions upon occupational enterprises because these are in line with their main objectives. Statutory undertakers may well restrict the use which tenants can make of their land to avoid adverse effects on the land use which is their primary function. The National Trust similarly modifies its management to attune with its essentially conservationist objectives. Such owners accept that their specific objectives can in certain circumstances reduce the value of their land; one could hope that this reduction in value does not disappear but is transferred to another asset, perhaps a clean water supply or a heightened public appreciation of the countryside. Yet other owners with other objectives may, by fulfilling those objectives, reduce the value of their land and in so doing transfer that reduction elsewhere. Defence lands, for example, used as tank training grounds, will have much of their value transferred to the unquantifiable asset of a nation secure from invasion.

These transfers of value are often neither appreciated nor understood by the public at large who see merely an inaccessible or devastated countryside or just one whose pattern of use is unacceptable to the not-understanding eye.

Regrettably this hope just expressed is not always realised, for management, in destroying one value, may indifferently fail to transfer it fully elsewhere. Thus a good supply of water may be obtained not only at the expense of other land uses but also to the detriment of the landscape. Pylons striding across a close countryside bring their own good in return for a diminution of some land value but for a diminution of landscape value too. Good land management on the other hand can lessen the impact of intrusions into the countryside, and where applied with care and feeling can sometimes entirely eliminate it. Statutory undertakers, however, governed by limited resources and limited terms of reference, are sometimes inhibited from taking the broad view of land management and of their responsibilities beyond the confines of the particular land use to which their immediate powers are directed. There are signs that this attitude is softening, particularly in the case of bodies responsible for the maintenance of water supplies whose new lakes and reservoirs are today frequently imaginatively conceived and managed.

Whatever its objectives land management tends to be a personal thing which often cannot be effectively, nor with understanding, exercised at a distance. The danger which lies in large-scale ownership is that of impersonal management unsympathetically applied from far away, and by rule rather than by an intimate knowledge of the enterprise and of the needs of the occupiers of the land. Impersonal management by rule might precisely regulate the countryside, but might do so with a suburban mind and therefore fail; for effective protection and conservation of so delicate an idea as landscape needs a deep understanding of nature and of the countryman himself upon whose continuing co-operation success must depend.

Should the pattern of ownership change then the pattern of countryside management may change also. If landownership moves into the hands of the nation, land management might be exercised more expansively (and possibly more expensively) with an eye generally on countryside use and development, but such management at the same time could be dangerously distant and impersonal. If, on the other hand, the number of farming owner-occupiers increases, then it may well be that the nation should accept some responsibility to exercise prudent management superior to that exercised by the owner-occupier, lest he fail to appreciate the need for proper land management as well as for proper enterprise management.

The effect of taxation and social policy

At the moment of writing a Labour Government's policy for land is not yet on the statute books; however estate duty is being supplanted by a capital transfer tax and a future wealth tax remains a distinct possibility. Social policy leans more heavily towards the redistribution of wealth through capital taxation and is likely to be effective. It is not possible to argue, because no research has been done, that the owner-occupied farm is a more or a less efficient unit than one which is tenanted. In consequence no argument against the break-up of large estates can hold water on efficiency grounds; but is agricultural efficiency the sole criterion of good management? The answer surely must be that it is not. Good management of the countryside should aim not only at the business-like efficiency of the enterprises run on it but also at the happiness and well-being of the inhabitants, and the maintenance of a landscape able to delight, or at least not to offend, the nation as a whole.

If capital taxation on the present and proposed pattern takes full effect, then it would seem that the ownership structure of the land is going to change and change quickly. Such a change will initially mean the break up of the large privately-owned agricultural estate and the dissipation of much of the capital which stands behind it and which is necessary for the maintenance of a prosperous countryside: but as such estates shatter they will re-settle into another pattern of ownership. It is this new pattern which matters. In the first instance it may be that the new owners will be the erstwhile tenants, so that, for example, a 5,000-acre estate may become ten 500-acre farms all in separate ownerships. Under the new structure of capital taxation it is unlikely that a single estate will pass into the hands of a new private owner, but it could pass into the hands of an institution as an investment or, ultimately, into the hands of the State. In the meantime, the number of owner-occupiers is likely to increase. But farming is an expensive business (and land has been valuable) so that the next owners are themselves likely to be hit by capital taxation until there comes about a further dissipation of ownership into yet smaller units. As has been pointed out above, the dispersal of ownership management in this way could result in a lesser overall concern for the landscape which would call for greater state control.

The future must not be left to care for itself and more effective control should be discussed now, and exercised as soon as possible. Landscape control might be in the hands of the planning authorities, but they are usually urban-based and some leavening of their make-up would be necessary. There are at the moment many separate authorities concerned with the use and management of the countryside whose functions sometimes conflict. The Ministry of Agriculture's prime concern is with food production, the planning authority's with some control of rural development, the Department of the Environment's, as a part of its functions, with landscape, nature, recreation and access: an authority responsible for landscape control would need to have ·powers to reconcile, and ultimately to over-ride, conflicting views; in the meantime perhaps a start could be made by giving the Ministry of Agriculture more responsibility for conservation and for encouraging positive acts of landscape improvement, perhaps in some way linked to its control over certain grants-in-aid. If estates now in single private ownership moved into larger hands, such as those of an institution, land use could continue to be exercised by tenants responsible only for the maintenance of their working capital and of their particular enterprise and ownership management would remain divorced from enterprise management. Capital taxation would of course hit these tenants, but they could occupy larger farms before it did so than they ever could as owner occupiers.

It is necessary to realise that about half the farms in this country are already run by their owners and that the capital taxation envisaged will adversely affect all those other than the very smallest. The effect will be, within a generation at the longest, to cause the break-up of these farms into smaller units with the consequent management problems already hinted at.

Indeed as farms shrink in size the new units created will need houses and buildings. Are local authorities to provide them and at what cost? Is it really possible to envisage a new countryside of small holdings peppered with new houses and buildings or of open fields worked from the villages, as of old?

Forestry

Little has been written above about the future shape of forestry in Great Britain. A number of taxation concessions given to woodland occupation and ownership have, over the past decades, encouraged private investment in forest enterprises, but here again proposed capital taxation, unless it is modified, must bring about a radical change of view. Ownership in forestry is likely to change even more rapidly than ownership in agriculture. In the main the institutional investor has not shown great interest in the ownership of woodlands nor in their exploitation and it is unlikely that such bodies will now be persuaded differently.

The effect of wealth and capital transfer taxes on private enterprise in woodlands must be either that the woodlands are abandoned to dereliction or that the whole pattern of forest management changes to encourage a rapid felling of hardwoods and their replacement by softwoods grown on as short a rotation as possible. If these taxes are altered so that they do not impinge on growing timber then the situation would be different again and private investment in traditional forestry still possible. It may be, on the other hand, that woodland ownership will move extensively out of private hands into specially constituted forestry companies whose enterprise management must be heavily commercial, for they would be in the business to make money or, more likely, the Forestry Commission would become the owner of most of the woodlands. The Commission has, in the recent past, shown commendable interest in the amenity aspect of its woodlands, as well as in their commercial success and, from this angle, an extension of the Forestry Commission's ownership and occupation of woodlands may not be a matter of great public concern. It is worth suggesting, however, that a variety of ownerships and of enthusiasms is of benefit to the woodland industry and even more to the maintenance of a varied countryside, and also that individual woodland occupation and management gives employment and interest to a large number of people.

The need for a policy for land use

It is possible to envisage therefore a new pattern of ownership of farm land and of woodland; the former being either one of owner-occupation scattered between blocks of institutionally owned land or, ultimately, of municipally or nationally owned estates farmed by tenants; the latter being in the main ownership of woodland by the state through the Forestry Commission. Whether the farm is owner-occupied or tenanted, capital taxation would seem to mean that the individual farms will themselves be much smaller than they are at present, being mainly family farms worked by family labour with few paid employees. Taxation itself would ensure that any farmer who prospered exceedingly would soon be cut down to size.

It is not possible however to build a prediction of the future structure of land ownership and land occupation on a foundation consisting solely of current taxation policies, for if ownership and occupation do not pay, then there is nothing left to tax. The countryside will not be covered by a multitude of small farm-holdings nor, on the other hand, by wide ranging mechanised farms of several thousand acres, nor by extensive and well-managed woodlands, nor by country parks and picnic sites, nor will it be prosperous, even though controlled, if there is no consistent strategy for land use. There is a desperate need for a well spelled-out and accepted policy for British agriculture and British forestry which is not subject to frequent change.

The use of land for productive purposes is of itself an operation which takes time to be effective, and which can be planned ahead. Investment in land and in the fixed equipment necessary for its proper use, must be long term. Production lines cannot be switched quickly and inexpensively as they may be in a factory. Crops and stock take time to grow and to mature. It may be difficult, but should not be impossible, for government to formulate a policy for British agriculture, even though it may to an extent depend upon the agreed policy of our EEC partners which must in the longer term be dictated by the world's demand for food. This will not lessen. Land ownership and land occupation cannot function in a vacuum and only when there is a defined and agreed policy for agriculture and for other rural land uses in this country, can the landowner (whoever he may be) and the land user properly plan for the future. Only if such a plan can be formulated will it be possible to assess the future shape of the countryside and of the rural landscape.

In the past a policy for land use was often individually formulated by the larger landowner, and perhaps copied by his neighbours, the object of which was to maintain the viability of the countryside for the benefit of present and future generations. Today country planning is not effective if ownership and occupation are to be only short term and in any event cannot be effective in isolation, for, despite our rifts and disagreements, we are indeed one nation in one world.

Public management control

It has been pointed out that there is a distinction between ownership management and enterprise management and that as, and when, the number of large-scale private landowners dwindles, then the number of owner-occupiers may increase; alternatively as the number of private landowners gets fewer the number of public or corporation landowners may increase. The owner-occupier must, in that event, recognise his responsibilities as an owner as well as an occupier and this he may find difficult to do. Impersonal owners may themselves leave in the hands of their tenants much of the erstwhile ownership responsibility, for they are not on the spot and may exercise their management at a distance. In either event therefore it is suggested that the strong arm of ownership management is weakening and if not only a viable countryside but also an acceptable one, is to be maintained, the state, or county or district councils, may have to take over ownership, or at any rate certain powers of management and direction which they have previously eschewed, and perhaps exercise them through a specially constituted agency.

These powers, which would apply particularly in the sphere of conservation and amenity, might have to put some restriction upon the enterprise of the land occupier, and, being exercised for the good and benefit of the general public, would transfer value from land to people. It would be inequitable to force such a transference without compensation. If the landowner puts an effective restriction on his tenant's enterprise, he already pays for it in reduced rents. In essence if the state, as even part landowner, places such a restriction on enterprise then the state should make good the loss. We must all pay for that which we snatch. Compensation could be in different forms, offered perhaps as a capital sum for the usurpation of rights, or as an annual payment so long as the restriction lasts, or as a grant of the cost of positive action necessary for the preservation or enhancement of amenity. In this way encouragement could be given to the planting of small areas of woodland or to the maintenance of rough uncultivated lands or to the special selection and siting of farm buildings.

Control of this nature is more than mere planning control (which of itself should now apply more rigorously than it has done), although it is a form of it, and would indeed extend the imposition of restriction on the use of land beyond the sphere of ownership into the sphere of occupation, thus, and to an extent, restricting enterprise. It would be a matter for discussion as to how far such control might extend; some already exists in the form of action which can be taken to prevent the spread of animal diseases, to prevent pollution of water supplies or to prevent maltreatment of livestock kept under intensive conditions.

In the formulation of any policy for the control of land use, such as of agriculture and forestry, a number of questions must remain unanswered, but not unput. Modern farming and forestry, like other industries, depend upon the availability of resources and upon the demands which the nation makes for the alternative use of such resources. For example, as and when fossilised fuels become even more expensive, and their availability less, the nation will not merely have to control their use but also to decide indeed where they are to be used. Upon such decisions the future pattern of the landscape depends.

Labour

Over many years there has been a drift of labour away from the land. This has taken place as farm wages have slowly increased and as farming itself has moved from a labour-intensive to a capital-intensive industry. It is doubtful if a dramatic increase in the agricultural wage would pull the labour back on to the land, for the drop in numbers has taken place largely through natural wastage and by a failure of farmers to replace men as they left. There has indeed been nothing to prevent the individual farmer offering high wages to keep a labour force of the size he requires. A smaller work force has emerged because machinery has to an extent been substituted for labour and been cheaper to use. It may be however that, if scarce energy restricts the use of machinery, men will have to come back on to the farms. Will they, and in what circumstances and subject to what conditions? If capital taxation causes a reduction in farm size then it may be that all the labour necessary can be provided by the family unit. It may indeed be that a scarcity of machinery as well as the impact of capital taxation will cause the size of the average holding to fall. From our present viewpoint it is difficult to envisage an increase in the number of farm workers. Cottages once occupied for farming have, in their thousands, been sold off the farm. An increase in the farm labour force would bring with it a demand for more housing and, in the light of present pressures, such housing is more likely to be provided by, and demanded from, the state than from the individual farmer or landowner. Such a demand could revitalise our dying villages and change the shape of the countryside again. It seems unlikely to happen.

Conclusion

This chapter has attempted to show that by and large it is not the structure of land ownership which imposes a pattern on the countryside but the structure of land occupation. Farming is a business. Landowning is a business which is dependent upon land use, and the prosperity of land use in turn depends upon the maintenance of a consistent government policy for all land uses including agriculture, forestry, recreation, mineral extraction, reclamation and development.

It would seem that the structure of ownership is likely to undergo a change towards a greater number of smaller ownership units (and almost certainly smaller farms) in which occupation and ownership merge. It is not always recognised that these two functions exist, particularly when they rest in one person, nor is it always easy for a farmer to distinguish between his responsibilities as occupier and those as owner. Confiscatory capital taxation could indeed shatter both the present ownership and occupational structures and within the next 50 years all land could be state owned and land use exercised only through leases. Whoever owns the land has responsibilities towards it which entail continually investing capital in its permanent equipment in order to enable profitable occupation to persist, a need to conserve the countryside and to look after the well-being of those who live in it. In other words land needs managing. The time is probably coming when, in any event, stricter control will be necessary by the state in the field of management because many of the functions of management which used to be exercised by the landowner are, with his demise, no longer exercised by anybody. Such control by the state may well extend beyond the field of planning into the field of enterprise management and this could mean the imposition of restrictions on certain methods of land use and the imposition of positive requirements of countryside management. If these restrictions and requirements are to be imposed the nation should be prepared to pay for them, gladly.

6

Agriculture in a Time of Inflation

TRISTRAM BERESFORD

There is one thing of which all men are equally ignorant, and that is the future.

IN this chapter I shall consider the recent growth and present state of the national farm, and attempt to predict the changes we may expect in the foreseeable future, and the effect these changes may have on the countryside. Although national agricultural policy does not distinguish between farming in England, and farming in the rest of the United Kingdom—Wales, Scotland and Northern Ireland—the English national farm has certain characteristics that are different in degree from the Welsh and Scottish farms, and from the agriculture of Ulster. I shall briefly describe these differences, and my tentative conclusions will apply more to the English scene than to that of the others. I shall deal only cursorily with the hills and uplands, since they are the subject of a separate chapter.

The last 40 years of agricultural history in these islands, and in particular the three decades that have elapsed since the passing of the first Agriculture Act in 1947, have been a period of unparalleled growth and development. The phenomenon—for it is nothing less than that—is usually spoken of as the Agricultural Revolution. The term is misleading. It implies upheaval, convulsion, radical change. But to date nothing in the nature of a mutation has occurred; rather what has occurred is a progressive release of latent powers, the flowering of a latent talent, an impressive response to need and opportunity, a *renaissance*. There has been nothing like it since the upsurge of emulative endeavour released by the enclosure movement of the eighteenth century; and what has happened under our noses in our own day has been reinforced by the adventitious aids of science and technology, so that not only has the rural scene been transformed—not always for the better—but behaviour and life-styles have evolved also. The farmer is no longer a peasant, but a capitalist. The farm worker is no longer a labourer, but a craftsman. As for the landowner, though he is now the weakest party of the three, he is no longer a sleeping partner in the industry, but has become a participant.

Not that the process of change has been continuous and unbroken.

As we might expect, there have been ups and downs; good weather years and bad weather years; periods when the net product index has been static; periods when it has soared. It is only on graph paper that trend lines are consistent. In practice, an industry as complex and diverse in structure as agriculture needs its rest periods, its pauses to draw breath, its times for recovery and consolidation before it again moves forward. And these the political and economic history of the post-war period have provided — not only for farmers but for secondary industry also, although their recuperative intervals have seldom co-incided. In general, times that are good for industry are bad for farmers, and vice versa. The nation's need is often the farmer's opportunity. However, in spite of Stop–Go, the underlying trend has been upward. Investment has provided for expansion; expansion has provided for investment — with the result that the United Kingdom, with a population of 56 million, has become about two-thirds self-supporting in supplies of temperate food. From being a labour-intensive occupation, with a million and a quarter people working on the land, our agriculture has become one of the most mechanised in the world, highly capitalised, with fewer than half a million whole-time workers, more than half of them farmers and farmers' sons and daughters. From these trends, the surge in output and the fall in manpower, is derived the assertion that, in terms of output a head, the record of British agriculture is as good as that of most growth industries in the country.

A Cambridgeshire landscape in 1975, bleak, featureless and an ecological desert — but highly productive of a limited range of crops. (*Photo: John Topham*)

These considerable changes have come about through a combination of favourable factors: greater technical proficiency on the part of farmers and farm workers; greater security of tenure, at the expense of the landowning interest; a massive increase and improvement in the resources at the disposal of agriculture, not the least of which has been the contribution of research, development, education, information and advisory services. In short, a larger volume of national resources is now devoted to food production than ever before; and arguments that arise from time to time about increasing still further the percentage of national self-sufficiency in temperate food supplies invariably turn on the cost/benefit equation—whether it is sound to commit an even larger share of scarce resources to agriculture than is devoted at the moment. It is a difficult question to resolve, because farming gives a low return on capital, and resources, once committed, cannot easily be withdrawn; and also because fluctuations in the terms of trade, and in supplies of primary products on the world market, can rarely be predicted with confidence.

Underlying the changes that have taken place in the scale, tempo and techniques of farming in the last 40 years, we may detect a series of changes in public attitude to the land. It is the latest of these attitudes that concerns us most, since it will have a certain bearing on the shape of things to come. But those that preceded it are not without significance, because they have left their mark on the present and are responsible for much of our present thinking.

During the war, and in the immediate post-war years, the land was regarded as a life-line, no less than the seas around our shores. Work on the land was tantamount to national service; and the interest of the farmer and that of the nation went broadly hand in hand, so that the Agriculture Act was passed without division through both Houses of Parliament, and few people, with the exception of notables like Geoffrey Crowther and Stanley Evans, had any doubts that digging for victory and digging for solvency were the proper policies for an impoverished Britain, even though they cost money. During the Churchill–Macmillan era, the attitude changed. The land came to be regarded as an investment, like any other business; the farmer, as a business-man—like his fellow entrepreneurs on the Grand Council of what was then the Federation of British Industries. It was a commercial era; the nation's standard of living was rising fast; economic growth was an aim to be pursued at all costs, a good in itself which we accepted uncritically as part of the conventional wisdom. It was during this time that many of the features of agribusiness imprinted themselves on the landscape: functional buildings, functional field-sizes, functional cropping. Efficient farmers could be sure of earning a steady, if modest, return on landlord and tenant capital; and some who were tenants found it profitable to buy their farms and turn themselves into owner-occupiers. But as the nation became wealthier, and prosperity more widespread, so demands on national wealth began to pile up. Prices rose, and as inevitably happens, the quality of goods and services declined. Agriculture too went into the mass-production business. Factory farming had arrived.

In the post-Macmillan era, the land became, for many people, a hedge against inflation. The scramble for security forced up the price. The supply of land was limited; demand was strong; and in the last year of the Heath government good arable land was making over £1000 per acre—about three times its value as a strictly agricultural proposition. The fact that farmers too were in the market for parcels of land with a view to enlarging their holdings; the fact that some of them, having sold land for urban development, had hot money to invest in order to defer payment of capital gains tax; the fact that prospects for most branches of agriculture were brighter, now that the United Kingdom (however disunited over it) had acceded to the Treaty of Rome—these were contributory causes of the steep rise in the value of freehold and tenanted land. But the prime cause was uneasiness in the stock market, the whiff of impending change, the something in the air that communicated itself to the nose of the nervous investor, and told him that now was the time to get out of equities and into assets that were tangible and inflation-proof. The land had become a raft, an ark in the rising flood. The rush to buy was reminiscent of the Florida real estate boom in the 1920s. Foremost among the bidders were the intitutional buyers. Some owner-occupiers, who had bought their holdings a few years earlier, took their capital profit, sold out to institutional landlords and stayed on as their tenants. This was known as lease-back.

We are now within sight of the present, when, for a variety of reasons, the public attitude to land—or should I say the ideological one—is changing once again. But whereas, up to 1973, the changes we have discussed followed a logical progression, each in turn shading off into the other, much that has happened since 1973 has made it exceedingly difficult to extrapolate from past experience. It is as though, in the Heath era, we came to the end of the road we know.

1973 was a watershed. We reached the crest, and began our descent into . . . what? The promised land? A land without promise? Let us say, into unfamiliar territory. The tomorrow we unconsciously took for granted, expecting it to be a continuation of today, became less and less predictable as the months went by. That markets would behave as we thought they would, that cargoes would come to port and be discharged on time, that wheels would go on turning, goods would go on flowing, growth would go on growing; that the terms of trade would ease and inflation be checked; that the law of probability would assert itself and Britain's luck would turn . . . one by one these expectations were disappointed. And perhaps it was not bad luck anyway; but a moment of truth. 'The fault, dear Brutus. . . .'

The oil embargo, and the four-fold increase in the price of crude—apart from heralding a decisive shift in the balance of world power—reminded us that there are built-in components in the structure of a high and rising standard of living that we are apt to overlook. One of them is energy. Another is food. Both, for as far back as memory takes us, have been abundant and cheap—except in wartime. Now, suddenly, they were neither. Economic growth, and all the material benefits it confers, was found to have depended, not on our technical skills, not on pride of place in the pecking order of the world, but on access to a gratuitous flow of energy. Now, all at once, the supply was found to be finite, threatened, precarious. First-class passengers on the deck of a luxury liner, we were suddenly confronted with trouble in the engine-room.

It was a moment of truth indeed—for farmers too. The growth of the national farm, that has raised output to three times the pre-war level, has been achieved not only by expertise, but by consumption of energy on a rising scale. As a direct consumer of oil, the national farm uses more than two million tons a year—two per cent of net imports. But there is more to it than that. An industrial agriculture needs lubricants, paints, detergents, plastics, synthetic rubber, fibres, nitrogenous fertilisers, insecticides, weedkillers—all products of the petro-chemical industry. It is also a consumer of steel, electricity and transport, which in turn depend on oil. Nor is oil the only source of imported energy entering into agricultural technology. There is, for example, the energy supplied by animal feed—protein as well as carbohydrate—anchovies, soya, maize and other coarse grains. As supplies dwindled, and prices rose (in line with other raw materials like coal, phosphates and potash), the farming industry was faced with a huge new bill of costs. In a single year, the price of these inputs rose by more than £500 million.

Higher raw material costs, whether for oil, coal or their derivatives, or for protein and coarse grains, are in the main attributable to an increase in effective demand on the world market. Sub-average harvests in the USSR, China, India; and harvest failures in semi-arid zones like the Sahelian belt, have helped to run down stocks in the surplus-producing countries—USA, Canada, Australia. But the state of imbalance in grain and feedstuffs may well prove to be temporary. There is normally a supply response to high prices. When wheat is good, farmers may be relied upon to grow more of it, if they can. In the United States, between 30 and 40 million acres of marginal land have been taken out of the land bank and brought back into cultivation. A year or two of above-average harvests in the USA and elsewhere should be enough to bring prices down—how far down will depend on the strength of world demand for animal protein, which is produced by feeding grain to livestock. But whatever may happen in the commodity markets in the next ten years, the lesson to be learnt from the events and the aftermath of 1973 is not so much economic as geo-political. The *Have-not* nations have taken a leaf out of the capitalists' book.

Though in 1972, agriculture consumed only 4 per cent of UK energy, the industry has grown steadily more capital-intensive in recent years. Machines—mostly oil dependent—have replaced men at an increasing rate.

(Photos: National Farmers Union and Godfrey Bell)

Hitherto dominated by the *Have* nations, they are now asserting them-selves. They have achieved monopoly status through co-operation. They have learnt to use their bargaining strength in world trade. They can dictate terms. With a steadily growing world population, they look like being in a seller's market for years to come.

For Britain, the rise of the Arab World has had two immediate consequences. In the first place, it has added several billion pounds a year to our import bill. It has meant that the kind of products we make in this country buy only three-quarters as much as they did of the goods we need to import from the rest of the world. This is a measure of the worsening of the terms of trade and of the weakness of the pound. In the second place, it has brought economic growth to a stop. Getting growth going again will depend on our success in mastering inflation — something we cannot do in isolation, for other nations are afflicted too, some more seriously than we are.

Inflation is not just rising prices. Rising prices are a symptom, not a cause of inflation. To understand the effect inflation has on an econ-omic activity like farming, a brief digression is necessary.

Adam Smith believed that the natural effort of every individual to better his own condition, when suffered to exert itself with freedom and security, is so powerful a principle that it is capable of carrying society to wealth and prosperity. His economic commonwealth consisted of a multitude of persons each seeking his own self-interest and in so doing unwittingly furthering the public good — thus promoting an end that was no part of his intention. The model served well in the eighteenth century, when Britain was embarking on the productive spree to which historians have given the name of the Industrial Revolution. Growth was an excitement in the air at that time. New frontiers beckoned. Freedom had been regained. Hanoverian security was a foundation on which it was possible to build for the future. Conditions were such that all who wished could participate in the productive process, and by that process the wealth of the nation would be generated. The wealth of the nation in theory would be shared by all, both for present enjoyment — that is consumption — and for future betterment, which would prompt the desire to save. In practice, however, self-interest proved to be a stronger passion than Adam Smith had allowed for. The wealth of the nation, instead of being common to all, became the spoils of the few. For so long as consumption remained the privilege of the rich, there was enough wealth left over to divert to savings. But in the long run, things change. The privilege of the few becomes the right of others; ultimately the right of all. The present age of mass-consumption is the expression of that right. In the course of a generation — the period that has elapsed since the end of the Second World War — we have witnessed the barely controlled, progressively less controllable explosion of mass demand — a claim on the wealth of the nation by all who are able to enforce it, as most of us are. The result is inflation. Because supply can never be equal to demand on this scale, some claimants, the weaker, are driven to the wall. The rest of us can satisfy our wants only if we resort to the dubious expedient of raiding the future—drawing on savings, running down investment, borrowing on the security of tomorrow's assets (such as North Sea oil), living at the expense of our creditors. Thus we see that inflation, though malignant in effect, may be no more than the expression of a desire for more equal shares in the common weal, a demand for more slices than there are in the cake.

Agriculture, the business of which is to produce food and fibre from the soil, is affected by inflation in more ways than one. In the most obvious way it suffers, as all industry suffers, from the augmentation of its costs. This is perhaps the least damaging effect, because people must eat, and if the farmer's costs go up, consumers in one way or another will have to pay the price. Whether or not the farmer is ever fully *recouped* for his increases in costs is a matter for endless argument between the farmers' unions and the Government, and (in EEC) between the COPA (Comité des Organisations Professionelles Agricoles) and the Commission. But as a rule, so long as agricultural output goes on rising, and so long as expansion is financed by adequate investment, the nation need not worry about where tomorrow's food will come from. It is when output stagnates, and savings are inadequate to finance growth, that anxiety arises, or should arise.

When the Wilson government came to power in the spring of 1974, this critical point had been reached in certain sections of the national farm—in particular in the livestock sector, which produces about two-thirds of total farm output. Determined to safeguard the nation's milk and meat supply, the government resurrected the device of consumer subsidies which, although they have serious drawbacks in an inflationary situation, are a means of doing two things at once: they supplement the farmer's returns, and stimulate consumer demand by making food cheaper than it really is. This remedial device was forced on government, not only by TUC pressure, but by the predicament of pig, beef and dairy farmers, many of whom were unable to make both ends meet. They had been exhorted to increase production. They had done so. Livestock numbers were at an all-time high. Unfortunately the market was weak because economic growth had stopped. It was unable to absorb a marginal excess of supply; and prices collapsed. Some farmers were ruined. Many lost heart. In the hills and uplands, where livestock farming at the best of times is a hazardous occupation, there was much distress. Government action was essential, and subsidies were reintroduced in an attempt to restore confidence. But because inflation has more pernicious effects in agriculture than the distortion of cost–price relationships, subsidies are unlikely to be the answer—although, by the close of 1974, they were costing £600–£700 million a year.

Farming is concerned with the long view. It does not flourish in a fore-shortened present. As Edwards and Townsend have observed:[1] 'growth is not simply a matter of doing better this year than last, but of

1. Edwards and Townsend: *Business Growth*, Macmillan 1966

93

doing things this year that add to strength over time'. This of course is true of other industries than farming, but it applies with special force to this oldest industry of all. Expressed in simple terms, it means that farming is a continuum; that it cannot tool up rapidly for quick results. Farmers build up the soil's fertility gradually, with practice and observation, and with the perception that comes from long experience. Fertility is their only real assurance against extremes, climatic or otherwise. As with land, so even more with livestock. To double the size of a

Modern food production has the appearance of a highly disciplined industrial process. Though there are fewer than half a million full-time agricultural workers in the UK, we are about two-thirds self-supporting in temperate foods. (*Photo: Nathan Keen*)

dairy herd, and to do it profitably, may take ten years. Even with poultry, where the reproductive cycle is conveniently short, doubling the stake takes time. Time costs money, which is where confidence comes in. But in a period of inflation, time becomes more expensive year by year. More and more confidence is needed before expansion takes place. In a period of rapid inflation, farmers with few exceptions cease to do the 'things that add strength over time'. They have their own ways of discounting the future. They will even sacrifice their breeding stock, which is like eating the seed corn. Therefore, although there have been calls from many quarters for a 10-year emergency pro-gramme aimed at making us 80 per cent self-supporting in temperate food, it is unlikely that resources will be provided in sufficient quantity to inspire confidence. It is not that the need is not urgent; but farming is a long-term business, and the mood of today is to live in the present. Moreover, in a society like ours, industrial re-investment will always take precedence over investment in food production because we are a trading nation, and because of the preponderance of urban jobs at stake.

Lest this be construed as political comment, let me make it clear that in my view a socialist government, if it can hold the centre, is the best hope we have of mastering inflation. But this is another thing than saying that a socialist government — especially one committed to a fundamental re-distribution of the nation's wealth — is the government best suited for getting results out of farmers. It is true that socialist governments have done so in the past: Tom Williams in the late 1940s and Fred Peart in the mid-60s were innovators who inspired confidence once their message was clear. But since that time, the political climate has changed. We have crossed the watershed. We are in unfamiliar country. Today, the public, or at least the official, attitude to agricul-ture is acquisitive and aggressive. Agricultural land — it is argued — is a primary resource. It represents a large part of the wealth of the nation. But it does not belong to the nation. It is in the hands of a tiny and privileged minority of farmers and landowners. The socialist party is the party of the towns, of the urban majority. More and more of their supporters are staking a claim to the land. They have the power to enforce their claim.

It is said that most farmers are conservative by instinct and persuas-ion. So they may be, although there are socialists who are farmers, some of them outstandingly successful at their job. But the real distinc-tion is that farmers are entrepreneurs within the definition of Adam Smith. They are self-seeking, and know themselves to be so, but they see themselves as vehicles of enlightened self-interest, and as servants of the public good. They will not take kindly — nor have farmers in any society taken kindly — to policies that will curtail their independence. They are the quintessential exponents of private enterprise capitalism within the state — virtually the only ones who have consistently avoided take-overs and managed to survive. Small firms have made the mistake of becoming big firms. They have been absorbed by yet bigger firms, and as a result have attracted the attention of the state. Small shopkeepers have been put out of business by powerful competitors, and seem likely before long to disappear without trace. But the farmer, until quite recently, has been protected by bi-partisan agricultural policies. He has remained much as he always was, despite his new lifestyle, his status, his income, his responsibilities. Nobody has envied him, although he has had his critics. Nobody has disputed his territory, although some have questioned his use of it. Nobody has grudged him his security as a tenant, as an owner of land, although some have argued that he had too much security. But inflation has altered things. It has made paper millionaires out of a number of owner-occupiers and landowners, and wealthy men out of a yet larger number. And wealth nowadays, especially when it is inflation-proof, is something that is bound to arouse the interest of the state. Profit may be a dirty word, but at least it is taxable. Wealth, according to the conventional wisdom, *is* a dirty word, and should be taxable too. The capital transfer tax, the wealth tax, the abolition of estate duty relief, will all be baneful in their effect on agriculture (as also on private forestry). Whatever their merits as fiscal measures, the best that can be claimed for them, from the working farmer's point of view, is that they have pricked the bubble of speculation in land, and by contributing to the sharp fall in values, brought land once again within his means. But these new taxes on capital will accelerate the break-up of estates, destroy much that is valuable in the relationship between landlord and tenant, reverse a twenty-year trend towards scale of enterprise in farming, and discourage investment in development and expansion. One of the vaunted strengths of British agriculture in relation to the agriculture of other Common Market countries is its structure. The land is farmed, not piecemeal, but in consolidated units of adequate size for effective management. In England, the average full-time holding (1972) is 210 acres—several times the average for EEC. For years past, successive governments have fostered improvements in farm structure, because of the notional correlation between size of holding and efficiency. Now, since 1974, there are to be penalties on size. The Country Landowners' Association has shown that a 350-acre farm could be reduced to bankruptcy by wealth tax debt in 35 years. From the budget of November 1974, it may be inferred that holdings of a thousand acres and over will cease to be viable as such after capital transfer tax has been levied. Farmers' sons will be unable to succeed their fathers without incurring heavy debt or selling off a part of the farm. Landowners will be compelled to break up their estates. The strategy is clear. From the proposal to nationalise development land, it is a short step to nationalise other land. This could be done (as has been suggested) by means of a land commission that would act as receiver for farms and estates caught in the fiscal net. The state as beneficiary becomes the state as landlord.

A further measure to which government is committed is the expropriation of tied (or service) cottages. For this step also there is justification on ideological grounds. The system is open to abuse. There have been occasions—fortunately less frequent of late—where farm workers and their families have been victimised by their employers, and turned out of their homes. But no system is perfect, and the vesting of farm cottages in, for instance, the local authority will make the farm worker independent of his employer, but will make the employer, especially the livestock or dairy farmer, less assured of his labour supply. It will also drive up wages, because employees, for the first time, will have a realistic rent to pay. Thus, a measure that is designed to enhance the dignity of the worker will at the same time temper the entrepreneurial and risk-taking spirit of the farmer.

All these steps—or strides—into an egalitarian future may be impeccable socialism, but they are not, in our present situation, conducive to confidence among farmers. Not only is there a sense of anti-climax, but there are deeper misgivings. The opportunity for expansion existed. It has been lost. The acts of government, dictated by higher priorities of state, if not by deeper disorders of the body politic, are in conflict with the farming interest, and therefore with the national interest in so far as the nation has a claim to a larger supply of home-grown food. It is ironical that, at a time when, on import-saving grounds alone, there is a case for stimulating the productivity of the national farm, government should be bent on killing the goose to get the eggs.

The milk churn at the end of the lane is one sign of the marginal farm—but for how much longer? *(Photo: Nathan Keen)*

The response of small businesses to inflation is less dramatic, and therefore less perceptible, than the response of big ones. If a big firm lays off labour, the market knows about it. But if a small firm sacks a single worker, it is not news. It is only when a lot of small firms take a similar step that their response is noticed, and becomes significant.

A small business reacts to uncertainty in other ways than laying off labour. Exceptionally, it will accept the challenge, and profit from defiance. There are always some who manage to keep their heads above water, swimming against the stream; but more often than not, there are special circumstances in their favour — youth and vitality, proximity to a market, or the unitary strength of a family concern. A more usual response is acquiescence in a deteriorating situation, making ends meet by running down assets, economising on upkeep, playing safe. Another response is the course of least resistance: to shut up shop altogether, or to keep open only that part of it that pays a subsistence income. All these responses may be expected, according to circumstances, from British farmers in the uncertain times ahead. But it is not only the farmer's actions that will tell. There are the farm worker's also.

In a recent article in *The Countryman*,[2] I showed that more than half the work in farming today is done by the farmer and his family. We are already on the way to having a do-it-yourself agriculture, as they have had for years in the United States and elsewhere. It is a trend that will grow if labour continues to leave the land, as it has been doing since 1946 at an annual rate of two per cent a year. Will this trend continue? I think it will, for several reasons. It is not simply a question of pay, which is lower in farming than in many other jobs. Nor is it only a question of hours of work, which are often longer or more unsocial, if we think of seven-day weeks with livestock, or seasonal peaks in arable farming. Nor is it a question of prospects, which are by no means bright for the keen young worker. No, it is something more fundamental; something to which rising wages are not an answer.

What we are experiencing in agriculture is not a drift from the land, but a flight from the dirty-hands job to the clean-hands job, from physical work to non-physical work, from exacting full-time work to less demanding temporary work. This phenomenon, which is peculiar to modern societies (and not only industrially developed ones) leads me to believe that for farmers in Britain the brief post-war period of gentility is over, whereas for the farm worker it is just beginning. As in the new Polders in Holland, where the employees live in the town and the employer does the weekend work on the homestead, so also in England the five-day week is with us. As the prospects of genteel occupations off the holding become more enticing, the younger married workers leave the land. There is already a labour shortage. In arable farming, and in horticulture where the labour requirement is high, men are reluctant to work overtime; and school-leavers are discouraged by the unpleas-

2. *The Countryman*, December 1973

antness of outdoor work in all weathers. On the livestock farms, key posts are hard to fill; good men are scarce and expensive; the indifferent worker, though less scarce, is more expensive still; and the young men are barely showing up at all. Some farms that formerly employed labour now employ none. This has meant scaling down operations, or falling back on a single activity that the farmer, with family help, and the services of a contractor, can manage on his own.

What does this suggest? Obviously, a future for the family farmer—one that he will earn by the sweat of his brow. The threat to his position is more illusory than real. He is a small enough fish to slip through the fiscal net, and he represents in any case the irreducible unit of enterprise. He tolerates the duties of his calling when no one else will. Farming is a hard life—whether or not it is also a good one. It takes from a man more than most are prepared to give in brain and brawn and care and hours of work. Machines have lightened certain tasks, but they have complicated them as well. They have added to the sum of resources employed and to the sum of skills required; and hence to the calls upon the human engine. Although his standing in society has improved, the family farmer knows his function has not changed. He is still *la bête humaine*—the human beast of burden. He accepts his role for reasons that few sociologists seem capable of perceiving, tied as they are to stilted concepts of 'intrinsic value', such as independence, or challenge, or open-air life, or job satisfaction. He accepts his role for motives he does not put into words—because farming is in his blood and in his bones, and because, if he has a son, it is also a future. Like Antaeus, he draws strength from earth. For this reason, he is no good at other things. Farming is the only existence in which vanity will not betray him. It is the only existence in which he can preserve life until the end.

These are truths from which we contrive to escape from time to time. While labour was plentiful, dependent and depressed, employers were able to ride round on a horse and leave the drudgery to others. Hard times broke them. Since the war, affluence has revived their kind, equipping the amateur with secondary skills and the pretensions that go with them. Scale is impressive, but it has its flaws. It is vulnerable to taxation, as we have seen; and when times are hard, it is short of staying power. Now, as labour slips through our fingers, and inflation makes us steadily more equal, and some less equal than others, we find ourselves once again face to face with the truth that the land is the last resort of the individualist, a job for the kulak, the yeoman, the family farmer—because none but he knows what it costs and is ready to pay the full price. This is where we seem to be heading. The signs are plain. The small farmer provides the essential element of continuity the big farm lacks—chiefly a matter of marrying a working wife, raising a working family, and leaving a pittance behind him. Small may be beautiful, as Schumacher claims. It is also a life sentence.

As I write these words, memory evokes a scene, and with the scene a chance word I had not long ago with a smallholder who farms on brick earth above the Vézère, in the Dordogne. After a climb, I found him with his wife and son bent double in a field in the hot sun. They were picking strawberries. He explained that the weather had been dry so long that the fruit was small and fit only for jam. We spoke of the prospects for farming in a society no less threatened by inflation than our own. He was not afraid, he said. His father had farmed the farm, and his father before him. As for himself and his son: 'Who will envy us our work?'—he asked. 'Look at these hands! No, *monsieur*. In bad times, we are the profiteers, the food hoarders, the survivors. In good times, we are a sociological problem.'

Mutatis mutandis, it could come to that here—a pruning back of leaders and side-shoots, not to say suckers, to the root-stock; except that we are more cushioned, more favoured, England especially. England has a main-stream agriculture, and produces, off 24 million acres— only half the area of the national farm—about nine-tenths of the arable output of the United Kingdom and two-thirds of the livestock and livestock products. Because of this, and because of proximity to the big consuming centres, farmers in England earn on average more than they do in Scotland, and nearly double what they earn in Wales and Northern Ireland. As things are now, about 60,000 of them, out of a total of about 100,000 full-time farmers, are employers of labour; and the land they farm is usually the better land, much of it in the top two grades of the Ministry of Agriculture's recent classification survey. But of all the farmers in the United Kingdom, they are probably the most under pressure from inflation—basically because of the ever-rising cost of a unit of time and a unit of space. They are closer to the hub of things. They have cities round them, expanding cities, cities bursting at the seams. There are few farms in England that are not in the catch-ment area of industrial towns, which compete for manpower, force up wage rates and exude urban standards and urban discontent. For these reasons, English farmers are caught more than most in the 'rat-race'. Every year they look a little less like farmers, a little more like indus-trialists. They work in open-air factories, subject to natural hazards; but their object, like the industrialist, is to maximise output from a steadily increasing volume of resources. It is these pressures that compel them to cut their corners. They grub out hedges, hedges that have been there for centuries, because modern machines are too large to man-oeuvre in small fields. In their search for labour-saving, time-saving, space-saving systems, they streamline their cropping, intensify livestock husbandry, replace farm buildings with omni-purpose umbrellas, burn straw, step up their reliance on fertilisers, sprays and other chemicals, and so far as nature allows, specialise in mass production. English farming is permissive; and since you cannot take liberties with nature without paying for them, it is at times excessive, as wild-oats, the eutrophication of water courses, careless straw-burning, unsightly buildings and the infrequent but undeniable abuses of factory-farming testify. But those who criticise should also recognise the achievement. Excessiveness is not the chief characteristic of English agriculture, only an occasional blemish; but the blemishes will spread as it becomes harder to earn an adequate after-tax profit, less feasible to run an adequate labour force, more imperative to keep within bounds the rising cost of food.

For farmers and their families, the future offers less leisure, not more. After a brief heyday, they are back in overalls—those who got out of them, as many did not. Longer hours, less relief; more tasks, less time to do them in. The average age of farmers in England is about 45. The older men have been through the mill, as the younger have not, yet. They have lost their spring. They are more stretched than they were. As times goes on, one would expect them to take the line of least resistance, shut up shop, or keep open only that part of it that pays the rent. When this happens, it is not only output that drops; but upkeep falls off as well. Farmers begin to consume their capital. Pride suffers; and emulation—which is one of the forces that keeps the country tidy—will suffer too. Some will retire, rather than let this happen; but others will not be able to, because of taxation; and others will not wish to. As for the young, they will discover that youthfulness burns itself out more quickly than it did. At the pace of change today, a man soon gets out of date; soon ceases to make the running, and falls behind. He will evolve a routine and stick to it. He will not be less dynamic; it will take more dynamism to do a single thing well.

This is what many of the farmers of the American Middle West have come to. They are operators, rather than innovators—closer to the type of the smallholder in the Dordogne. They depend on their own brain and brawn; and with family help, they repeat their operation year by year, improving, simplifying, streamlining, but staying in the groove. There are no grace notes. There is a monotony about the Middle West that is imposed by the landscape—a monotony that our own finite landscape does not impose, unless it be in the fens. But there is also a sameness imposed by utilitarianism, by the frugality of the family farm. This sameness we shall see more of, before long. The same determinants of change are driving us to the same solutions. There are no other solutions for an agriculture that is pressed for capital and short of labour. The best farming will be no less resilient, but different: in the lowlands, stockless arable systems and landless livestock systems; in the uplands, ranching styles instead of traditional husbandry. Marginal land will go out of production and revert to forest.

But I see no reason to share the deep concern of the Countryside Commission about our changing landscape, nor do I find their pessimism wholly justified by the facts elicited in their recent report.[3] To

3. 'New Agricultural Landscapes', Countryside Commission, CCP 76, 1974

me it seems inevitable that with increasing state participation in the industry, the obligation conveyed in Section 11 of the 1968 Countryside Act will have increasing influence. 'In the exercise of their function relating to land under any enactment, every Minister, Government Department and Public Body shall have regard to the desirability of conserving the natural beauty and amenity of the countryside.' An age of leisure, if we had been able to achieve it, might have conserved the rural heritage with the minimum of interference from officials and the maximum co-operation of the farming community. But it seems as if we have lost our chance—as if the age of leisure may elude us. Therefore in the years ahead we should expect no more than a working landscape, governed by what the state demands from its farmers, and more specifically by what it leaves in their pockets.

Changes in farming practice mean changes for the landscape. Between 1960 and 1966, UK farmers removed hedges at a rate of approximately 10,000 miles a year; since 1970 the rate has fallen to 2,000–3,000 miles a year. (*Photo: John Topham*)

7

Open Landscape and Hill Farming

GEOFFREY SINCLAIR

AsK one of those long-distance walkers, a naturalist, a motorist or just a man in the rush-hour bus queue, where the best open country is, and you will get a list which almost certainly contains one of our national parks. Each individual in the sample will start with his own favourite and will enthuse so variously about the wilderness, the plant life, the views or the peace and quiet, that it may be a while before it hits you. All these places and qualities have something in common which no-body mentions—hill farming, and the hill farmer. Hills they know about, but hill farming and the life of the hill farmer mean nothing to the man in the queue or his friends. So let me shatter some illusions. The last thing I want to do is to analyse away the enthusiasts' enjoy-ment: but, the wilderness is not really wild, the vegetation is only semi-natural, the views are of a landscape farmed and forested by man; and as for peace and quiet—were you there on shearing day?

Over large areas of England and Wales typical open landscapes have received official recognition (though not much protection) by the unfortunate misnomers of national parks and areas of outstand-ing natural beauty. The central features of the parks are large tracts of semi-natural vegetation, mostly in private ownership, and used as rough summer grazing by hill farmers. It is this grazing, and as-sociated management practices like burning, which keep the vegetation down to a low cover—hence the 'open' landscape. It forms the *raison d'être* of the 'open country' designated for conservation by the 1949 National Parks and Access to the Countryside Act, which defined it as 'mountain, moor, heath, down, cliff or foreshore'. There are some superb undesignated open landscapes, such as Upper Teesdale, and some parts of the national parks are quite uninviting. But take away the best vegetation, and where would the uplands be?

Simply to equate vegetation, which is a landscape cover-type, with rough grazing would be misleading, for some vegetation has other uses, such as nature reserves or grouse moors. And some very rough grazing can be found on run-down pastureland. My definition of 'vegetation' is 'semi-natural plant communities formed by non-woody species', and 'agricultural land' means farmland not covered by vegetation.

Clearly, if open landscape derives from vegetation, which is condi-tioned and maintained by grazing, you have to understand hill farming to understand that landscape. The principle behind the traditional system of hill farming is that the winter carrying capacity determines the summer stocking rate. When sheep are on the hill in summer, the lower and better in-bye land is used to grow grass or other crops for winter keep. The 1946 Hill Farming Act introduced hill cow and sheep subsidies—currently £24·50 and £1·75 a head—and provided irresistible incentives to the farmer to make full use of his undergrazed hill land in summer by increasing his winter carrying capacity. For present purposes, the most significant method of boosting subsidy income is for the farmer to improve hill land by cultivation, re-seeding and enclosure, all aspects of which are grant-aided at 50 per cent. In 1971–2 this package of aid (as can be seen in Table 1) amounted to £29·6 million exclusively for hill farmers, who also shared in other grants totalling £124·6 million, of which their portion cannot be identified.

TABLE 1: *Grant and subsidy support for hill farming, U.K., 1971–72*

Support	Total (£ million)	Important to hill farms	Exclusive to hill farms	Details
Price guarantees covered by CAP	97·9	—	—	—
Price guarantees not in CAP	43·0	16·4	—	Sheep
		6·9	—	Wool
Other grants and subsidies	185·6	1·9	—	Brucellosis eradication
		35·1	—	Fertilisers
		5·2	—	Lime
		58·1	—	Capital grants
		1·0	—	Structure
		—	14·7	Hill cows
		—	9·8	Hill sheep
		—	5·1	Winter keep
Totals	326·5	124·6	29·6	—
		154·2		
Administration	15·6			

Without this support hill farming would wither away; improvements cannot be made without grants, and the extra stock they permit cannot be sustained without subsidies. It is intrinsically non-viable, unless farmers manage very large areas in the traditional manner. This is not a realistic option because it would abet depopulation and produce an inadequate return on capital: yet some form of livestock farming is the only agriculture the uplands can sustain.

The townsman may ask why, if we pay so dearly for our relatively small supply of food from the hills, we do not write off the hill farmers, even though they may be fine people, whose way of life is an important part of our national character. Without hill farming the landscape and

A typical hill farm in Teesdale, on the Yorkshire–Durham borders. Hill farming provides the sustenance for the upland landscapes in many national parks and areas of outstanding natural beauty. *(Photo: John Topham)*

the community would change fundamentally, whether through neglect or afforestation (which is the subject of Chapter 9). And the resource on which the hill farmer is based, three million acres of rough grazing, supports about six million sheep and a million cattle. This land is the nation's ultimate food reserve for an extreme emergency. The stock and the men are an indigenous and inseparable part of that reserve, without which the hills could not play the role they did in two world wars.

But 'meat from the hills' is, to change the metaphor, a red herring. No economic case can be made for hill farming solely on the grounds of food production. If it could be, there would be no need for special hill farming grants and subsidies. True, the hills will always produce some beef and lamb, but unless there were transcending social and political reasons, such extravagant sidelines as the hill farming support system would have felt a Beeching axe long ago. The system is necessary, not really because it produces more food, but because it is better to keep the community and the landscape alive by supporting a worthwhile activity than by contriving some artificial and irrelevant occupation in an open-air museum. What is basically wrong with the present system is the muddled thinking which permeates its administration. Financial support is dispensed by the Ministry as if it were an agricultural answer to a food production problem. This hides the fact that in reality, by footing the bill, society has accepted responsibility for perpetuating an uneconomic way of life, and makes it difficult for the hill farmers, the National Farmers' Union, the Country Landowners' Association and the Ministry itself to realise that their responsibilities to society extend beyond food production to the conservation of wildlife and the landscape. Since hill farming, in response to official incentives, has to some extent taken an undesirable course by reducing the appeal and the accessibility of landscape, society has the right to alter the pressures and incentives, so as to secure more acceptable results: provided always, that farmers are no worse off financially. This does not mean that all open landscape should be sacrosanct; in fact there are many areas where improvement should be even more actively encouraged.

This confusion of purpose explains why in the last 30 years hill farming legislation has given the MAFF a charter to operate a so-called agricultural support policy which, in any context other than a national emergency, is illogical and irresponsible. Because it is presented as a food policy, the farmers and their organisations back all their claims with the assertion that 'the nation needs more food' when what they really mean is 'we need more money'. But the right way to raise the hill farmer's income is not to encourage him along an anti-social course which may spoil a precious landscape.

The farmers' resentment of Stanley Evans' famous accusation of 'feather-bedding' was understandable. But the real case against hill farming subsidies, put by Cheshire and Bowers in 1969,[1] is that they deprive industry of capital which it could put to better use. And, if

1. 'Farming, conservation and amenity', *New Scientist*, vol. 42, p. 13

Fyldon Common, in the Exmoor National Park. Once a superb heather moor, commanding superb views from the Exmoor ridge towards Dartmoor; ploughed up and fenced with Ministry of Agriculture grants in the 1960s, it has since reverted to rushes and has become an eyesore. *(Photo: David Doble)*

hard-working farmers dislike being misrepresented as lazy good-for-nothings, they should refrain from speaking as if some kind of divine right attached to their operations. In its evidence to the Countryside in 1970 Conference, the CLA stated that the decision to use land for any purpose was, and should remain, at the discretion of the owner. The formidable farming lobby, the only one with its 'own' Minister in the Cabinet, makes great play with agriculture's post-war achievements, which are superficially considerable. What other industry could make such vast increases in output, and yet shed so many men for other work? The answer is, of course, 'none'. Governments know this well, and in return have resisted attempts to subject agriculture to planning control, full rating and other forms of bureaucratic interference. The result has been a 'special relationship' unique in British politics, from which outsiders and broader national interests tend to be excluded.

Witness the alliance in action. The designations of national parks have been opposed almost automatically by the CLA, the NFU or the local authorities (which often amounts to the same thing). What they could not stop they have weakened in practice. Sir Jack Longland's report to the Countryside Commission in 1971 revealed the feebleness of the national park authorities, and the Sandford report[2] belatedly confirmed his findings, but only after the Local Government Act of 1972 had continued the basic arrangements unchanged. The Countryside Act of 1968 contains two conflicting provisions. Section 37

2. Report of the National Park Policy Review Committee, HMSO 1974

requires the Countryside Commission, and all public authorities, to have due regard to the needs of agriculture and forestry. Of course they should, but in practice this conflicts with the reciprocal obligation in Section 11, on the same authorities, to have regard to the 'desirability' of conserving the natural beauty and amenity of the countryside. The reality is that Section 37 muzzles the authorities, degrading the Commission from a watch-dog into an underdog, while Section 11 is simply disregarded by the Government departments at which it was aimed. In the 1960s the MAFF had to accept evidence that upland landscapes on Exmoor were being irretrievably damaged by cultivation and enclosure as a direct result of its support policies. Yet the Ministry still declines to modify its grant policy or to co-operate meaningfully with the national park authorities. In 1974, the Sandford report, although guarded in its references to agriculture, made several recommendations designed to prevent MAFF policies from 'insidiously transforming the character of a wide area'.

Manifestly, amenity is in an unenviable position. The primary responsibility of the Countryside Commission is 'to conserve and enhance natural beauty', a particularly difficult task in open landscapes whose scale, character and physique make them disproportionately vulnerable to alien development. Its budget, which only passed the £1 million mark in 1973–4, is less than the MAFF spends each year on persuading farmers to retire or amalgamate their holdings. Unfortunately, too, the vital local pressure groups often present an extraneous, middle-class, self-interested image, which the farming community (itself not disinterested) tends to resent. The landowners on national park authorities, although often personally sympathetic to conservation, inevitably attach over-riding importance to the needs of agriculture and forestry as they see them.

There is a fundamental and unresolved conflict. The support policies of the MAFF provide local benefit to farmers, but (Section 11 notwithstanding) the Ministry declines to shoulder responsibility for interests other than farming. It seems to regard conservation, although promoted in a national interest, as basically prejudicial to the rural community. The farming lobby claims, and not without some justice, that conservationists are ignorant about agriculture, would impose penal sanctions on it, and would turn the countryside into a museum.

Yet the differences are far from irreconcilable. They are only made to appear so because the institutional arrangements promote the conflict rather than the solution, as separate agencies pursue mutually incompatible objectives. With give and take it is possible to conserve the best landscape without imposing a dead hand on genuine hill farming husbandry. It is possible, too, without destroying the finest stretches, to enable the hill farmer to enjoy a standard of living that will keep him where he wants to be—on the hills, farming in the traditional ways.

The paradox is that, although some farming practices must be controlled, neither scenic beauty nor lively communities can be maintained if the hill farmer is not prosperous. The dilemma has its origin in the thinking of the 1940s, when post-war agricultural policy and the machinery for planning and protecting the countryside were both introduced. The assumption, made explicit in both the Scott[3] and the Dower[4] reports, was that the best way to conserve the traditional landscape was to farm it. For this reason, and because the nation was short of timber and food, farming and forestry were virtually exempted from planning control (as Adrian Phillips shows in Chapter 8). Agriculture is the only industry with its own Minister in the Cabinet, thus being free to push its policies through with scant regard for the protective planning machinery which looks so impressive on paper.

As a result, the Countryside Commission has never been able to take the agricultural bull by the horns. The chairman, John Cripps, made a forceful plea at the 1973 National Parks Conference for the integration of farming and conservation policies, but the Minister of State for Agriculture's contribution was merely to assert the over-riding needs of food production. So the Commission has continued to concentrate on minor but useful details, like visitor control, farm visits and country parks. Its most constructive effort has been the Upland Management Experiment in the Lake District and Snowdonia, which encourages farmers to 'undertake small tasks on their property for the enjoyment of visitors'. This has now resulted in the appointment of Agricultural Liaison Officers and has the merit of involving farmers in constructive landscape measures. In 1974 the Commission published a report on the impact of farming on lowland landscapes[5] and has commissioned another on the uplands, both of which try to deal with the existing situation. I cannot but sympathise with the Commission's difficulties, but the fact remains that the measures it adopts can only treat the symptoms of a disease it is powerless to cure. It is pre-occupied with recreation and seems unable to discharge its statutory responsibilities to conserve the countryside.

This can best be illustrated by the ploughing up and enclosure of Exmoor, which has earned the nickname (not yet entirely deserved) of Ex-moor. The Exmoor Society commissioned me in 1965 to survey changes in moorland vegetation. The report, published in the pamphlet 'Can Exmoor Survive?' in 1966, showed that 710 acres of moorland had been 'lost' each year between 1957 and 1965. This prompted the (three) national park committees to define a 'critical amenity' area of 43,567 acres over which ploughing should be controlled, subject to compensation. The snag was that the committees, as planning authorities, had powers neither to control cultivation nor to pay the compensation. Their efforts to secure the insertion in the Countryside Bill of 1968 of a clause to establish amenity conservation areas within which

3. Report of the Committee on Land Utilisation in Rural Areas, HMSO 1942

4. 'National Parks in England and Wales', by John Dower, Cmnd. 6628, HMSO 1945

5. 'New Agricultural Landscapes', Countryside Commission, CCP 76, 1974

changes in agricultural practice would be subject to planning control were resisted by the farming interests and by MAFF. Only when the national park committees asked to be relieved of their impossible responsibilities for conserving the landscape, was a last-minute and badly conceived amendment rushed through the House of Lords. This is now Section 14 of the 1968 Act. It empowers the Secretary of State for the Environment to make an order prohibiting the occupier of specified 'moor or heath' in a national park from converting it to agricultural land without giving six months' notice. The experience of Exmoor shows that Section 14 is almost valueless. No blanket order has been made for the whole 'critical amenity' area, but there were two hurried orders when the committee learned that ploughing was intended. Any farmer is free to plough without giving notice, and the MAFF still abets him by refusing to notify the national park committee of grant applications and paying half the cost of ploughing and enclosing the land. The maximum fine of £200 is quite inadequate. On the one occasion when agreement was reached on compensation to be paid for

The heart of Exmoor: Mill Hill, the ridge beyond Weir Water, is owned by the Somerset County Council and managed by Exmoor National Park Committee to conserve the moorland. But three-quarters of Exmoor's 40,000 acres of 'critical amenity moorland' are not protected against conversion to agricultural use. (*Photo: David Doble*)

an access agreement, on the basis of loss of profit, the national park committee jibbed at paying. The Sandford report — still to be implemented — recommends that this situation should be remedied.

The Sandford committee, taking up an earlier proposal by the Commission, has recommended that the park authorities be given power to conclude landscape management agreements, which would require owners and their successors in title to refrain from cultivation, and to maintain the existing vegetation. This is a step forward, but agreements are voluntary and, as the Sandford committee noted, powers of compulsory purchase are only available on open land to secure access, and not to conserve the natural beauty.

What about purchase? There can be no doubt that the owner of the land is in a far stronger position to enforce a management policy than a planning authority. But with compulsory powers as a last resort, land has usually first to come on the market; and the mere threat of acquisition could provoke a spate of pre-emptive ploughing. Ironically the capital transfer tax seems more likely to discourage ploughing than any of the measures so far suggested.

It is hard to visualise either the planning or the national park authorities developing a consistent purchase policy to cover all conservation land, but the fact is that, whether land is publicly acquired or not, the concept of 'free amenity' will have to go. When all hill farming practice was aesthetically acceptable, and the visitor's casual *de facto* access (to which he had no legal right) was no hindrance to the farmer, there was no problem. But once farmers began to change the landscape and to restrict access, as they were perfectly entitled to, there were howls of anguish from preservationists who took their privileges as a right, and saw farmers' rights as an infringement of theirs. The suggestion that landscape conservation must involve some form of compensation produced startled cries that this would be paying farmers for sitting on their backsides.

The argument is misconceived, of course. By maintaining rough grazing, voluntarily or compulsorily, against economic inducements to plough it up, farmers would be still farming it, but at a vastly reduced profit. They would be — and many already are — effectively subsidising amenity and the tourist industry out of their own pockets. The amenity interest will never win the collaboration of farmers, on which so much depends, if it requires them at financial loss to produce less food by conserving a landscape which many people will never visit and some never appreciate.

Society has a moral right, in return for its financial support, to attach some conditions. But can this be done by planning control? I accept the argument of Adrian Phillips in Chapter 8 that what is needed in the countryside is not less planning but more, but the problems have to be faced. If conversion is to be treated as a change of use, and subject to development control, it would be a costly and novel extension of bureaucracy. Without compensation for refusal of permission this could not be made acceptable to farmers; but such a precedent would have awkward repercussions throughout the planning system. And compensation would be indiscriminate, with large sums wasted on owners who had no intention of ploughing amenity moorland; or it would be selective, and open to abuse by insincere applications made solely to collect the money. Yet control without compensation would not only be unfair; it would drive farmers out of business to the damnation of the landscape and the deterioration of our ultimate food reserve.

While, therefore, planning control and ownership may have their parts to play, the solution is a commitment by the Ministry of Agriculture and the Department of the Environment to conservation agriculture in the uplands. This aims to conserve landscape, and the emergency food resource, and to maintain farmers' living standards by providing farming incomes rather than compensation. But before discussing in detail how this might work out in practice, I must first challenge the wrong-headed philosophy that we *always* need all the food we can produce.

'It's all very well for these amenity people to holler,' a hill farmer once told me, 'but they'll never get anywhere because we'll always need more food.' And he started off on what you might call the Great Food Production Argument. Its devotees are not one bit impressed by what amenity people *can* prove, that in straight food production economics, modern hill farming is virtually paid for by the state. They argue that the hill farms reduce the demands on lowland farms, form part of an indissoluble food production chain by raising stock for finishing on the lower ground, and so reduce the deficit on the balance of payments. We should, the argument runs, maximise production on the hills by cultivation, surface treatment and enclosure on the grand scale.

The surprising thing, considering the encouragement given by a single-minded Ministry to enthusiastic hill farmers technically prepared for expansion, is that the uplands have not been exploited even more. The controlling influences have been the diseconomy of hill farming and the limitations on available capital and income support. These clearly show that the Cabinet and the Treasury, which control the Ministry's purse strings, are far from believing in food at any price. The MAFF incentives to improve hill land have been nicely calculated to produce salient changes in land use and landscape only in the more favoured areas, where the return on capital *after grant* would be highest. The tragedy is that of all open landscapes, the most beautiful are often also the most vulnerable. It is no comfort to the amenity cause to know that the destruction of world-class scenery on the Exmoor coast (for example at Kipscombe Hill) has produced a neglible quantity of food at a relatively modest loss to the taxpayer. The Ministry's policies have not been purposely designed to destroy the landscape, and individual farmers are not to blame, but together they have succeeded in wounding it.

How much open landscape does remain, and what have we lost? An authoritative answer would require a national survey of land use trends similar to the work already done on Exmoor[6] and the North York Moors,[7] using as its basis the unique record of vegetation cover compiled by the Second Land Use Survey. The MAFF's returns of rough grazing, which are only approximately accurate, and say nothing about vegetation content, suggest a determined trend downwards since the 1946 Hill Farming Act was passed (see Table 2). After allowing for afforestation, which cannot be done with any accuracy, I estimate the annual average loss of rough grazing in England to improved agricultural use to be 11,530 acres for the period 1946–72 or 0·31 per cent p.a. of the rough grazing area. For the period 1957–65, the Exmoor Society documented a loss of 710 acres p.a., or 1·21 per cent p.a., compared to 8,333 acres or 0·25 per cent p.a. for England. This estimate suggests that the loss on Exmoor was proceeding nearly five times as fast as the national rate—so that exceptional open landscape, supposedly protected by national park status, was being lost much faster than land of a generally lower landscape quality. There are, moreover, signs that the problems which were once thought to be peculiar to Exmoor are now spreading to the rest of the country, in particular to Dartmoor, Cleveland, Shropshire and Northumberland.

TABLE 2: *Estimate of rough grazing conversion to agriculture England, 1946–72*

	Rough grazing: acres
MAFF, 1946	3,705,244
MAFF, 1972	3,090,943
Reduction, 1946–72	614,301
Estimated afforestation, 1946–72	314,530 * SUBTRACT
Estimated conversion to agriculture	299,771
26 year average	11,530

* = A 90% estimate of the combined Forestry Commission new plantings and the Forestry Commission's estimate of private plantings.

Sources: MAFF Agricultural Returns. Forestry Commission Annual Reports.

The situation I have analysed arose from yesterday's conditions, when supplies of imported grain and protein were readily available, farm labour was cheap, energy in all its forms (including fertiliser) was not only cheap but plentiful, we had more good land, inflation was calculable, capital was available, land prices were relatively low and

6. *The Vegetation of Exmoor*, G. Sinclair, Exmoor Press, 1970

7. 'Land Use Changes in the Moorlands of the North York Moors National Park', D. C. Statham, Centre for Environmental Studies Working Paper No. 16

our context seemed to be firmly fixed by a cheap food policy based on Commonwealth agreements and preferences.

But the post-war period of British agricultural policy, from 1946 to 1974, has ended. Not only does our energy come from food, but our food comes from energy. A crisis in one is a crisis in the other. The assertion that we produce 70 per cent of our temperate food, and nearly all our poultry meat, pork and milk, is simply not true. For we do not grow much of the food our animals eat, nor do we produce all the energy which grows the rest. The time has come to re-think our overall food strategy. We waste much of our best land by growing cereals for the livestock industry, when we could be producing more for direct human consumption; beef and lamb are over-subsidised and under-priced: they are really luxury foods. We must halt the decline in agricultural research expenditure, and expand work on nitrogen fixation by plants, land capability and plant breeding.

The short-term effect of the crisis which hit the farmer in 1974 may be to slow down the conversion of hill land. But in the longer term we can expect a worsening food situation and stronger pressures for 'food at any price'. What would happen then, if we had no policy for planning the best use of our land resource? The easiest target would not be the radical reorganisation of lowland production but the improvement of open landscapes with the greatest apparent potential, the bracken,

Fencing on Dartmoor. How can this be reconciled with the primary purposes of national park designation—to conserve natural beauty, and to promote its enjoyment by the public? The fencing destroys the beauty and denies access. (*Photo: Simon Warner*)

gorse, Festuca/Agrostis grasses and drier heather habitats. Unless MAFF could make grants discretionary, many agriculturally unwise schemes would be subsidised only to deteriorate, as in the past, to rushes. Heavier grazing and enclosure of the remainder would, by reducing variety in vegetation, extinguish many rare species, deplete fauna, diminish heather and generally spoil the appeal and accessibility of the landscape. In some areas, overgrazing might eventually reduce output by encouraging unpalatable grasses like the unlovely Nardus, or by turning steep slopes into scree.

Technical progress would be much easier, and a bit cheaper, if various impediments to raising output were removed. The Countryside Commission, The Nature Conservancy Council and the national park committee authorities would be among the more obvious casualties. The 'inviolable' status of National Trust land, already breached by the Offshore Petroleum (Scotland) Act of 1975 could hardly survive. Common land status, which has protected much open country, would also have to go.

The moorlands of the south-west, the southern heaths and the Welsh Border hills offer the most attractive prospects. Next come the North Yorks Moors, extensive areas in Northumberland and favoured parts of the Pennines and the Lake District. Mineral extraction would be encouraged anywhere, particularly potash in Cleveland, and lime in the Peak, the Lake District, the Craven Pennines and the Mendips. The military could be moved off potentially good land in Dorset and Salisbury Plain to the barren slopes of Snowdon, Scafell and Skiddaw.

I may have exaggerated. I hope I have. But what worries me is: by how much? And how extreme would a food emergency have to be to justify, either morally or economically, such severe measures?

An assured future in the EEC is not without its problems, but we shall be part of a free trade area whose food supply will be more closely related to its demand. Yet at the time of writing the situation is absurd and paradoxical. The EEC as a whole has over-production, is resting good land, encounters social and environmental problems related to the under-use of land, has relatively inefficient farmers and has Ministries of Agriculture with broadly based responsibilities for landscape and conservation. It has the potential both for increasing production and for solving some of the problems. Yet we are fully stretched to produce an illusory 70 per cent of our temperate needs with the best farmers in Europe, experience social and environmental problems of the over-use of land and confine our Ministry of Agriculture to food production. Our capacity for increasing our own production without incurring high costs and exacerbating our problems is very limited.

There is no present justification, particularly now that we have voted to remain in the Common Market, for spoiling our best open landscapes. The future is less certain. The UK population is now almost static, but all kinds of world-wide developments, such as war, famine, setbacks in European oil production or our inability to market exports, may affect our capacity to import and increase the pressure to grow more food at home. With less energy it would, given present techniques, take more land to maintain existing production, unless agriculture once more becomes labour-intensive.

I expect the domestic priorities for open landscape to swing from one extreme to the other in sympathy with the rise and fall of the pressures for food production. The important thing is to avoid the extreme of destruction for the needs of a moment. For this it is essential to reconcile and to integrate our own hill farming and environmental policies and place them in (at the least) a European context. We cannot afford conflicting strategies promoted by competing agencies, each given narrow objectives and unable to take a comprehensive view. The two main competitors to be reconciled are the Ministry of Agriculture and the Department of the Environment, whose principal agency for this purpose is (or should be) the Countryside Commission.

Whatever the political and administrative machinery required for its preparation, the need is a common policy, a joint plan of action that is sufficiently flexible to reflect the needs of society both for conservation and for food production. Only by securing parity of influence between the two departments, coupled with a gradual integration of their ideology, policy and practice, can we ensure that neither is in a position to over-ride the other.

On past performances the prospects do not look too good. The Ministry of Land and Natural Resources did not last long. The Rural Development Boards in England and Wales were killed by vested interests which resented the planned use of privately owned resources. Even the Department of the Environment is a fashionably mis-named administrative umbrella. Multiple use is unattainable unless land is planned for a multiple purpose as part of an integrated administrative policy. We have got to get beyond shot-gun marriages of departments which continue to lead their old lives under new names, or the high-minded injunctions of the Countryside Act to respect other interests which are themselves unwilling to consider any interest but their own.

The combined crisis of energy, finance and the balance of payments can only make it more difficult to protect the environment; correspondingly it makes it more urgent to integrate the conflicting policies and put a brake on environmental irresponsibility. It is unfortunate that the Countryside Commission's brave attempt to tackle the causes rather than the symptoms of land use conflict was not made when the climate was more favourable to conservation. By suggesting in its discussion paper, 'New Agricultural Landscapes', that landscape conditions should be attached to agricultural grants, it goes to the heart of the political or institutional problem. Such conditions might have little effect in the lowlands, but in the uplands, where farming practice is still determined by grant aid, it could prove very useful. The question is whether the MAFF can be persuaded or required to attach meaningful conditions to its grants, whatever the Commission may say.

To summarise: the rationale for the integration of landscape and hill farming policies derives from my view that:

(1) There is at present no intrinsic economic justification for the production of additional food from open land;

(2) Government support for hill farming can be justified socially to conserve communities, landscape and the emergency food resource;

(3) The present institutional arrangements foster conflict between agricultural and conservation policies and are a waste of public money.

My analysis leads to three main conclusions.

The first is that resource conservation policy should be the joint responsibility of the Ministry of Agriculture and the Department of the Environment (through a Countryside Commission with greatly enlarged powers and budget). Its intention, in the uplands, would be to produce food by maintaining the essential core of the best open landscape through traditional, low-density rough grazing. This would have to be accompanied by an understanding on development and agricultural policies (along the lines suggested by Adrian Phillips in Chapter 8) by which the Department of the Environment would protect the better farmland from urban uses, and the Ministry of Agriculture would encourage increased production of crops for direct human consumption. The integrated policy would be implemented by grant and subsidy support to hill farmers. The present headage subsidies for hill sheep and cattle would continue, but at higher rates designed to make the major contribution towards incomes. The rate would be regulated annually to reflect economic conditions, and each holding would have a maximum quota beyond which no headage payment would be paid. A sliding scale would reflect the economies enjoyed by the larger units, and there would have to be some special additional arrangement for the smaller farms. The headage subsidies would be conditional on the occupier concluding a management agreement with the planning authorities which would require him to refrain from enclosure, cultivation or destruction of vegetation on defined 'conservation land'. This would be unlikely to include all his rough grazing.

Capital grants for improvement or enclosure should be suspended until the landscapes have been graded. Aid would then be resumed for land graded as having a low amenity value and a reasonable agricultural potential. Access should continue to be restricted to a *de facto* basis, and compensation should be readily provided for physical damage done by visitors. Local authority help—such as national park ground staff—should be available, as an alternative to grant aid, for work such as dry stone walling, hedging and banking. The role of the MAFF advisory officers should be strengthened and enlarged in its scope. Such a policy would not necessarily cost much more than the present system. How it would be worked out, financed and conducted, is an administrative problem, which can be solved if the political decision is first taken by Cabinet and Parliament.

My second conclusion is that there should be a joint resource evaluation exercise, to assess the relative priorities for landscape conservation and food production. This could be done by bringing together the unfinished 'Hills and Uplands' section of MAFF's Agricultural Land Classification, and a comparable survey grading amenity values to be undertaken by the Countryside Commission as an extension of its current upland landscape study. The joint exercise should grade specific land; taking samples or merely suggesting national or local percentages is not good enough. Disregarding administrative boundaries it should define 'conservation land', and within it a higher grade which might be called 'conservation heartland'. The concept is different from the 'heritage areas' of the Sandford Report, because it is specifically related to the integration of farming and environment policies. In the heartland conservation would have an absolute priority over improvement, but in the conservation land the management agreements must be flexible enough to recognise the problems of individual farmers.

This leads me to my third conclusion, which is that neither grade of conservation land should be improved beyond the terms of its management agreements unless the country faces an acute and enduring food shortage which requires increased output from every acre of productive land—at almost any price. To facilitate this the government should have power to declare a state of agricultural emergency. This would permit MAFF progressively to direct support into phased increases of food production, in the areas and the order indicated by the joint resource evaluation. These phases would be:

first, remaining marginal agricultural, reverted or non-amenity vegetated land;
second, graded conservation land;
third, recreational open space, such as golf courses and parks;
finally, the conservation heartland and the commons, where, even at this stage of the emergency, there should be a strong presumption against any form of cultivation.

This is, admittedly, a desperate policy for an emergency that, one hopes, will never arrive. But it attempts to clarify the problem and to show the advantages of an integrated policy and a joint evaluation of resources. Only in an almost unthinkable emergency should the conservation heartland—which currently may be grubbed up or converted by any farmer with a mind to it—lose its protection. Integration, of course, applies equally to forestry, which Colin Price discusses in Chapter 9, and in neither case is there any more time to lose. We are looking, in this book, as much as 50 years ahead. But if we look back 50 years, to the foundation of the CPRE, we can see, all too clearly, how much can happen in that time, and how long it takes to achieve essential reforms.

8

Too Much Planning
—or Too Little?

ADRIAN PHILLIPS

ANYONE who is concerned about the future of the English countryside, especially the conservation of its landscape, has good cause to be discouraged by what has happened in recent years. Since the war some 50,000 acres of countryside have been lost annually to urban uses (63,000 annually between 1968 and 1973;[1] new roads and powerlines have sliced up the countryside; larger reservoirs have been built and bigger mineral workings opened up than ever before; there have been new, and often damaging pressures from recreation; extensive coniferous afforestation has taken place; and more radical changes have occurred in the appearance of the farmed countryside than any since the enclosures, perhaps since man cleared the primeval forests. These are the outward signs of far reaching economic and social changes in rural Britain; welcome as most of these changes are, their impact on the countryside has been largely destructive.

It is ironic that the countryside should have suffered so much when, for the first time, development and conservation have, in theory, been made subject to overall control through the town and country planning system. The failure of the planning system to develop as a really successful vehicle for change and conservation in the countryside has led many to despair of it. But this is to misread the signs: the problem is not too much planning but too little. In reality the countryside has been largely deprived of the planning it needs.[2] This neglect must be remedied because by almost any social, economic or physical measure the rate of change in the countryside is now without precedent, as is the uncertainty which observers feel about where these changes are leading. Unless there is better and more planning than hitherto we shall lose all control over what happens to the countryside.

1. *Hansard*, 20 November 1974, col. 422

2. Unless the text indicates otherwise, the terms 'planning' and 'planning system' are used to mean something rather wider than just those activities deriving from Town and Country Planning legislation; they embrace also the actions of central government and of regional bodies which affect the way in which local planning authorities exercise their planning powers. It is appreciated, though, that even this is a relatively narrow definition, excluding, for example, all the resource planning done by different arms of government and the estate planning done by public and private landowners.

The changes which will affect the countryside

Events outside Britain will have a growing impact on the English countryside. In international affairs a notable feature of the 1970s has been the emerging awareness, prompted by such traumas as the energy crisis, that a 'one world economy' has arrived; global interdependence is the dominant theme of our times. This interdependence has already begun to be felt in rural areas, for example in the rise in the costs of fuel, animal feedstuffs and timber, and in the impact of 'imported' inflation.[3] Our current difficulties are not deviations from the norm, but the precursors of a new and lasting situation with profound implications for the countryside. Britain will have to grow much more of her own food and perhaps timber, aim at self-sufficiency in energy and adopt conservation policies—including recycling—towards such resources as she has.

Clearly such considerations have profound implications for planners and planning; land use issues in the countryside will become even more critical than hitherto. As in wartime, the emphasis on maximising food production from the land is likely to take precedence over other considerations. The planning system will need, more effectively than hitherto, to protect productive farmland from the other demands put upon it, and future generations will judge us as having been extraordinarily shortsighted in allowing so much post-war development to take place on good farmland, with the implicit assumption behind such decisions that we could always import the food we needed. Self-sufficiency in energy is also likely to be pursued at almost any cost; the coasts of Wales and South West England may well have to accommodate some of the oil-related developments which have arrived in Scotland; opencast and deep mining for coal may occur in areas previously unscarred. Likewise with minerals, particularly those which we import but which are also found, albeit as low grade ores, in our finer areas of countryside.

While Britain led the world as an exporter of manufactured goods and imported food and raw materials cheaply, the imbalance between population and the productive capacity of the land and surrounding areas could be ignored. But now she must become more self-reliant. Conservationists fear that it will be the environment, especially the rural environment, which will suffer as more effort is put into exploiting our own resources; they are also apprehensive lest politicians and others become impatient with what they may regard as the selfish antics of the environment lobby when national survival is at stake. This argument can already be heard and needs to be refuted. The financial costs of protecting the countryside are, in terms of gross national product, infinitesimal. The impact on the output of food and timber would be similarly insignificant. And disregard for the rural environment is shortsighted as it implies a readiness to bequeath an impoverished

3. These events have had a more profound impact on economic activities in the countryside than the politically more controversial issue of decisions taken in Brussels.

countryside to our descendants—for landscapes and wildlife are not restored quickly and historical features once lost are gone forever. Finally, it means discounting the strongly-held views of a large part of an increasingly environmentally-literate population who care about what happens to the countryside.

So against a worrying global perspective and uncertain long-term prospects, we must grapple with conflicting claims on the countryside and find ways of meeting a variety of objectives, social, economic and environmental. The planning system is the only democratic way we have of doing this. The challenge therefore is not to replace the system with something else but to analyse its shortcomings, and those of the planners who work it, and to suggest how improvements could be made. Such an analysis follows, by reference to four levels of countryside planning (the national, regional, county and local), and to the training of rural planners.

Planning at the national level

At the final Countryside in 1970 Conference the then Prime Minister, Mr Heath, said that the newly-formed Department of the Environment would help conserve the countryside.[4] But he left his listeners mulling over two questions: how would the DOE relate to the other departments of government whose duties had, as the Prime Minister put it, secondary environmental aspects? and how successful would be the integration within the DOE of the functions such as local government, the regional machinery, physical planning, housing and pollution control, transport, the construction industry and the management of the government's own estate which were formerly the responsibility of three separate departments? Five years later, we can attempt some assessment of the DOE's performance.

First, it has done well just to survive in broadly its original form; indeed it has, by bringing nature conservation and sport within its orbit, shown a capacity to enlarge its functions still further; contrast the fate of its twin sister, the Department of Trade and Industry, whose functions have been substantially pared down. Given the passing of two general elections and the economic and social difficulties facing all governments since 1970, it is probable that had either the concept or the functioning of the Department of the Environment been found conspicuously wanting, it would not have lasted unscathed.

But the mere presence of the Department has fostered a misplaced complacency: that the environment is adequately allowed for in the process of government by establishing a powerful department of state whose prime responsibility it is to be concerned with the protection of the environment. This may be true for urban planning where so many of the considerations which relate to how towns develop, such as housing, transport or local government, fall within the DOE's scope but it is

4. 'Proceedings of the Third Countryside in 1970 Conference', p. 166, The Royal Society of Arts, 1970

most certainly not so in the countryside. The land uses associated with some activities, such as urban expansion, transport, mining, water storage and recreation fall within planning control (subject to certain conspicuous omissions where statutory undertakers and minerals are concerned), and there is close DOE involvement in these at the national level. But the two activities which have the greatest impact on the countryside, farming and forestry, are very largely outside the ambit of planning and, at the level of central government, are wholly separate from DOE. Emphatically this is not an argument for including the Ministry of Agriculture within the DOE, nor for the inclusion of all agricultural activities under planning control. But there is a need for a thorough examination of the potential and real conflicts which exist between the prosperous agriculture which it is MAFF's duty to promote and the countryside which DOE, the Countryside Commission and local planning authorities aim to conserve.

The Ministry of Agriculture is already powerfully influential in determining how the countryside is used; under the impact of the pressures outlined above, the influence of its future policies on the countryside will be all the greater. Though many recent changes in farming and forestry practice have worked against conservation interests, it is by no means clear that this had to be so or must be so in the future. For example with a creative approach on the part of farmers and the Ministry to landscape,[5] new and attractive landscapes could emerge in areas of intensive farming. But this depends upon a contract between the planning of the Ministry of Agriculture and that of the local planning authorities and the DOE. Under the terms of this contract, the planning authorities, backed and guided by DOE would be more diligent in protecting good farmland from urban development, and for their part, the Ministry of Agriculture would promote policies of conservation in harness with those designed to raise agricultural productivity. Steps to this latter end might include: the recruitment of professional ecological and landscape advisers with the Ministry; the establishment of a group of independent advisers to the Minister of Agriculture to consider any topic of common concern to agriculture and the environment referred to them, and to publish their findings; the setting up of a working party of senior MAFF and DOE officials upon which the Nature Conservancy Council and Countryside Commission might also serve, to identify areas of potential conflict between their respective policies and consider how these should be resolved; and the production of joint MAFF/DOE advice to local authority planners and farmers on matters of common concern. Unless this is done, unless, so to speak, MAFF, is 'environmentally fertilised', a widening gap will emerge between the environmental expectations of local authority planners and the reality brought about by further developments in intensive farming; and responding to future global developments, we shall most assuredly destroy the environmental quality of our farmed

5. 'New Agricultural Landscapes', The Countryside Commission, CCP 76, 1974

landscape. If there were no other way it would be a price worth paying to survive, but if we organise our institutions and policies properly, it is not a price we *have* to pay.

Though recent experience and foreseeable developments suggest that the greatest single threat to the environmental quality of the country-side comes from the agricultural industry, much of what is said above about the need to take organisational steps to inspire a greater environ-mental awareness in MAFF is true of other government departments. In this respect it is not enough to rely on the requirements of Section 11 of the Countryside Act;[6] its purposes are wholly commendable but it has had about as much impact on the course of events in the countryside as a 'no litter' sign in a London street market. For example it is unlikely to have much effect on a Department of Energy which aims to make Britain self-sufficient in fuel. Decisions taken in that department, which exercises closer control over the industries for which it has responsibility than MAFF can over individual farmers, will be momentous in their significance for the countryside. Though the Department will wish to avoid a repetition of the environmental mistakes of the nineteenth century in exploiting coal, oil, gas and other sources of energy for the twenty-first, this will only come about if the officials there think envir-onmentally; they will be greatly helped in this if environmental exper-tise is lodged in the ministry. DOE's employment of landscape architects as advisers on road design is an encouraging model. The Department of Energy will need to heed the advice of landscape architects, ecologists and experts in rural sociology.

Returning now to the Department of Environment: there have of course been individual decisions which rankle with those concerned about countryside conservation, for example the decision to press ahead with the A66 improvements in the Lake District; and there are individual decisions which please. But more important than these, and the cause of much of the concern about the DOE, has been a certain detachment on the part of the Department towards the countryside. True the Countryside Commission exists to cover landscape and recrea-tion issues and has recently had a small staff increase, but the guidelines agreed between the Commission and the Department make it clear that the Commission is to have only limited involvement in other issues affecting the countryside. This leaves many rural topics with DOE, e.g. policy towards green belts, rural transport, rural settlements, second home ownership, retirement and holiday development, rural mineral resources, the uplands and so on. But in few of these fields have local authorities received much guidance from the centre and little encour-agement to adopt an active role, for example through the purchase of land for conservation. In two or three areas, second homes and disused railway lines for example, it was not until after the Commission had

6. 'In the exercise of their functions relating to land under any enactment every Minister, government department and public body shall have regard to the desirability of conserving the natural beauty and amenity of the countryside.'

itself sponsored studies to focus public attention on the issues that the DOE took an active interest.

The need for a strong lead from central government on countryside policy issues was felt by the authors of the CoEnCo report[7] who proposed a Royal Commission on the countryside to 'consider changes which are taking place, the consequences and uncertainties associated with these changes and [to make] recommendations upon the ways in which [the countryside] should be planned, in order that it can realise its optimum use as a resource for production and recreation and an area for satisfactory living'. It was implicit too in the report the Sandford Committee[8] on national parks which by making 48 recommendations, mostly directed at government, was partly a criticism of the previous neglect of these areas. Whether a Royal Commission is established — and the attraction of having such a body to provoke debate on the future of the countryside is considerable — and whatever may be done about the individual Sandford recommendations, the DOE is likely to have to take a more active role than hitherto in identifying the problems of the countryside and promoting the policies to solve them. Of course social equity alone requires that the Department continue to give priority to the problems of the urban environment; as Mr Crosland's Fabian pamphlet reminds us,[9] this is the environment which concerns most people most of the time and much of it is in dire need of improvement. Even so it might be helpful if the Department of Environment were to devote more of its resources to rural planning; after all the countryside is 80 per cent of our environment.

Not that the countryside is a planning vacuum. Over the years central government and its agencies have developed a pattern of defences for the countryside through the zoning of national parks, national nature reserves, ancient monuments and so on. It could be the basis for a comprehensive and sensible national strategy for the protection of the countryside. This, of course, is not exclusively a matter for the Department of the Environment; other ministries and agencies in resource planning are involved. Can they work so closely together that their policies harmonise rather than conflict?

The danger of a profusion of agencies with advisory or executive functions in the field of countryside recreation and conservation is the waste of valuable manpower and scarce financial resources, the difficulties of developing national policies and the possibility of contradictory advice being given to local planning authorities. At present there are, in England alone, seven such bodies.[10] What is required here is as near

7. 'Urban Pressures on the Countryside', Committee for Environmental Conservation, 1972

8. Report of the National Park Policies Review Committee, HMSO 1974

9. Anthony Crosland, *A Social Democratic Britain*, Fabian Tract 404, 1971

10. The Countryside Commission, the Forestry Commission, the Sports Council, the Nature Conservancy Council, the British Waterways Board, the Water Space Amenity Commission and the English Tourist Board

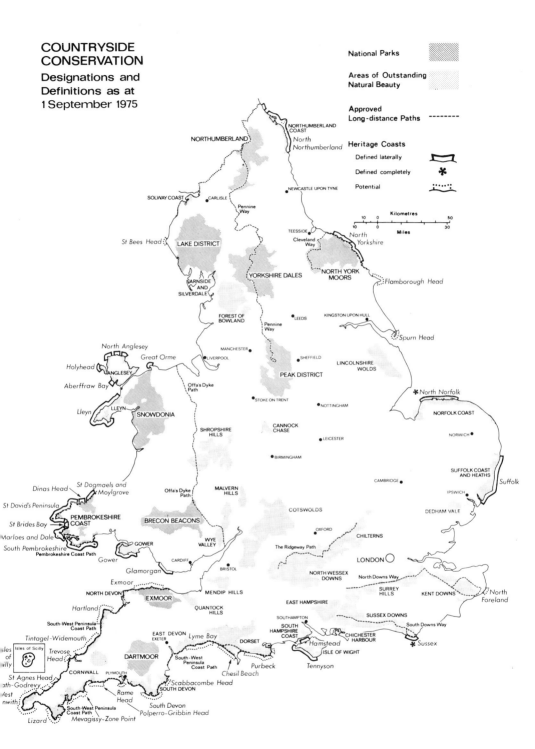

COUNTRYSIDE CONSERVATION

Designations and Definitions as at 1 September 1975

National Parks

Areas of Outstanding Natural Beauty

Approved Long-distance Paths

Heritage Coasts

Defined laterally

Defined completely

Potential

Kilometres

Miles

NORTHUMBERLAND COAST

NORTHUMBERLAND

North Northumberland

SOLWAY COAST

CARLISLE

NEWCASTLE UPON TYNE

Pennine Way

St Bees Head

LAKE DISTRICT

TEESSIDE

Cleveland Way

North Yorkshire

ARNSIDE AND SILVERDALE

YORKSHIRE DALES

NORTH YORK MOORS

Flamborough Head

FOREST OF BOWLAND

LEEDS

KINGSTON UPON HULL

Pennine Way

Spurn Head

North Anglesey

Great Orme

MANCHESTER

LIVERPOOL

SHEFFIELD

LINCOLNSHIRE WOLDS

Holyhead

ANGLESEY

Aberffraw Bay

Offa's Dyke Path

PEAK DISTRICT

STOKE ON TRENT

North Norfolk

Lleyn

LLEYN

SNOWDONIA

NOTTINGHAM

NORFOLK COAST

SHROPSHIRE HILLS

CANNOCK CHASE

LEICESTER

NORWICH

BIRMINGHAM

Dinas Head

St Dogmaels and Moylgrove

Offa's Dyke Path

MALVERN HILLS

SUFFOLK COAST AND HEATHS

Suffolk

St David's Peninsula

PEMBROKESHIRE COAST

COTSWOLDS

CAMBRIDGE

IPSWICH

St Brides Bay

DEDHAM VALE

Marloes and Dale

South Pembrokeshire

Pembrokeshire Coast Path

BRECON BEACONS

WYE VALLEY

OXFORD

CHILTERNS

GOWER

CARDIFF

The Ridgeway Path

LONDON

Gower

Glamorgan

BRISTOL

NORTH WESSEX DOWNS

North Downs Way

North Foreland

Exmoor

MENDIP HILLS

EAST HAMPSHIRE

SURREY HILLS

KENT DOWNS

NORTH DEVON

EXMOOR

QUANTOCK HILLS

SUSSEX DOWNS

Hartland

SOUTHAMPTON

SOUTH HAMPSHIRE COAST

CHICHESTER HARBOUR

South Downs Way

South-West Peninsula Coast Path

EAST DEVON

EXETER

Lyme Bay

DORSET

Hamstead

Sussex

Tintagel-Widemouth

Trevose Head

DARTMOOR

South-West Peninsula Coast Path

Purbeck

ISLE OF WIGHT

Tennyson

Isles of Scilly

St Agnes Head

Chesil Beach

CORNWALL

PLYMOUTH

Scabbacombe Head

SOUTH DEVON

Bath-Godrevy

West Penwith

Rame Head

South Devon

Lizard

South-West Peninsula Coast Path

Mevagissy-Zone Point

Polperro-Gribbin Head

a guarantee as a government department can give of several years' continued existence for all the bodies currently in being. This time should be used to carry out a joint central government/agency review to evolve a sensible national and regional structure for countryside agencies over a period of, say, 10–15 years. In this way each agency would have, in the short term, the assurance of continuity, yet each could contribute towards formulating the long-term pattern of government agencies with countryside responsibilities. This should enhance morale and ensure that the agencies' experience is made available to government.

The regional level

Over the last five years, government has repeatedly stressed its faith in regional strategies as guidance to the counties preparing structure plans and to government departments in planning their own investment in the region, thus bridging the gap between decisions taken at a national level which have an impact on the environment and the plans of the local planning authorities. The concept of a regional role for government, which was a very tender plant ten years ago, when George Brown set up the regional economic councils and boards, has become well-established; a surprising success when the fate of most advisory bodies is recalled. With more political devolution to Wales and Scotland now under active consideration it is hardly conceivable that the regions of England would diminish in importance. In countryside affairs, therefore, a higher level of activity in central and local government should be complemented by a strengthened input by the countryside agencies in the regions.

There is evidence, for example in the South East Strategy and the plan for the North West region, that the joint central-local government teams have begun to think constructively about the countryside, recognising its vital economic role, especially through the production of food and timber, and its aesthetic and restorative value for our largely urbanised population. This is a welcome departure from earlier attitudes, typified by the expression 'white land' which implied that the countryside was a *tabula rasa* upon which urban forces could be given largely free rein. However the analysis of the issues which arise in planning the countryside, and the development of appropriate policies in the strategies are capable of much improvement. For example the strategy for the South East was thin in its treatment of regional recreation.[11]

11. It was for this reason that the Countryside Commission, the Standing Conference on London and South East Regional Planning, the Greater London Council and the Economic Planning Council for the South East joined together, after the publication of the Strategy, to study current and future countryside recreation patterns in the region and come up with the basis of strategic policies which might be incorporated in the planning authorities' structure plans.

The effective coverage of countryside matters in regional strategies will depend in part upon the government agencies with responsibility for countryside recreation and for conservation developing a regional voice. Whereas at national level several points of contact exist for these bodies,[12] there is no comparable machinery for joint working at regional level. Most of the bodies have a regional structure, but the boundaries of their 'regions' differ; the Countryside Commission has no real regional set-up at all,[13] only internal divisions in its one English office at Cheltenham.

The agencies should co-operate at regional level so that they can work better with each other, give co-ordinated and better informed advice to local government (especially the counties), and supplement and, if necessary, counter-balance the powerful regional voices of government departments such as DOE and MAFF. But such co-operation will not come about without organisational changes designed to foster closer working between agencies. Because these changes will impinge on complex and sensitive matters about which agencies and government departments are likely to have strong views, a thorough analysis of the ways in which agencies can and should co-operate at the regional level is needed; hence regional structure should fall within the terms of reference of the joint review suggested above.

County level

With the coming into being of the 45 new county councils in England on 1 April 1974, and in particular with their responsibility to prepare structure plans, it should be easier to incorporate the countryside into strategic planning. Of course some counties had shown themselves forward looking in this respect before 1974, but too often the coverage of rural matters in the development plans of the former counties was disappointing, with conceptual thinking which was frequently poor. Will structure planning authorities undertake a systematic examination of the likely future pattern of demand and the resources available to meet recreation demands? Are there effective methods of landscape evaluation which can be used, and will it be possible to implement the admirable statements of intent towards landscape conservation which will doubtless be made?

In the past deficiencies of technique, typical of the intellectually weak base to much rural planning, have stemmed in part from a lack of authoritative guidance, and in part have been a consequence of the previous local government system. Many of the former counties, especially the rural ones, adopted a defensive posture towards the pressures which fell upon them from the adjoining cities for housing land,

12. For example, in meetings chaired by the Countryside Commission, by the Countryside Recreation Research Advisory Group and (the English Tourist Board and the Forestry Commission apart) through their parent body, the DOE.

13. Since this chapter was written it has been announced that the Commission will have a presence in the new Regional Councils for Sport and Recreation.

for recreation and so on. Many of the county boroughs looked upon the surrounding counties as extensive reserves into which they should be permitted to expand at will. Creative planning rarely flourishes in a community which adopts a hostile attitude to change, nor are many good planners attracted to serve in such areas. So most of the planning departments of the former counties concentrated on development control, an activity which accorded well with the essentially conservative attitudes prevalent in many rural areas. Of course development control is a vital part of planning but if it is not harnessed to serve the purposes of a good plan it can be arbitrary and sterile.

It is important not to overstate the case nor to parody what happened. In nearly every county planning office there were men and women of vision and they had their counterparts on the committee; in some areas they carried the day. Often the most forward looking members of planning committees were those with the deepest roots in the past, whose inherited sense of stewardship towards the land they owned and their tenants made them far-seeing members of the planning committees. But even so the 1974 reforms should help planners in the counties to think strategically about town and country without the distraction of boundaries—although this problem will remain where metropolitan counties are concerned since they are still cut off from their hinterland. There have also been significant developments in the style of local government; because the environment is one of those topics which has its impact upon, and is affected by nearly all the functions of local government, it is a consideration which should benefit from corporate planning in county halls. So, while the passing of the old counties carries with it dangers that the rural voice may be drowned when it should be heard and that the relationship between counties and districts may often be difficult, a better chance exists now than before 1974 to accord the countryside the standard of strategic planning it deserves.

The statutory vehicle for strategic planning is the structure plan, which provides the framework for public investment in the county and for major land-use decisions; it also guides districts in development control and local plan-making. Structure plans are only approved by the Secretary of State after a thorough period of public discussion and participation. Public debate about plans serves two purposes: the authors of the plan can learn from those who will be affected by it, and those for whom the plan is being prepared are enlightened about the problems the planners face; the result should thus be a better plan and a better-informed public.

County planners preparing the structure plan need guidance from an advisory countryside committee. Some counties may choose to set up sub-committees of the county with co-opted members; others establish broadly based consultative committees. Whatever their precise terms of reference and composition, countryside committees should always provide a meeting point for groups as far apart as the National

The extent to which the motor car has influenced English land use planning is revealed by this aerial view of Downham, Kent. *(Photo: John Topham)*

Farmers' Union and the Ramblers Association. They provide a channel for ideas from within the rural community which planners can work on, a device which can be used to harness voluntary effort in the countryside, and a convenient test bed for the planners' proposals while still in draft.

In the past there has often been a wide gulf between planners and land users; each has viewed the other with suspicion if not outright hostility. In part this reflects policy differences at a national level; for example, the dispute over ploughing of moorland in Exmoor National Park arose because it appeared that the intentions of national park legislation were in conflict with the policies of the Ministry of Agriculture. There are similar ambiguities in national policy with regard to forestry in national parks. The land users' attitude is no different from that of anyone else who senses that his freedom of action is constrained by planners. But feelings run high because there is a fundamental difference of temperament between the two groups. The officials have a professional background that leads them to assume the inevitability and rightness of public control over private actions which affect the environment. But land users are essentially an independent-minded body of men, whether they be small hill farmers or 'barley-barons'. They tend to regard the planning machine as an ill-informed and unwarranted intrusion upon a task made difficult enough by the vagaries of the market and the climate. Indeed so wide apart are these two groups that they sometimes have a wholly different perception of environmental conditions; thus studies have shown that farmers derive more aesthetic pleasure from an intensively farmed area, largely devoid of trees, hedges and wildlife than from a more neglected farmland, but scenically and ecologically more diverse, and which the community as a whole would probably consider more attractive.[14]

The preparation of the structure plan offers an opportunity to close this gap. Planners should use these occasions not only to explain their thinking but, even more important, should involve land users in the formulation of policy, give them the confidence that their views are listened to and, where possible, allocate to them a role in the plan; for local and special plans can be a help to landowners who wish to provide for recreation, re-organise the footpath network or plant trees on their land. In this way planners will improve the chances of a harmonious relationship when it comes to dealing with individual cases which are potentially disputatious, such as the siting of a large farm building, the clearance of small areas of woodland vital to wildlife, or an attempt to close a footpath. The scope for conflict between planners and land users will increase in the future and some friction will be unavoidable; but planners must redouble their efforts to reduce this to the minimum without, of course, sacrificing the rural environment which it is their responsibility to conserve. Some rebuffs are to be expected but it is a welcome sign that the National Farmers' Union should now be encouraging its members to be active in public participation about structure plans.

District level

This is the new front line of planning; whatever the reservations of the planners about the wisdom of giving such a wide range of planning powers to such relatively small authorities,[15] the present disposition of powers is likely to stand for many years. So profoundly traumatic has been the experience of local government reform that there is little likelihood that even the most palpable shortcomings of the new system will be corrected until a new generation of local government members and officers have taken power and new officials are at their desks in Whitehall.

The quality of development control and local plan making will vary widely between districts. This is likely to occur just because more and smaller local authority units make for variability; it may also happen

14. 'New Agricultural Landscapes', *op. cit.*

15. The concern of planners and other professionals on this score was never a popular cause. In so far as there was an identifiable public view in rural areas on the subject, it was distrust of the proposed new districts on the grounds that they would be larger and more remote than their predecessors, the Urban and Rural District Councils and Municipal Boroughs, even though few of these had significant planning powers.

because the total of talented planners is limited and they will probably group themselves around the better district planning officers; and it may also occur because local plans, prepared by district councils, will be subject only to the most limited supervision by the county or the Secretary of State. In this situation countryside conservationists would be well advised to encourage an articulate and informed public opinion, to press for improvements to the development control machinery, and to argue for better protection for nationally-designated areas.

Public opinion is often more persuasive in a small local authority than a large one, perhaps because the elected are personally known to many electors. Rural conservation groups should exploit this factor. No apology is needed for this plea for lobbying; for certain, there will be other groups, many of whose interests may be hostile to countryside conservation who will argue their own cause. Conservationists will find planners and councillors more receptive to participatory planning than formerly, even though there is the occasional frustrating reversion to the Jurassic age of local government secrecy. This creates exciting new

More than a quarter of a million people live in Britain's ten national parks, many of them in villages like Thwaite (*left*) in the Yorkshire Dales. From time to time conflicts arise between the economic health of such communities and their status as areas statutorily protected for their beauty.

(*Photo: Barnaby's Picture Library*)

opportunities, especially at the district level, for partnerships to be forged between local government and the voluntary movement. But in voicing their concern for conservation, amenity groups should show themselves both well-informed and broad-minded, innovative but realistic, politically mature and drawing their support from all ages and classes. These high standards are required if the opportunities opened up by participatory planning are to be taken; nothing is more disheartening than to hear an amenity group, under the specious guise of conservation, advance narrow, selfish arguments, display misanthropic views towards visitors to the countryside, or air ill-informed opinions about farmers. The constructive role that voluntary groups can play is considered by Dr Roy Gregory in Chapter 13.

Outside national parks, where control is the responsibility of planning boards or county council national park committees, all but a few categories of planning applications are determined by district councils

Contrary to popular belief, the designation of areas of England and Wales as national parks (*above*) has had no significant consequences for patterns of land ownership. And although planning is the responsibility of a national park planning board or county council national park committee, the main land uses—agriculture and forestry—lie almost entirely outside control. (*Photo: Countryside Commission*)

who will be judged largely by their performance in development control. Here a distinction should be drawn between the shortcomings of legislation, which may not allow the planning authority a satisfactory measure of control, and the shortcomings of the authority itself, that is in making 'bad' decisions. One cannot legislate for good decisions, only provide the right training for the professionals who advise, and members who take decisions, foster a public opinion which cares, and so create the conditions in which wise development control flourishes. But the legislative weaknesses can be removed.

Development control has always invited easy jibes, for example Lord Goodman's witty but one-sided observation that 'we have in this country a system of planning that would have made the Ottoman Empire drool with envy'.[16] A more balanced comment is to be found in the interim Dobry report:[17] 'Although it is dangerous to generalise, my present impression is that control is sometimes liable to be exercised in far too rigid and bureaucratic a manner and too slowly.' Dorby sees no case for a *substantial* relaxation of controls on a national basis, though he has a lot to say on the details of the development control system. Considering that his report arose from a climate of hectic concern, almost panic, that the rising pace of applications, very evident in 1973, coupled with the upheaval of local government reform could lead to the collapse of the entire system, this conclusion that no fundamental changes are called for in the system is sobering. But in three areas there is a need for selective tightening of controls: over the special position enjoyed by farmers and foresters; over that of statutory undertakers; and in national parks and areas of outstanding natural beauty.

The relationship between land users and planners in the countryside is a recurring theme in this chapter. At district level planners and land users need to come to terms with each other and to accept two dominant realities: that we shall have need of our farmers as never before in peacetime; and that the scenic, wildlife and historic resources in the countryside will be endangered on an unprecedented scale by the activities of land users. This is why planners must take agriculture and forestry as fully into their thinking as, say, transportation; and landowners must accept a greater degree of control over their activities than hitherto. This is not the place to explore in detail the arcane wonders of the General Development Order but the absence of planning control is most serious in three areas: the siting and design of farm buildings presently exempt from control; the ploughing up or afforestation of formerly open country often vital to the landscape; and the clearance of hardwoods important to the appearance of the countryside. The objections to extending planning control into these areas are not without force; certainly there are dangers in so doing. But against them should be set the difficulties planning authorities find in conserv-

16. *The Observer*, 27 October 1974

17. 'Review of the Development Control System'; interim report by George Dobry QC, HMSO 1974

ing the countryside when these activities are not subject to control, and the inequity of a system which, for example, imposes a requirement for planning permission upon an urban householder wishing to build a garage in his garden but permits a landowner or forestry interest to enclose and afforest many hundreds of acres of much admired moorland. Farmers and foresters currently hard hit by inflation, and worried by the effects of a capital transfer and possible wealth tax, may not respond to this argument with enthusiasm, but they have better reason than most to be confident about their long-term future; people will always need what they produce.

Even so, the control by planning of farming and forestry should be limited; it is not normally the best way, for example, of preserving individual trees in the countryside nor of controlling most day-to-day land use or management actions of farmers and landowners. However, new legislation is needed to make it easier for local authorities and land users to enter into management agreements for conservation purposes. Such agreements could certainly supplement planning control in rural areas and help attain the objectives in development plans but there is a need also for extensive experimentation in this field before we can be sure how widespread their uses should be.

Local authorities and statutory undertakers also enjoy some exemption from development control. For example minor—and sometimes not so minor—road improvements can be carried out without any form of supervision by the planning authority even though the cumulative environmental impact of minor road widenings and straightenings is considerable. Regional water authorities have wide discretion to carry out river improvement schemes involving dredging, straightening and dumping waste material which can largely destroy the individual character of waterways. To bring such activities within planning control would check the worst excesses while achieving high standards of design and encouraging landscape treatment where works are essential. A prize should be given to the first district council which can banish concrete posts and chain-link fencing from their countryside.

The operation of the General Development Order (GDO) may be likened to a fishing net; little items find their way through the mesh where the GDO automatically grants permission for certain classes of development. It is surprising that there should be no finer-meshed net in those areas of countryside (or towns for that matter) of special environmental significance, such as national parks or areas of outstanding natural beauty, except in the rare cases where an Article 4 Direction is in force. In its absence minor permitted developments, which may be acceptable in more robust environments, can, over time, have a serious impact on the quality of countryside which is supposed to have a special degree of protection. Thus, whatever may be done throughout the countryside, there is an especially strong case for a more restrictive approach in these areas to give them added protection and reassure a

The most beautiful landscapes may be protected by more than one formal designation. Beachy Head, Sussex (*left*) lies within a statutory Area of Outstanding Natural Beauty, as well as being on a Heritage Coast. The South Downs Way, a protected long distance footpath, passes along the cliff top. Kynance Cove, Cornwall (*below*) is similarly designated. But the protection afforded by designations is often more illusory than real.

(Photos: Leonard and Marjorie Gayton; E.W. Tattersall)

public sceptical of the significance of designation. The mechanics for this might be a National Parks and Areas of Outstanding Natural Beauty Special Development Order by which some GDO exemptions would be selectively withdrawn in such areas. The lead has come in the Dobry report.[18]

National parks have received much attention recently; legislation in 1972 and 1974 has built a new basis for administration and finance, and the Sandford report has aired the policy questions. The special status of the parks is now recognised in several ways; for example their planning and management are a county or planning board responsibility. For a decade or two at least the existing concept of national parks seems likely to hold good. However, a lively debate seems probable on the desirability of retaining the other special areas of countryside, e.g. areas of outstanding natural beauty, green belts and heritage coasts where conservation will be left largely with the district councils.

That debate has begun. At the Countryside in 1970 Conference,[19] for example, Sir Colin Buchanan repeated the argument that by giving some areas of countryside special status—by 'docketing' them—we threaten by neglect the remaining unremarkable areas which give our countryside its quality. The green belt has been much criticised; indeed to denounce it as a weapon of middle class hegemony has become obligatory for membership of the neo-Marxist school of urban planners. Special areas are also likely to be criticised by some of the district councils affected, resenting what may appear as rather arbitrary designations which could restrain economic activity. There are even amenity groups who will criticise the concept on the grounds that, judging by past performance, the delineation of special areas appears to have little effect on the policies followed by planning authorities or to influence Ministers on appeal, and that they could indeed be counter-productive by attracting visitors. And certainly there will be developers, landowners and others who will always fear that the policies applying within such areas will circumscribe their freedom.

There is truth in some of these arguments; certainly a government-led study of the purposes behind the green belt is long overdue. But we should retain areas of outstanding natural beauty (though a less cumbersome title could surely be devised, one that omits the inaccurate word 'natural') and identify other special landscape and conservation areas. The more we understand about our environment, the clearer becomes the need to select and apply different policies in different areas, and to rank policies as of national, regional, county or local significance; thereby plans can be made to reflect the essential diversity of the environment at the appropriate level of significance. Theory apart, it is clear from the report of the Countryside Commission 'that the AONB concept is widely supported by local planning authorities, as

18. 'Review of the Development Control System'; final report by George Dobry QC, HMSO 1975

19. 'Proceedings of the Third Countryside in 1970 Conference', *op. cit.*, pp. 63–6

well as amenity interests . . .; there is increasing evidence that government, local government and developers accord these areas respect in
considering where new development should be located'. They also
argue in support of new designations that 'there are several tracts of
undesignated countryside which, by common consent, are at least as
attractive as some of the areas already designated'.[20] The question then
is not whether we should protect some areas of our countryside by
singling them out for special attention, but how to persuade the district
councils, whose day-to-day responsibility they will be, to give them the
care they need.

These are the kind of questions which need answering:

(a) How can counties and districts be encouraged to work together in
    drawing up and implementing policies for these special areas so that
    they are planned as one unit even when they cross administrative
    boundaries (all but five of the existing 32 areas of outstanding
    natural beauty will be divided between two or more districts and
    several will lie across county boundaries)? Do they require special
    committees?

(b) How can district councils bring landowners, farmers, amenity
    bodies, recreation interests, developers and so on together and
    obtain their support for conservation of such areas (here it may be
    worth watching the Countryside Commission experiments in
    selected heritage coasts)?[21]

(c) Should there be a special emphasis on management policies in these
    areas to supplement planning policies, as is proposed for national
    parks in the Sandford report? And if so, what administrative struc-
    ture do they require?

(d) What should be the role of central government and its agencies in
    giving financial support to districts which incur costs in protecting
    these areas?

Local government reform assigned the day-to-day planning of our
environment to the care of 326 district councils. In rural areas some of
these councils are responsible for countryside and coast of national
importance, areas like the Sussex Downs, the Cornish Cliffs and the
Shropshire Hills. The way in which they look after such areas—how
they handle development pressures, cope with visitors, protect farming
interests, involve the local community in schemes of conservation and
so forth—should be watched closely by conservationists.

Training the rural planners

More and better planning at each level, from central government to
the district councils, requires more and better planners. Unfortunately
rural planning has been neglected in the training given to most planners; the subject has never become fashionable among those who design

20. Annual Report of the Countryside Commission, 1972–3, HMSO 1974
21. *Ibid.*, pp. 12–13

and teach curricula. By comparison with the study of inner city problems, of methods and techniques of planning or of transportation, rural planning has, generally, been given little attention. There is still a tendency to look upon rural planning as a 'soft option', as an appropriate backwater for the less talented and less ambitious. Yet, as many of the younger planners in central and local governments now appreciate, countryside planning raises difficult and complex social, political, economic, even ethical questions; indeed, in one sense, it is wider in scope than urban planning because it requires a major input from the natural sciences.

The Countryside Commission have sought to raise the level of discussion on rural planning; thus they have sponsored research and experiments, published the results and held seminars on various topics. But they have neither the remit nor the resources to delve deeply; they study symptoms not causes. In any case there are many fields of rural planning for which they have no mandate.

Even if the Department of the Environment gives a more forceful lead in rural planning than hitherto, something else is needed if more teachers and students are to pay it the attention it deserves; what is missing is an intellectually respectable 'voice' to speak for rural planning, which could explore in depth topics of current or likely future concern and disseminate findings through papers, seminars, etc. This could be provided by a national centre of rural planning studies.[22] It would need to develop close working relations with the national and local government bodies who could make use of its findings, but also to awaken in other educational institutions an interest in rural planning. A small core staff would be required, drawn from several disciplines, to which would be attached temporary staff on fellowships, principally from national and local government. To extend its influence to the full, it might also provide short, intensive in-service refresher courses to local authority officials in counties and districts. As to finance, at least some of the funds could come from the government departments and agencies with the principal interest — the Department of the Environment, the Ministry of Agriculture, the Countryside Commission and the Nature Conservancy Council.

However, the argument running through the chapter is that we need particularly by broadening the professions represented in the planning office. Agriculturists, estate managers and ecologists should contribute to the making and implementation of plans for the countryside. Of course it takes time for a multi-disciplinary team to jell and for the habits of mind to evolve which allow each skill to make its distinctive contribution, but the increasingly active role for rural planning sketched out above calls for a range of professional comprehension which is not represented in any one discipline.

22. A School for Advanced Urban Studies at Bristol University, set up in 1973 with the financial backing of the DOE, provides an instructive precedent.

Conclusion

This chapter began on a pessimistic note in summarising the changes in the countryside since the war. Is there any reason to end by looking forward more optimistically? The prospect is sombre because Britain's social and economic problems conspire to threaten the future of the countryside, particularly in the pursuit of food and energy.

However, the argument running through the chapter is that we need to use the planning system more, and more wisely, because it provides the best means of reconciling the conflicting claims upon the countryside and ensuring the conservation of its vital assets for future generations. We have in the planning machine one of the few British institutions which can still be described as the best in the world.[23] But the advantages it offers have nowhere been fully realised. True, in local government there are encouraging signs of an awakening interest in rural planning; and, once the dust has settled, local government reform will be seen to have improved the prospects further. But success depends on a lead from the centre. If government departments with the principal responsibilities grasp the need for comprehensive rural planning at all levels, there is a good chance that we can conserve the countryside while, at the same time, following national policies designed to make us more self-sufficient in the production of essential resources. If not, we shall pass on to our children a vastly poorer countryside than we inherited.

23. See footnote 16 on p. 133

9

Forestry

COLIN PRICE

FORESTRY in Britain takes two rather distinct forms. In the lowlands the traditional pattern is of small-scale hardwood blocks, extensive conifer forests being generally confined to the infertile heaths. In the uplands, there is little forestry tradition, but in the last 50 years substantial areas have come under large-scale conifer afforestation. It is arguable that this, of the many recent changes in the uplands, has done most aesthetic damage.

Vociferous opposition from amenity groups has generally met either puzzlement or complacency. Foresters have argued that they know their job, have a 'feel' for the land and so will give landscape due regard. More recently, the Forestry Commission has appointed a landscape adviser, and incorporated aesthetic aims in forest design. While this is all to the good, the relatively minor reforms of practice hardly go far enough. The aesthetic problem of upland forestry is not just a matter of detail, resolved by a gratuitous clump of hardwoods, or the inflection of an odd boundary. Rather, because the topography of the uplands reveals land use in plan-like view, it turns upon tracts of textures and colours, and upon the impact of masses on spaciousness. An unfortunate tendency of afforestation has been to occupy the middle and upper valley-slopes; not only imparting a top-heavy, unstable appearance, but also revealing the maximum extent of forest to view from the opposite valley-slope.

When the forest is so displayed, even a single-species crop of hardwoods would grow monotonous: and the flow of the landscape may become confused when forest sprawls over watersheds and valley-bottoms. To this monotony and confusion, the gloomy, unvarying coloration of most conifers adds an inability to take light and shade. Consequently, subtle undulations of topography become entirely invisible, and even significant ridges tend to merge. Finally, Sitka spruce, the major species of upland afforestation, displays a singular and unattractive texture, abrasively barred, and, even in maturity, a harshly rigid spire never outgrowing the Christmas tree image. On a larger scale, the aggressive striations recur in line-thinnings and grids of fire-breaks. Whenever Sitka is seen on a downward perspective, the eye is concentrated on the gritty texture, and only the most assertive topography can create any differentiation. This is the essential, the unavoidable problem of upland afforestation. Clever landscape architecture can reveal

Forestry Commission plantation near Tregaron in Central Wales. Lines of conifers, monotonously regimented and covering hundreds of acres of formerly open country-side, are also still an unfortunate feature of tracts of the Commission's 610,000 acres of conifer plantation in England. *(Photos: Forestry Action Group)*

the topography and relieve the geometry of boundaries and fire-breaks. But no cosmetic treatment can pleasingly accommodate spruce-tracts to an unreceptive landscape. Subterfuges like hardwood planting in groups or bands tend only to underline the monotony. Retention of existing hardwoods is welcome for wildlife and internal amenity, but the charm of broadleaved softness is spoiled when hemmed within rectangular conifer blocks in external view.

141

Unattractive in itself, the coniferous forest also displaces spacious landscapes, and, unless carefully confined by topography, impinges on an area far beyond its physical boundaries.

The problems of the lowlands are not so intractable. Owing to the preponderance of flat perspectives, masses and harsh geometry make less impact, and there is more possibility of integrating commercial forestry into existing patterns by tinkering with the margins. Cosmetic treatment (hardwood clumps and belts, small clearings, boundaries curved to topography) has more to contribute.

Concern has centred on the traditional hardwood cover, now threatened by neglect, clearance and especially conversion to conifers. In the lower-rainfall, more fertile areas of the Midlands and the East, there are less stringent limits on species that can be grown. Larches, Corsican pine, western hemlock, the cypresses and even Norway spruce, all softer-textured than Sitka, may replace it as the dominant conifer. Nevertheless, transition from hardwood, or even indigenous Scots pine, to these exotic conifers will be detrimental to wildlife and internal amenity.

Frustrated by the failure of aesthetic arguments to reduce the rate either of upland afforestation or of lowland coniferisation, annoyed by foresters' complacency, some amenity groups have broadened their attack to include economics. The singular position of forestry investment is that it takes several decades to mature: upwards of 50 years

Increasingly, in lowland England, soft-textured variable hardwoods are giving way to more commercial conifers. Here, on a Forestry Commission plantation in Herefordshire, ring-barking of immature hardwoods clears the way for conifers, to the inevitable detriment of wildlife and amenity. (*Photo: Forestry Action Group*)

under normal regimes in Britain. Over such a period, the compound effect of the Treasury's 10 per cent discount rate[1] reduces the expected output of timber to an insignificant present value. Since the implication is that British forestry, with rare and special exceptions, is hopelessly unprofitable, it is not surprising that the amenity groups have been attracted to this argument.

But use of a high discount rate in economics is largely due to a conceptual confusion among economists between *rate* of output and *timing* of output. Alternative investments might yield (in simple interest) a social value of 10 per cent of the investment cost per year: but this gives no immediate reason why values a year hence should be depreciated by 10 per cent. Indeed, there are very strong reasons, not least of which is the shortage of raw materials, nor *not* automatically devaluing contributions to future resources. When the timing element is removed, forestry's output compares quite favourably with that of other investments.

This viewpoint, based on a concern for the future, is, admittedly, unconventional, and incomprehensible to most economists. Their arguments against it rest on the (irrelevant) preference of present generations for their own welfare, and on the (unfulfilled) expectation that revenues from Government projects will be reinvested in totality.

The amenity groups, then, cannot legitimately argue high discount rates against afforestation. If they do so, they will find the 10 per cent rate unkind to long-term conservation in other spheres. The case for a long-term outlook being clear, economic objections to forestry must have a less treacherous and illusory foundation than high discount rates. Nor, in a situation of limited resources — especially of energy — does it make sense to assume synthetic substitutes for wood.

There are, of course, other sources of wood. Other countries have better climates for timber production and, all things being equal, would grow the raw material more cheaply. But claims of massive reserves of available timber have been naively made. North American and Russian supplies are likely to be curtailed by rising home demand and decreasing area devoted to forestry. In the tropics too the expansion of agriculture and home demand make plantation forestry and exploitation of virgin forest uncertain sources for 50 years hence. Britain cannot *rely* on being able to import all the timber wanted by then — certainly not at present prices.

Given, then, a concern for the future, and a realistic view of alternative supplies, a case can be made for basic self-sufficiency in timber. But 'basic' does not mean consumption at present, or, even less, at projected levels. Present use of wood products is wasteful, some would

1. Discounting is arithmetically the reverse of compound interest. Instead of converting £100 invested now to £110 in a year's time, discounting at 10 per cent implies that £110 in a year, or £121 in two years, or £11,739 in 50 years is equivalent to £100 today. By working in physical units, such as volume of timber, one may evade the difficulties raised by inflation. The Treasury's discount rate of 10 per cent is supposed to be derived from the rate of interest earned in private investment.

say mindless. A vast amount of paper packaging and printed advertising serves no social end, indeed, encourages consumption of other scarce resources. Demolition and rebuilding requires great quantities of sawn timber. Much of it would never happen if the full cost of raw materials were taken into the reckoning. The timber of old buildings is burned unproductively on site: there are sawmills where the fate of all off-cuts is the same. If circumstances demanded, substitutes for newspapers, disposable wood packaging, even toilet paper could be devised, using much less raw materials. A mend-and-make-do mentality—an integral part of conservation—would have quite modest timber demands: replacements for decayed structural timber, wood to build necessary new homes, some paper for those communication functions that could not be taken over electrically. Present forests are estimated capable of supplying 25–30 per cent of present national demand by the end of the century. By re-use, recycling and restraint, this seems adequate to meet basic requirements without further afforestation, and without reliance on imports or substitutes.

The reduction of supply would, of course, lead to higher real timber prices: indeed, such a rise would be a major incentive towards the economies suggested. Then, further timber-growing would undoubtedly be profitable; provided all other prices remained the same. This latter condition is unlikely to be fulfilled. If pressure on the land resource is expected to increase the price of timber in the world market, price increases should also be expected for agricultural products, for which the possibilities of substitution, re-use and recycling offer little margin of adjustment. The claim that forestry adds to, rather than detracts from agricultural production can be ignored. It is based on experiments where careful estate management has gone in parallel with afforestation, and it is to the former that improvements in agricultural yield should be attributed. It is a reasonable speculation that still higher yields would have been possible if afforestation had been limited to a few shelterbelts.

The decision to afforest should not be taken, therefore, without considering potential needs for agricultural products and the difficulties of re-establishing a stock-farming community and tradition, once these have been eliminated from an area. Furthermore, while the sheep is self-harvesting, the planting and harvesting of timber requires roadstone, machinery and fuel, all of which it is safer to assume will grow scarcer, and thus count more heavily against the net benefit of forests. For technical reasons too, a low discount rate increases the ascribed cost of capital. The enhancement of forestry's prospects by a long-term outlook cannot therefore be assumed proven.

Should the world survive in reasonable order, some timber in excess of the basic home-grown supply might be imported from countries with a more favourable climate. Many potential suppliers are Third World countries who would benefit greatly from labour-intensive export trade. Taking a wide view of welfare, then, the objective of self-sufficiency ought not to be taken further than a basic supply: for efforts to maintain employment in the British uplands actually reduce opportunities for employment in poorer nations. Free trading may not be the complete policy for a world of uncertainty and political stratagems: but it has significance outside the margins of a safety-first supply.

Recent forestry policy

No such long-term or broad-view considerations influenced the policy statement of 1972.[2] Instead, the Government tried to justify its continued support of afforestation by referring to social benefits. Of the evidence offered in favour of its view, little can be substantiated.

It is almost certain that the cost to *society* of employing labour in the uplands is less than the wage rate, partly because of the lack of alternative employment there. This itself, however, is far from establishing the case for forestry, since many other forms of employment are possible. If the employment objective is framed in terms of national productivity, creation of jobs in highly profitable industries seems the best line. If it is a regional matter, then light industry might well be attracted to the uplands by the low labour cost ascribed by the Treasury in assessing forestry. The wording of the 'Forestry Policy' document stresses the community aspect of upland employment, yet large-scale afforestation may displace the sheep-farming community and tradition. The new community itself is subject to dissolution too: productivity and improvements, use of outside contractors and concentration of processing industries continually reduce the number of permanent jobs. Many Forestry Commission houses now stand empty, or are occupied only as second homes. So, while forestry relative to unemployment may look attractive, the comparison with *alternative* employment is less favourable.

If forestry is to be justified in the uplands, it must be because it is productive in the widest sense. If it is not, it cannot form a secure base for a community.

Much use has recently been made of an estimated 15 million day-visits to Commission forests in 1968. The figure is less impressive when compared with 20,000 million visitor-days *not* spent in Commission forests in the same period! Of course, neither statistic has much meaning. As the largest owner of access land in Britain, the Commission would be expected to supply much of the requirement for informal recreation, simply because such land is scare. As for the forests, the 15 million visits prove nothing about them, beyond that they are not *intolerably* unattractive.

The current emphasis on recreation in justifying afforestation hangs on this failure to distinguish *land* from *land use*. Recreation facilities are used because they have been provided, not because they are in a forest. Other land uses might have served as well. Benefits due specifically to forestry (screening of cars, absorption of crowds, shelter from wind) could be achieved with a much smaller area. They certainly cannot

2. 'Forestry Policy', HMSO 1972

add to recreational value of plantations far from roads in the uplands. Here, forestry *sterilises* a recreational resource with barbed wire, drainage ditches, impenetrable vegetation and mysterious roads to nowhere.

The claim made for afforestation that it enhances the beauty of the landscape, or creates it where none existed, has three separate foundations. The first stems from an idea of mature, soft-textured, variable hardwood forest. It has little relevance to either the form or the context of upland afforestation; while in the lowlands it is just such a landscape that commercial forestry replaces. Second, the functional aesthetic states that what is useful and efficient must be beautiful; a pure assertion, which necessarily assumes perverted perception on the part of hosts of commentators on aesthetic values. Third, questionnaires at some sites have seemed to show a public preference for conifers. But no matter how carefully questions are framed, questionnaires are subject to numerous biases; and in any case it is perilous to transfer results from one site to another. Using the rather less bias-prone method of counting heads, I have found a markedly greater patronage of open birchwood than of open pinewood when the option is available.

It can be conceded to conifers that, from within the mature stand, the towering trunks are impressive. Unfortunately, maturity is reached by progressively fewer stands as, under the influence of rising discount rates, impenetrable youth yields to gloomy adolescence and back to scrawny infancy on an ever-faster cycle. Externally too, mature conifers can perform valuable scenic service: but it requires a sympathetic discretion that has rarely marked recent afforestation. The association of forestry with good conservation again springs from the mature hardwood image. In the lowlands the case is clear. Conifers support a far smaller assortment of wildlife than, say, even a monoculture of oak. The effect of wholesale coniferisation of mixed hardwood forest will unquestionably run against wildlife conservation.

The practical issue of the uplands is harder to resolve. While hardwoods can and do grow at high altitude on poor soils, they are not commercially attractive. As far as plantations are concerned, then, the choice often lies between open moorland and conifers. Because conifers do attract certain species not found in open moorland, some afforestation will increase diversity locally. As the scale increases, however, the proportionate length of favoured edge habitats is reduced, and open habitats, especially the valley-slopes, may be entirely annexed. The replacement of natural hardwood habitats will be particularly damaging.

In the broader sense, conservation goes beyond immediate effects on wildlife. There is an opposite of the functional aesthetic alleging that species not native to Britain, and ill-looking in its landscape cannot be 'good for the ecosystem', and so will ultimately upset the utilitarian functions of land. Such generalisation is unhelpful. There is no solid body of evidence that conifers downgrade the majority of soils. On the other hand, it is not clear that they generally improve upland soils, and

Fine mature beeches in a National Trust wood at Slindon Park, Sussex. (*Photo: Forestry Commission*)

certainly not to the extent that selected hardwoods may do on selected sites. Again, diversity seems desirable, to provide a basis for judging long-term effects of different land uses, to maintain options in an uncertain world, and to provide an insurance against a comprehensive attack by pathogens.

On one matter the weight of evidence is conclusive — trees consume more water than grassland or heath under British conditions. The effect is of sufficient magnitude that the large-scale afforestation of a catchment might require the building of an extra reservoir to maintain reliable yield. Claims that forests have a beneficial effect on water quality in Britain are based on the results of felling a catchment, rather than those of leaving it unafforested: if anything, the detrimental effects on quality should be attributed to commercial forestry practice.

Instruments of policy

Given these technical, economic and aesthetic observations about forestry, it should be possible to devise an approach that would better meet objectives. Unless the forester can be accepted as the sole arbiter of different interests, some form of control is implied.

The arguments against bringing forestry into the arena of planning are usually general ones against any form of control. However, the close-guarded right of the owner or manager to order affairs on his own land become disputable as soon as they impinge on other people: and it is just such effects that foresters claim as an important feature of forestry. Though foresters assert that regulation of external effects could be left to them, they have a natural bias in favour of forestry as the solution to problems, and often do not think of recreation, amenity, wildlife or employment in any other context. Given this bias, and a lack of formal training in these specialist spheres, the forester can hardly claim to be the best person to make impartial decisions. The argument that forestry is a complex and dynamic process applies equally to many activities over which planners exercise some control. That control does not extend to day-to-day activity in houses or factories: why should forestry be treated differently?

The need for control is especially great in the private sector. The Forestry Commission, as a Government body, has social objectives: but at present little influence other than moral pressure can bear upon private forestry. The lowland estates, with a strong aesthetic tradition, are of less concern than upland afforestation, which has accelerated dramatically in response to fiscal incentives. The system whereby income from forests can be realised free of all but nominal taxation of land under Schedule B has received much publicity. Its tendencies are to increase private afforestation and to redistribute income towards the richer. Less well-documented are effects on quality of forest. High rates of return, and relief of planting costs shorten rotations. Large profit expectations inflate hill land prices and so increase the cost of 'carrying' open spaces or slow-yielding hardwoods. Conifer planting to the edge of the acquisition is thus encouraged, even though the estate follows no natural site limits. The pleasing patchwork of divided ownerships as it is seen in the perspective of the lowlands becomes disjointedly harsh in the uplands. It is hard to determine to what extent these unplanned incentives have exacerbated scenic degradation. Yet their effect is to reward the despoiler and to penalise those landowners who do modify their forestry to serve wider social ends. Capital transfer tax seems to avoid the worst deficiencies of the former estate duty concessions, but the wealth tax as proposed would only reinforce the pressure towards short-rotation conifers. This illustrates the difficulty of achieving appropriate control over private forestry by fiscal means. Grants are probably more equitable, and have more favourable qualitative effects. Even so, an effective system would be costly, and could not influence location of forests without direct control.

One cautionary note should be sounded. The planning process is subject to political pressures. In the nature of things, pressure groups represent present interests, with the future figuring only if its interest reinforces some present sectional interest. Thus future generations' requirement for timber supplies is likely to be under-represented politically unless it is explicitly recognised.

Positive policy

Bearing in mind the claims of the future, whoever is charged with planning forestry should take a positive attitude to it. In so far as summary is possible, the economic facts suggest mild pressure towards further afforestation of land whose alternative physical productivity is low. But the case is neither so overwhelming nor so unequivocal that aesthetic considerations can be ignored. While it would be going too far to undertake new afforestation only for aesthetic purposes, some configurations of land and land use will accommodate forestry far better than others. Because of this variable capacity, catch-all or expedient approaches should not be countenanced, and a less opportunist, more discriminate attempt to plan land use is desirable.

In the lowlands, conflict between the aesthetic and productive goals of *society* is not acute. Most land will still be needed for agriculture, but many parcels of land will remain whose timber productivity justifies a continued patchwork land use pattern. Lower rainfall makes the productive margin between conifer and hardwood narrower. The longer rotations indicated by low discount rates would not only increase the proportion of mature woodlands, but also make hardwoods financially viable, especially if a high-value product can be achieved. Pressure on supplies should also lead to more intensive utilisation of hardwoods' copious branchwood, e.g. for pulp or fuel. For the latter purpose, it is significant that the greater density and calorific value of hardwoods show them in a better light than the volume comparisons invariably used to judge their performance.

Increasingly, scarcity of land should favour more intensive systems of silviculture. Greater emphasis would be placed on selecting species matched to the individual site, on using natural rather than geometrical stand boundaries and on replacing mass-production methods and mentality by sympathetic treatment of individual stands. It is likely that such a silviculture, bringing workers closer to the land, will better promote stable rural communities.

Although the long-term viewpoint makes aesthetic goals and productive ones more compatible for society, most lowland forests remain privately owned. It is unlikely that the individual will readily pay the initial high cost of hardwood establishment and intensive silviculture, with no prospect of seeing the crop mature, and every likelihood of taxes on wealth penalising him for his pains. Planning control cannot force a landowner to plant hardwoods. Replanting with hardwoods could be written into approved management plans, or be a condition on felling licences. But it would be hard to forbid neglect, premature felling to meet tax liabilities on a high-value crop, or the disintegration of coherent management as estates are broken up. If the ownership of land is to be devolved, new institutions will be required to ensure continuity of management through time and across space, to retain scope for individual creativity and to allow that the legacy already created may continue its evolution.

The heaths of the south and east pose intermediate problems, offering the perspectives of the lowlands and the scale of the uplands. The Scots pine is a long-familiar tree in such landscapes, and the more productive Corsican pine has an acceptable outline too. Unfortunately, planting is constrained neither by altitude nor by agricultural use, and the case for leaving open spaces must rest on the recreational and aesthetic needs of a large urban population crowded close at hand.

For the private forester, the unintentional incentives to short rotations and conifer monocultures work particularly well in upland conditions: the conflict between commercial and aesthetic goals is accordingly strong. This fiscally-aggravated divergence of private and social interest reinforces the case for withdrawing the nominal Schedule B tax option. Without major tax advantage, existing estates would sacrifice less by making concessions to amenity, while further upland afforestation would largely revert to the more socially-oriented Forestry Commission.

Even in the long-term social view, conflict persists; but in the case of new afforestation, planning control could effectively represent aesthetic interest. One major function would be to define a limit for afforestation both more natural and (partly for that reason) more aesthetic, cutting if necessary across ownership boundaries. The hope would be that agreements on and incentives to positive management could achieve a co-ordinated afforestation programme.

Shaping forest boundaries to topography is gaining acceptance. Location and quality of boundary is an equal problem. The upper limit of a plantation often cannot be defined by any topographical or climatic 'tree-line'. In the lower-lying areas, the whole valley-slope may be productive, and no logic can be perceived in suspending afforestation, say, two-thirds up the slope. A rocky plateau-edge escarpment may both provide a natural limit and break up the hardness of the boundary. In high mountains, declining yield sets an upper limit. This is often heterogeneous country, and, even when crag and scree do not enforce a scattered boundary, to provide one is only to give the land its due. At intermediate levels, the problem may be intractable, especially where valley-slopes occupy a large proportion of the land area, but yield no topographical limit. To plant up to the ridges may not be productive, and produces a multi-valley blanket. To suspend planting in mid-slope is arbitrary, and looks it. This is the problem of afforestation in the Yorkshire Dales. The obvious solution is not to afforest on a large scale.

Getting the boundaries right is only the beginning. Unless planting is in small groups, the most expertly delineated forest in the uplands presents the problems of the mass—texture and colour, monotony, blanketry and space invasion—demonstrated most acutely by Sitka spruce. Unfortunately, Sitka has been held superior to alternatives over such a range of sites that even a more selective approach might not obviate its extensive monoculture. If aesthetic considerations are given more weight, the first improvement would be to keep Sitka out of prominent positions. The only sites in the uplands that are really immune from plan-like exposure are those plateaux and ridges high enough not to be overlooked. Productive conifers that might look better are lodgepole pine on the visible plateaux, silver firs and larches on the valley-slopes, and Douglas fir and western hemlock on the more fertile soils of the valley-bottom and margins. Some of these species, and others less well-tried like redwoods or Weymouth pine, almost equal and sometimes exceed the performance of Sitka when site is carefully chosen. In a state of uncertainty, a wider range of species might be justified simply as an insurance. Various textures, outlines and colours are represented, all improving on Sitka. The cypresses, while good producers, are too reminiscent of suburbs or municipal parks to look right in the uplands, to present generations at least.

But even the gradual banishment of Sitka to sites where the impact of its texture and colour would be minimal does not mitigate the effect of the remaining spruce, which would continue as the dominant species of the uplands for decades, even if planting were discontinued in sensitive areas. Nor does it obviate the monotone or the blanket. Relieving these ills with species variation or felling patterns would create internal boundaries, which themselves need careful conformation to topography, appropriate line quality and a scale of variation decreasing towards landscape focuses and points of high visibility. The contrast of larch and hardwoods with gloomier conifers is usually unpleasant unless softened by flat perspective or scattered intermingling. Felled areas seem to me a productive source of variation, creating inner pattern and, in the exposed trunks of remaining trees, a texture to divert the eye from the compulsive grapple of the spruce canopy. They can be left to merge with open land, to modify insensitive outer boundaries, but will retain their relieving function for many years even if replanted.

If planning were extended to cover forestry, general conditions relating to these points could be attached to permission to afforest. Where forestry is the existing land use, only patience on the part of the planner and open-mindedness from the forester will fashion a more pleasant forest. For private forestry, some modification of the proposed wealth tax seems necessary if attractive forest is to be financially viable.

All these points of aesthetic principle do not, however, add up to ubiquitous credentials for forestry. The best-landscaped forest affects a familiar scene and a familiar kind of scenery, so that changes should be made slowly and with sensitivity. Furthermore, methodical application of principles alone entails danger of creating 'uniform diversity', in which all the uplands, for example, are conformed to a standard scenic package of sailing-dinghied reservoirs, landscaped quarries and inflected spruce plantations. Aesthetic susceptibility is perhaps more vulnerable to indifference than insult. There is something beyond rules, difficult to generalise about, a belongingness in the landscape, which is only partly a matter of scenery as we are accustomed to it. It is significant of the present approach that in the controversial Langstrothdale afforestation the concessions to landscape, even in a national park, were confined to minor adjustments. If the national parks are to have any meaning, the approach should start from the land, to see what additional constraints its form and nature put on the aesthetic qualities of land use. Ideally, we should like to plant only where the landscape seems positively to enjoin it — to create focuses and flows of line, under escarpments and in tight hollows. As I have argued, however, there is more pressure than that, and the positive planner should be seeking in addition areas where forestry *could* fit in.

The constraints are likely to be the attractiveness of the existing ground-cover, and the importance of the sense of space. For example, Northumbria might seem acceptable country for large-scale forests. 'There are no radiant colours they can mask, no exquisite skyline they can break, and the contours show kind discretion in revealing their unnatural geometry.' Yet with the planting of Irthing Basin one of the last few wilderness voids in England is vanishing. A new landscape appears in Northumbria: how long before an old landscape disappears from England?

Given that the material output of forests is not trivial, proposals to favour amenity at the expense of timber production will increase pressure for afforestation elsewhere, whose effects must also be considered. This kind of overall planning, including evaluation of alternative aesthetic impacts, is a necessary complement to local initiation of acceptable afforestation. Then, if production amenity must suffer, it will at least be easier to minimise losses.

10

Energy

ROBIN GROVE-WHITE and NIGEL LUCAS

RURAL England has reason to fear the energy industries. The provision of oil, gas, coal and electricity has a dramatic impact on the landscape. On the scale required to sustain the UK's present industrial and social commitments, energy provision is highly obtrusive. But the prospects for the future look worse still.

The benefits of high energy consumption appear obvious. Our prosperity has historically been linked to it, and industrial activity has grown as energy consumption in all sectors has increased. Rural life relies on energy inputs—agriculture and food production are dependent not only on fuel, but also on the high energy contents of chemical fertilisers. Our domestic comfort depends on the conversion of fuel to produce heat. So too with transport systems and with the settlement patterns to which we have become committed. The consumption of energy is growing and shows no sign of abatement.

But the price to be paid for this commitment is also growing. In many parts of the country it is already apparent—oil refinery complexes and oil terminals of many hundreds of acres in once-unspoilt areas; remote coastal and estuarial sites dominated by nuclear power stations, open-cast coal mines searing through rolling countryside; electricity transmission lines (the 'grid') proliferating in almost every corner of the country. Locally such developments may have caused dismay; but so far, in towns and cities, to satisfy whose demands the developments largely take place, the impact has been dismissed as of trivial consequence. The wider national interest, the argument has run, has to take precedence over such parochial considerations as the impact on local amenity.

However, we are reaching a point at which the impact of the energy industries on rural England can no longer be so lightly regarded. Pressures over the next 30 or 40 years could lead to such colossal extensions of these industries that impact on the landscape ought to be seen as a significant factor in energy policy decisions themselves. For if present trends continue, not only will the physical impact on the landscape be extensive, but the very statutory framework within which crucial land-use decisions are taken in the UK will alter for the worse. Indeed if our assumptions about energy supply and demand do not change, the pressure for extension of the existing supply system could lead to severe abrogations of public rights, so that the coal and electricity industries, for example, could become increasingly exempted from the procedures for public challenge which exist within present legislation. This possibility is just as important to those concerned for the future of rural England as the possibility of power stations and oil industry developments on our few remaining stretches of remote coastline. For the statutory framework of Britain's land-use planning system protects us all; if, in a democracy, its piecemeal erosion takes place because of short-term political expediency, substantial public and private interests will be in real jeopardy.

In the past, UK energy supply decisions have been based almost entirely on economics, albeit within a political and geopolitical framework. This cannot be expected to alter, but there could be important shifts of emphasis, if a will to change direction emerged through our political institutions. For this reason, to understand the possible impact on the environment of the energy industries in the coming decades, this chapter examines two possible scenarios. Each involves different assumptions about the political choices which could be made in the immediate future.

The first alternative assumes a continuation of our present underlying political and economic priorities up to and beyond the year 2000. It suggests that the UK's system of energy supply will become increasingly centralised and based on electricity generated by nuclear fission. By contrast the second alternative postulates significant changes in present assumptions, giving a higher priority to local control and local self-sufficiency. The decisions determining which direction will in fact be pursued will be political rather than technical. But there are already very great economic, institutional and even intellectual pressures towards a commitment to the centralised system—a gloomy prospect for rural England, as we shall see.

The first alternative: centralisation

The present UK system of energy supply has been and is crucially wedded to economies of scale—big oil refineries, big coal mines, big power stations and a big grid for electricity distribution. However, even if these economies are realised in practice—and there is growing evidence that the unreliability of large generators may be eroding them in the UK—they also have great disadvantages. Sheer physical impact on the environment is one of them.

Before the Arab oil embargoes and price rises of October 1973 it was commonly estimated by authorities all over the world that national energy consumptions would double or perhaps treble by the year 2000. The gradual depletion of fossil fuels, especially oil, was planned to be matched and exceeded by an increase in the supply of other forms of energy, particularly nuclear power. The UK was no exception to this general rule.

The high prices and restricted production enforced by the OPEC cartel have given an even greater stimulus to a search for secure supplies of energy through special relationships with suppliers or by making the most of indigenous resources or through the development of new sources of energy.

It is now widely assumed that, North Sea oil and gas notwithstanding, Britain will become increasingly dependent on electricity generated from thermo-nuclear fission. The supply curve for world petroleum is expected to peak in about the year 2000, and North Sea oil production will probably begin to decline between 1990 and 2000. Although it is impossible to predict with precision the date at which demand could outrun supply, there can be little doubt that replacement of oil by other sources of energy will become critical over the next 30 years. Coal reserves are greater, but it will be difficult for the coal industry to sustain production at much above an output of 120 million tons p.a. To achieve the overall energy consumption growth rate of two per cent p.a. forecast for the period up to the turn of the

West Burton power station in Nottinghamshire—a coal-fired station of 2,000 MW, it is one of the CEGB's largest. As with all such stations, approximately two-thirds of the energy content of the coal is lost as waste heat through the cooling towers. The arguments for making better use of this waste heat are strong. (*Photo: CEGB*)

century could thus require a growth rate of up to five per cent p.a. in electricity production—which would depend on sustained production by the oil and coal industries to provide the fuel for steam-raising in fossil-fuelled power stations. The proportion of power stations which would be nuclear-powered would have to grow steadily through the 1980s and 1990s. Estimates of electricity demand have changed over the past three years, but the Department of Energy is now assuming that additional generating capacity of perhaps 90,000 MW might be needed in the UK by 2001. This means a total of 45 or more very large power stations, most of them nuclear—almost a trebling of total generating capacity in 25 years.

What could this mean for rural England?

A single 2,000 MW power station is an enormous undertaking. A coal or oil-fired station may extend half a mile and occupy up to 400 acres; it will have eight 375-ft-high cooling towers and a 650-ft-high chimney stack. Fuel must be moved in bulk requiring the laying of new roads or railways. The site for a nuclear station, while holding smaller buildings, will be even larger; that at Bradwell, Essex extends over 730 acres, for example. It is the limited life of a nuclear reactor which dictates this remarkable requirement; when obsolete (after 30 or 40 years), the reactor can be partially dismantled but the core is best left alone, covered in concrete and grassed over. Further reactors would simply be built on adjacent ground if output were to continue. In addition new power stations bring with them a need for transmission lines to link the stations' output to the national grid. Such lines are at present 400 kV, but on present trends, an enlarged system of 1,000 kV lines with more massive pylons might have to be introduced by the turn of the century. Experience with objections to the 400 kV grid suggests that the Central Electricity Generating Board (CEGB) would require unprecedented skills of political persuasion to make such an enlarged grid palatable, or even acceptable, to the public.

If by the 1980s the Fast Breeder Reactor (FBR) is introduced, the Generating Board will increasingly be faced with the problem that they have already taken the least controversial sites for power stations. Future new sites for nuclear reactors will cause serious conflicts as they will tend to be situated in rural areas of greater and greater amenity value. Hitherto in the UK where there have been worries (real or imaginary) about the safety of nuclear plant, they have been appeased by requiring such power stations to be located on 'remote' sites, away from centres of population, although certain reactors, for instance Advanced Gas Cooled Reactors, have been considered safe enough not to be sited remotely.

The great advantage claimed for the Fast Breeder is that it can make more economical use of uranium than other (thermal) reactors. There is therefore great pressure to introduce it quickly to avoid the shortages of cheap uranium predicted for the early 2000s if reliance on non-breeder reactors develops internationally. However, the FBR still

400 kV lines from Sizewell nuclear power station in Suffolk. With electricity generated in ever larger power station units, the national grid has also steadily expanded. On present patterns, the long-term prospect is for transmission lines on a still larger scale — say, of 750 kV or 1,000 kV capacity, radiating from 'nuclear parks' many times the size of Sizewell. (*Photo: CEGB*)

presents very substantial safety problems, and after 25 years of development, the design has still to advance beyond the phototype stage. To appease public concern over safety there might be a need for remote sites for at least 25 FBR stations by 1995, quite apart from sites for other (thermal) nuclear and fossil-fueled stations. The CPRE, in evidence to the Royal Commission on Environmental Pollution in 1974, has already warned of the acute conflicts with amenity to which the provision of such FBR sites could give rise, for they would almost certainly have to be on coastline or river valleys valued for their remoteness, their beauty or their wildlife. Moreover, if present thinking prevails, the use of these sites would ensure that two-thirds of the energy converted would automatically be dissipated in waste heat or lost in transmission.

A further problem for the countryside arises from the fact that growth in nuclear power in the generating system would create a concomitant need for electricity storage capacity. This might take the form of pumped storage plant — a form of installation for which suitable UK sites exist only in mountainous national parks.

Prototype fast breeder nuclear reactor at Dounreay, Caithness. This could be the model for far larger commercial fast breeders in the 1980s and 1990s. The UK Atomic Energy Authority has indicated that 50,000 MW of such capacity (literally dozens of fast breeders) could be needed by the year 2000. But where in rural England could they be sited acceptably? (*Photo: UKAEA*)

The problems of nuclear fuel demand special attention, for they go a long way towards explaining why antipathy to new nuclear power proposals can be expected to grow steadily. In the first place, fission products of the thermonuclear reaction in the reactor core of the power station must be kept from the environment for several hundred years in order to avoid radioactive contamination. Second, the transuranium elements which are also produced in the reactor core are separated from the fission products for re-use as fuel. Certain of these elements persist in a very radiotoxic form for very long periods. Plutonium is the best known of these; it must be kept from the environment for at least a quarter of a million years. Processing and transport of plutonium (from reactor to fuel processing plant) is thus a difficult and dangerous operation because of the material's high toxicity. A number of recent reports from the USA and UK suggest that even the stringent regulations and strict monitoring so far enforced may not be adequate. Thirdly the plutonium produced from nuclear power is a convenient material for thermonuclear weapons. This makes military standards of security — over literally tens of thousands of years — absolutely vital.

One way of minimising the problem, in the Generating Board's view, would be to concentrate a number of reactors on the same site: investigations are already under way, for instance, to establish whether up to 10,000 MW of nuclear capacity could be located at Orford Ness, a site within the Suffolk Coasts and Heaths Area of Outstanding Natural Beauty and on designated Heritage Coast. The euphemism 'nuclear

Undergrounding of 400 kV cable now costs more than £1,700,000 a mile, but in a case like this — at the river Wye near Ross on Wye — the expense is worthwhile. Hedges and fields will grow again and nothing will be seen.   (*Photo: BICC*)

park' would be applied to such a concentration of capacity; 400 kV and later, probably, 1,000 kV—power lines would radiate out from it through the AONB. Other coastal sites are also being surveyed. Nuclear parks would create enormous environmental intrusions in those areas in which they were located, but the concentration of facilities—including waste disposal and fuel processing plant—could bring benefits for the supply authorities.

All of these problems would be aggravated if a rapid commitment were made to nuclear power. Experience suggests that quality control and security would also become more difficult to guarantee if the nuclear power station construction programme accelerated over the coming decades in line with the UKAEA's expectations.

But in this scenario nuclear power stations would provide only a proportion (albeit a large proportion) of new electricity generating capacity. Indigenous coal would also play a substantial role, as could oil for as long as supply could be guaranteed. But neither of these resources could be exploited at the required rates without very substantial upheaval to the environment.

After a long period of decline the National Coal Board now has plans to achieve an annual production rate of 120 million tons p.a., perhaps increasing this in the 1980s. Investment of £600 million over the next decade will, it is hoped, provide 42 million tons p.a. of new mining capacity by 1985; 22 million tons of this would come from extensions to

Tips at an open-cast coal working near Widdrington, Northumberland. The National Coal Board aims to increase the number of its open-cast workings in the next decade—but the Board shows increasing skill at restoring and landscaping such sites.

(*Photo: Simon Warner*)

existing mines, while 20 million tons would come from new mines. The most promising new areas seem likely to be in the Selby region of Yorkshire, various sites in the Midlands and, in Oxfordshire, where reserves extending into the Cotswolds are known to exist.

New collieries take up to five or six years to complete. To bridge the gap between the increase in demand and the mining of coal from new deep mines the Coal Board plans a rapid expansion of open-cast mining, which can be initiated more quickly than deep mining. It is unfortunately a very ugly operation which cannot be disguised while working is in progress. The operations at the beautiful Druridge Bay in Northumberland which are visible from any point in the bay and many other parts of the coastline show the typical despoliation of the landscape. Characteristic of the new pressure for open-cast mining is the Board's proposal to mine at Morpeth, Northumberland, in an attractive agricultural and residential area. Two thousand acres are involved, somewhat more than the area of the town itself.

On the other hand it must be said that when open-cast mining is adopted in abandoned mining areas there is little doubt that the land can be restored to a better condition than the old tips and colliery workings. There are many examples of this, especially in the North. But it hardly needs stating that any proposal for coal workings in the Cotswolds would certainly cause great controversy.

The prospective contribution of oil to UK energy supply is dominated by petroleum deposits in the North Sea and, very likely, in water off the coasts of South-west England and Wales. However, if present rates of growth of energy demand continue, it is unlikely that North Sea reserves could provide a long-term source of supply for the UK. It has been estimated that even if recoverable North Sea resources proved to be twice as great as those in official Government estimates (in the 1974 'Brown Book'), UK requirements beyond the mid-1990s could not be met. Nevertheless, industrial development associated with exploitation of these deposits has already had a drastic impact on long stretches of Scottish coastline. There is also evidence that the comparatively mild environmental restrictions in the UK are encouraging oil companies to site refineries here to process oil for export.

To supervise the rapid development of terminals and platform construction sites, and also to facilitate such development, the Government has taken powers in the Offshore Petroleum Development (Scotland) Act 1975 enabling it to acquire land for oil-related purposes by an 'expedited' procedure. It was the Government's original intention that the Act would have gone even further—by drastically circumscribing Parliament's discretion to scrutinise the exercise of the executive's powers under the Act. It was only after intensive lobbying by the CPRE that the Government was defeated on this occasion by an amendment moved in the House of Lords. But the Government's original attitude was significant and will recur. Landscape considerations are not to be allowed to stand in the way of energy developments.

It is already clear that the coal industry also considers its problems to be such that some similar kind of dispensation is called for. In January 1975, the Chairman of the National Coal Board told Parliament's Select Committee on Science and Technology that 'the problem of open-cast (mining) is the difficulty of getting planning consents. If we want to expand open-cast quickly . . . . we have to short-circuit planning procedures.'

In the circumstances, it is by no means fanciful to imagine that if a nuclear power station programme on the scale described above, with an expanded national grid, gave rise to widespread amenity opposition, on grounds of either safety or amenity, government would seek to reduce the opportunities and outlets for objection to that also—'in the national interest'.

Such facts illustrate the single most alarming feature of the scenario we have described: that if a steady growth in energy consumption in the UK is taken as an absolute requirement, other important priorities (such as the conservation of rural England) will suffer grievously. The commitment to meet an overall energy 'demand' expanding at upwards of 2 per cent p.a. into the next century, by means of a largely centralised supply system based on electricity will encourage consumers of all kinds to plan on that assumption. The recent preoccupation with energy conservation—manifest in the creation of entities such as the Advisory Council on Energy Conservation, the Energy Technology Support Unit at Harwell, the NEDO 'Energy Conservation' unit—has explicitly avoided the implication that we should fundamentally change our expectations about the availability of energy; users are simply encouraged to make *more efficient* use of available fuels. Investment in industrial plant and consumer goods which have high energy requirements is not to be discouraged. We are to continue as before, if slightly less prodigally.

But to meet the growing energy demand expanding at upwards of two per cent p.a. from indigenous and nuclear-based sources will strain our democratic institutions, including those affecting the look and care of English landscape, as we approach the end of the century. If this scenario is realised, something will have to give—and it seems more likely to be public rights than the energy supply programme. The political power of agencies embodying massive concentrations of technical expertise—the National Coal Board, the Central Electricity Generating Board, the UK Atomic Energy Authority, the oil 'majors'—further strengthens one's fears for rural England. The landscape's interests will increasingly run second, in the face of pressures rationalised as 'urgent' immediate needs for energy in 'the national interest'.

The alternative: decentralisation

The scenario described above is broadly that favoured by policy-makers in the industries and in government. It is claimed to be the

162

cheapest way of supplying the UK's energy needs. Whether or not such a claim is justified is itself debatable, but in any case the mathematical analysis of investment projects, although a useful way of allocating resources once social aims are clearly established, should not be allowed to pre-empt initial political value judgements. The aims of energy policy and general strategy for achieving them are and should be political decisions. If the political will could be found to lay the main stress on local self sufficiency, decentralisation and on minimising environmental impact then the technological response would be different. Economic analysis would still be an important way of choosing between projects, but it would operate within a different framework.

The electricity supply industry provides the clearest case of the disadvantages of a rigid adherence to artificial rules; technical anomalies have been created and future options are being closed off unnecessarily.

As little as 25 per cent of the calorific value of fuel burnt in power stations finishes as electric power for the consumer; the remainder is discarded as heat into the air, rivers or oceans. Cooling is indeed becoming more difficult with every station added to the existing network. This tendency forces stations to gather near existing sites or to be pushed into regions so far protected on amenity grounds. The split between electricity and heat corresponds closely to the proportions of the national demand for electricity and heat. There is therefore a *prima facie* case for generating electricity on relatively small sites close to centres of demand, so that the rejected heat can be used. This possibility has long been recognised and many schemes have been devised for different situations.

For example, electricity can be generated by gas turbines and the exhaust gases used for drying or for firing kilns. Steam for industrial processing or space heating can be taken from steam turbine sets or raised in the exhausts of gas turbines or diesel engines. Process heat for the steel industry or for coal gasification might be taken from nuclear reactors. The fluidised bed, a sadly neglected British invention, makes it possible to burn low-grade coal in urban areas both for heat and for electricity. But few schemes for heat and power generation in the UK have been successful, partly because the CEGB charges a high price for standby capacity and pays a low price for privately generated electricity delivered to the grid. It is unfortunate that the Board can adopt pricing policies which inhibit efficient use of energy throughout the country.

The pricing system severely discourages industry from generating its own electricity in total energy schemes, while the CEGB's statutory monopoly prevents local authorities from using the waste heat from local generating plants. There are few large towns in the UK more than five miles from a CEGB power station. The CEGB, in developing its supergrid supplied from remotely situated stations, is closing down the local stations, often small and inefficient, that are suitable in size and siting for conversion to combined-cycle turbines that would supply heat to the district, for homes or industry, and generate power for the grid.

A genuine technical problem with combined generation of heat and power is that the balance between the two is not always easily met when the plant is first installed and not easily maintained thereafter. The great advantage of the grid as a means of transmitting energy, partly offsetting its obvious disadvantages, is that any form of energy can be converted to electricity at the defined frequency and voltage and fed into the grid. This advantage would make it possible for local plant to concentrate on meeting the heat load and either putting its electrical surplus into the grid or taking its deficit from the grid. The grid would have more of a distributive function. The electricity supply industry would still supply power, but mostly for the base load that persisted when electricity from local stations was not available and for any extra demand made on the system that the local services could not meet. Nuclear reactors would be suitable for the base load, but the need for them would be restricted and they would be installed over a much longer period of time, permitting the highest standards of safety, security and engineering.

A useful source of surplus electricity could be produced from district heating schemes. The electricity would be generated at precisely the time of day and season of the year when temporary demand for electrical power embarrasses the supply industry. It takes 20 to 25 years to build up a district heating system. Hence it is often argued that it is too late to start in the UK because fossil fuels will not be available in 30 years time. If accepted, this argument would mean (as our first scenario indicated) that space heating in the year 2000 would be largely provided by electric power from nuclear fission. But heat from nuclear reactors can be transported to the district heating network, if necessary over long distances. Because it requires up to four units of heat to provide one unit of electricity it follows that by the year 2000 a district heating system begun now would reduce the installed nuclear generating capacity required for space heating substantially. If the present proportion of energy used for heating water and space persisted until the year 2000 then district heating by steam or hot water instead of by electricity might reduce the total installed generating capacity in the country by 25 per cent. District heating is therefore both a useful measure to conserve fossil fuels and a useful investment in a nuclear economy. It is however necessary to start now. It is only because planning started long ago and has proceeded without interruption that heating mains have been laid almost throughout Stockholm. The UK compares badly with several other countries in this respect; in the USSR two-thirds of all buildings in cities are supplied from a district network and all new towns are designed for heat and power generation. In Denmark one-third of all dwellings are district heated and 90 per cent of towns have a district heating network.

It is sometimes argued that the mild British climate is unsuitable for district heating, but Britain's mild winters last longer than the severe European winters; this provides a comparatively constant high load factor which, far from being an argument against district heating, weighs strongly in its favour. The capital costs of district heating mains would be met by the reduction in the nuclear programme; the technology of district heating and local generation are both known and reliable.

If the desire for local autonomy were to be recognised, new institutional arrangements for energy supply, now inhibited by the CEGB's monopoly, would have to emerge. This demands a shift in priorities, and would have to find expression in Parliament. But a whole new range of options would then open up, and would play an increasingly significant part by the turn of the century. What these options might be is an open question. Experiments by small communities with solar heating and wind or water power and other forms of alternative technology have evoked widespread sympathy and enthusiasm. It seems unlikely that the sources of power tapped by such alternative arrangements could provide the hardware on which the alternative technologies themselves depend or could supply the facilities of modern urban life, or the convenience now expected in rural society. Renewable sources are often unpredictable, or out of phase with demand and

Old windmill near West Burton power station in Nottinghamshire. Since the oil price rises of 1973 there have been signs of renewed interest in such untapped sources of energy as the sun, the wind and the waves. *(Photo: CEGB)*

tend like the wind or sun to be diffuse. But a decentralised system of the type we have described would provide both the time and opportunity to explore options going far beyond those that can yield immediate results. Specifically, in the context of renewable sources of power, the problems of their unpredictable nature can be reduced by making the grid available to receive these fluctuating inputs and by encouraging the state of mind that will recognise them as useful.

A decentralised system of power supply would require chemical fuels long after the reserves of fossil fuel were exhausted. Again several sources of synthetic fuel can be described. Fermentation of organic matter can yield methane and various methods have been studied for converting solar energy to hydrogen. Perhaps more commonly suggested is the liquefaction and hydrogasification of coal in association with nuclear power to provide heat and hydrogen for the process.

The second plank of our alternative scenario, complementing the decentralised generation of power, would be a serious approach to energy conservation. Resources at present are only allocated to saving energy if it can be shown to be economic in the very short term. A review is needed of the way in which such benefits as housing, communications and food are provided—not to seek short-term profit, or to deal with a temporary balance of payments deficit but to anticipate fundamental changes in the availability of energy. It would be easy to carry over the existing provision of services which grew up around cheap energy into a situation of expensive energy and yet to persist in meeting high demand at high cost because of an obsession with short-term gains.

The existing building stock in the United Kingdom has the poorest thermal performance of any industrialised country. An enormous quantity of energy (estimates suggest up to 20 per cent of our total primary demand) could be saved by standard techniques such as insulation, draft-stripping and proper maintenance of heating installations. The administrative problems involved are complex, involving a variety of groups who are not easily co-ordinated, small builders for instance. But there are no great technical problems: the issue has little appeal to a centralised government department such as the Department of Energy.

At best such a programme would only take up the slack which generations of architects and builders, oblivious of energy, have produced. But if the guiding philosophy changed radically, the benefits could be permanent. Well-insulated buildings can still show a low thermal performance if they are poorly designed. They ought instead to be designed from scratch to require as little energy input as possible and to use where possible the input from renewable sources. While there is no shortage of ideas in this sphere, there is a great shortage of both practical work and of research and development backing. Building design needs the freedom to fail as does any other form or research. Too often excellent work has not been followed up because the first attempt was not perfect. The best example of this is St George's County

School at Wallasey which was designed to do without any heating system. The building is massively constructed, well insulated and has a high solar gain. The building has faults; it is stuffy, smelly and noisy, but instead of following the lead and designing out these faults the initiative has been abandoned. Money and a concentration of research effort are needed; it is unlikely that they could emerge under existing statutory arrangements.

Changes in patterns of communication would also follow from the commitment to local autonomy in energy supply. The continuation of high fuel prices and advanced system of telecommunications could point in the direction of, simply, less mobility. The movement of less mass, more slowly, would be a consequence, with urban and rural public transport greatly strengthened for the movement of both freight and people. Many benefits that are not easily costed would emerge. The steady erosion of local cultures might be stemmed if not reversed. Energy-intensive agriculture and greater local self-sufficiency in food might mean that our choice of foods would be narrowed, with less seasonal choice, less meat and more vegetable protein grown for direct human consumption. Life might seem poorer; it could also be healthier.

The effects of these changes on the landscape are hard to predict in detail because obviously the full extent of the impact of any system of energy supply is dictated by the level of demand for energy in the community at large. Some siting problems would be brought nearer the consumer. Local generation is a likely cause of noise and air pollution, but such effects can be reduced to an acceptable level, at a price, by acoustic insulation and desulphurisation of oil products. The number of estuarine and coastal sites required for power stations could certainly be reduced, perhaps to one-half for any specified level of comparable services.

Again, the financial costs of adopting this scenario are hard to gauge. The apparent short-term convenience of muddling along, with one eye on the profit and loss account and the other eye on fast breeder reactors at the end of the road, must be traded off against the long-term benefits of providing a flexible system of energy supply designed not only to suit the convenience of the supplier but also the needs of the community. The authors are firmly of the opinion that the long-term benefits of district heating, insulation and urban public transport justify strategic investment in these areas. A large degree of local generation of electricity with heat recovery can be shown to be attractive financially for the country, but because of the institutional constraints described earlier, not for the owner of the local generator. This should be corrected by making the appropriate changes in the structure of the industry.

This alternative scenario may or may not be financially attractive in the short term, but the long-term advantage of a flexible system of energy supply are immense. The important point is that under present institutional arrangements, options are being closed off. The present concentration of energy supply duties in centralised (largely) statutory bodies pre-empts a range of possibilities which could lead to quite different consequences for rural England to those implied by the scenario we described first.

Conclusions

So what is the prognosis for the next 30 years? What can we expect by the turn of the century? Will we be faced with a consolidation of the existing institutional framework—centred on a unified national system of electricity supply, the elements tightly controlled by government? Or will political decisions have been taken which will by then be leading to a greater flexibility and reduction in the scale of units on which energy supply depends? If the one is to be seriously attempted, it seems unlikely that we can also attempt the other. A scarcity of manpower, capital and physical resources will ensure this. After all, in the past decade there has been a remarkable concentration of research and development funds into the nuclear option. In times of economic stringency, it is unrealistic to suppose that there could be a sudden diversification of research and development effort into a number of new areas simultaneously.

There are formidable obstacles to any move away from the nuclear-based centralised system. The apparently inevitable desire of established statutory and corporate entities (such as the CEGB or the UKAEA) to expand their influence and rationalise this expansion in terms of 'consumer demand' and technical efficiency is a block to change. The fact that nuclear power is the mode of electricity generation which fits most conveniently into the existing technical and administrative framework of the national grid is another. Another factor is Parliament's present reliance on technical expertise in the Department of Energy and statutory agencies; this makes it both difficult and unlikely that effective political challenge to the present institutional framework could be mounted. Indeed a 1973 report of Parliament's own Select Committee on Nationalised Industries argued strongly in favour of less political interference with the nationalised industries rather than more.

Such apparently ineffective political control reflects an unpleasant new fact: increasingly sophisticated technologies require 'lead' times (from initial research commitment to actual consumer use) which far exceed the lifetime of a Parliament. The fast breeder reactor, for example, after more than 20 years of research and development, has still not got to the prototype stage; but the maximum life of a Parliament is just five years. Political oversight, and therefore control, of the programme has been token. For there is, in the words of J. H. H. Merriman[1] 'a fundamental conflict between the life cycle of

1. In his Inaugural Address as President of the Institute of Electrical Engineers, 1974.

Parliamentary activity and that of long lead-time, high technology enterprises of crucial importance to the infrastructure of society'. The disturbing feature of such a statement is that the interests of 'high technology enterprises' are likely to be better protected than those of 'Parliamentary activity' if present trends continue. Yet the interests of the countryside, like other unquantifiable features of our lives, are critically dependent on the health of 'Parliamentary activity'.

The price to be paid for following the centralised, demand-led option would be severe—both to the landscape and to public rights. The programme of upwards of 45 large nuclear power stations by 2001 described above, with fuel processing plant, waste disposal and plutonium storage facilities and massive extensions to the national grid would be accompanied by extensive open-cast coal mining and offshore oil-related development.

The single most likely constraint on the postulated programme of centralised expansion of energy supply could be simply that the programme proves to be physically too ambitious. Quite simply, the demands it makes on the construction and engineering industries could prove to be too great. A doubling of electricity capacity could make extravagant demands on human, physical and capital resources, while enormous technical problems still await solutions. Shortages of manpower seem likely to arise in the UK in all branches of engineering by the mid-1980s. And all precedent suggests that a crash programme of power station construction would involve expensive labour disputes, materials shortages and component failures.

Nevertheless the energy industries' threat to rural England is daunting. For significant alternatives to emerge before the end of the century colossally powerful institutional, administrative and intellectual forces would have to be overcome. There are signs that this is possible, but perhaps they flatter to deceive: all recent government-inspired energy conservation initiatives, vital though they are, rest on the assumption that if waste can be minimised we can proceed with the same institutions in pursuit of the same political and economic priorities. They are not initiatives conceived as elements in an alternative programme to that described above as potentially so damaging. In such a context, energy conservation is largely a technical dodge, to get the most from a centralised nuclear-based electricity system.

A system is needed which gives more tolerance and encouragement to different approaches to the problems of both energy supply and demand—to decentralised systems, high efficiency systems, and a reduced commitment to nuclear-based electricity. For the sake of democratic prerogatives as much as for rural England, such a change of outlook must emerge soon.

11

The Development of Water Supplies

JUDITH REES

THE reservoir construction programme advocated by the Water Resources Board in April 1974, just before the Board was abolished, threatens, if implemented, to have a considerable effect on the English countryside. It also requires a massive investment that the nation may be unable to afford. The public is continually being told that unless extensive investment in new storage capacity is made to meet a demand for water that will double by the end of the century, a serious water shortage—even a crisis—will result. The case for the projected scale of reservoir development is however questionable, and it is possible that much unnecessary inundation of land, and capital expenditure, could be averted by measures which cost less money and do very much less damage.

The Board's water development strategy[1] is based on the prediction that in England and Wales currently available supply would fall short of demand by 2·9 million cubic metres per day (m³d.) by 1981, rising to 12·1 million m³ d. by the year 2001. The scale of these estimates can be seen from the fact that the apparent deficiency in 2001 is 29 per cent of present total use. The Board's suggested solution is the traditional one of undertaking an extensive construction programme to increase storage capacity. The sheer size of the apparent future water needs is so great that only a small portion can be met from local reservoir or ground-water schemes. For much of the country it will be necessary to develop large-scale regional projects, which involve considerable transfers of water from one area to another.

The impact of this policy on the landscape is very great. As ground-water sources are already heavily exploited, the expansion of inland surface water supplies by the construction of new, or expanding existing, river regulating reservoirs plays an important role in the Board's development programme. In the short period up to 1981 three large new reservoirs are to be constructed at Kielder (Northumberland), Carsington (Derbyshire) and Brenig (North Wales) and several existing reservoirs are to be enlarged, including the highly controversial case of Craig Goch in the Elan Valley. After these projects are completed, the capacity expansion programme is scheduled to continue with a number of schemes, which are likely to promote considerable public debate; a

1. *Water Resources in England and Wales*, Water Resources, Board, HMSO 1973

Haweswater in the Lake District, one of the reservoirs scheduled for expansion under the Water Resources Board's long-term strategy. An enlargement scheme would raise the water level virtually to the top of the wooded peninsula (*above*). When fully drawn down—as in this unusual photo (*below*) taken on 30 November 1973—Haweswater presents a depressing prospect within the national park.   (*Photos: Geoffrey Berry*)

'bunded' reservoir is to be constructed in the Dee Estuary, two further inland sources built at Aston (near Derby) and Longdon Marsh (Gloucestershire), and yet more existing reservoirs enlarged, including Haweswater in the Lake District National Park, and Llyn Brianne in Wales.

In making these proposals the Water Resources Board was following the convention in water supply management of relying on technical solutions to all shortage problems. Public water undertakings have tended to develop storage capacity, transport and cleaning facilities, irrespective of the relative costs and benefits, to meet all foreseeable peak requirements in their supply areas. In fact the only criterion used for deciding whether new investment in capacity is required is that projected consumption requirements at peak periods exceed present dry weather supplies. Costs are introduced into the investment analysis only when choosing between alternative schemes or strategies. Few, if any, attempts have been made to relate the costs of the chosen projects to the benefits derived from extra supply. It has always been assumed that the value of the additional water must exceed the cost of the supply; this attitude is typified by such statements as 'Water is cheap at any price'.

Capacity has normally been developed well ahead of public needs, since managers have put a high value on security of supply and have been extremely averse to the risk of shortfalls. Not only have attempts been made to provide large safety margins against unexpectedly high increases in water requirements, but in addition efforts have been made to guard against the exceptionally severe droughts that may be expected once or twice in a century. It is normal to attempt to guard against the one in 50 year drought and some authorities have even tried to develop enough capacity to be able to supply peak requirements even in a one in 100 year drought. Given present attitudes towards water such behaviour is entirely understandable, as the engineer who fails to provide enough water can expect to be criticised when its use has to be restricted. On the other hand, the costs of developing surplus capacity are so widely spread as to go largely unnoticed by the individual; most consumers have little awareness of the real costs involved in developing capacity which will be used fully only once in a lifetime, if that. In fact rather than being criticised for the over-provision of storage facilities the water manager is likely to be praised for his 'prudence'.

These tendencies to provide ahead of apparent needs, and for exceptional droughts can once again be exemplified from the Water Resources Board's national plan. In the first place, when calculating the potential supply to be derived from existing and future storage, water flow levels in the driest period since records began were used. This clearly underestimates the supplies now available under average weather conditions and so increases the level of extra capacity needed in the future; as a result, in most years developed storage facilities will greatly exceed peak needs. The practice of developing storage well

Alton Water reservoir will soon cover this attractive countryside near Tattingstone, Suffolk. A scheme that will flood more than 400 acres of high-quality agricultural land, Alton Water is a storage reservoir designed by the Anglia Water Authority to serve only local water needs. The adoption of a national water strategy, as proposed in 1974 by the Water Resources Board, would diminish the need for many schemes of this kind, by facilitating inter-regional transfers of water. But regulation of demand could have a still greater impact. (*Photo: CPRE*)

ahead of requirements is clearly shown in strategic programmes published by the WRB, relating the demand anticipated to the capacity to be provided. At each point in time capacity expansion keeps well ahead of the estimated supply shortfall. By 1981, for example, it is planned to provide five million m³ d. of extra water, whereas, as has already been seen, likely requirements are only expected to rise by 2·9 million m³ d.

Given this traditional 'supply' or 'requirements fix' approach to water management the possibilities of reducing the size of the needed extra capacity have rarely been considered. There has been considerable neglect of methods designed to improve the efficiency in use of existing supplies, although in recent years the greatly increased costs of new construction schemes, and the public opposition they arouse, have made engineers much more aware of the savings that could be achieved

173

by leakage control and the integrated operation of supply networks. Still less attention has been paid to the possibility of managing future demands for water as an alternative to increasing the supply. Neglect of these alternatives is by no means confined to Britain, for similar situations occur in many countries, including Canada, Australia, the United States and even water short Israel.

It is clear that the introduction of a more questioning approach to water resource development in Britain is long overdue, with a shift of emphasis required from managing supply to managing demand. In particular it is necessary to reappraise the real future needs of municipal consumers, comprising all industrial, domestic and commercial users of piped water from the public water supply authorities. This reappraisal is crucial since past and proposed large-scale supply extension schemes have almost exclusively been designed to cater for the requirements of this sector. Any increases in water used for private abstraction by manufacturers and irrigators, or for effluent dilution will 'ride on the back of' expanding municipal needs through the re-use of the public water supplies. To date a fundamental assumption of the water industry has been that all projected municipal needs must be met, but the costs of adhering to this policy are great and have become increasingly obvious in recent years.

In strictly financial terms water supply is no longer a minor item of expenditure. At 1972 prices the capital and running costs of the Water Resources Board's construction programme was estimated to be between £1,400–£1,510 million. These costs will escalate (at least by £120 million) if each of the ten new regional water authorities in England and Wales develop their resources independently, which at present seems likely unless the administrative and financial problems of inter-regional transfers are not rapidly solved. On top of these costs must be added the extra capital investment in storage facilities in the 'self-sufficient' areas (see map) and the increased local treatment and distribution costs. There appears to be no justification for incurring these expenditures, particularly at this time of capital shortage, if the costs involved exceed the value of the additional water to the consumer.

Consideration of the development costs in purely financial terms, however, omits several crucial elements of which the most important are, the loss of agricultural land and other land use or development potential, the social disturbance resulting from some schemes, and any adverse effects on the ecology or landscape of the affected areas. Because there are few upland sites suitable for large reservoirs emphasis has recently been placed on pumped-storage reservoirs in lowland areas, such as Graffham Water near Huntingdon and the very large Empingham Reservoir now under construction. These schemes have considerable impact on the environment since they lack depth and must inundate large areas of land to achieve the required capacity. The ecological changes resulting from such developments and from the

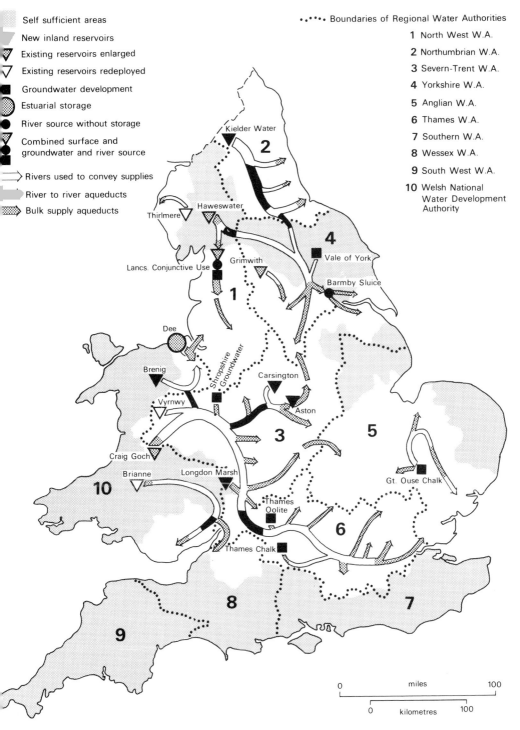

Self sufficient areas

New inland reservoirs

Existing reservoirs enlarged

Existing reservoirs redeployed

Groundwater development

Estuarial storage

River source without storage

Combined surface and groundwater and river source

Rivers used to convey supplies

River to river aqueducts

Bulk supply aqueducts

Boundaries of Regional Water Authorities

1 North West W.A.

2 Northumbrian W.A.

3 Severn-Trent W.A.

4 Yorkshire W.A.

5 Anglian W.A.

6 Thames W.A.

7 Southern W.A.

8 Wessex W.A.

9 South West W.A.

10 Welsh National Water Development Authority

Kielder Water

Haweswater

Thirlmere

Lancs. Conjunctive Use

Grimwith

Vale of York

Barmby Sluice

Dee

Brenig

Shropshire Groundwater

Carsington

Aston

Vyrnwy

Craig Goch

Brianne

Longdon Marsh

Gt. Ouse Chalk

Thames Oolite

Thames Chalk

| 0 | miles | 100 |

| 0 | kilometres | 100 |

suggested major transfers of water between river basins need much more careful consideration. To some people the intrusion of a man-made lake detracts from an area's natural beauty, while others find the water feature an attraction. However, particularly in the case of shallow reservoirs, the draw-down of water in the summer months, which leaves substantial areas of mud exposed, can diminish or destroy the attractiveness of the new landscape in the very season when most people wish to enjoy it. The unsightliness resulting from the low water levels that often occur in summer, when the rainfall is low and the demand for water is high, is exacerbated by the fact that the evaporation losses from large, shallow reservoirs are very high.

To some extent the social and environmental losses are offset by the great potential of reservoir sites for water based recreation, particularly as changing attitudes among water engineers has led to the opening up of many supply reservoirs to the public. But it is clear that existing sites are as yet not being used to full advantage, access to a number of reservoirs is still strictly limited, and the practice of selling exclusive recreation rights on some sites to private clubs, chiefly for sailing, immediately debars the less favoured sections of the community from ever enjoying the water space provided.

Two other types of cost associated with the present policy of automatically extending capacity ahead of needs must be mentioned. Firstly, public opposition to new schemes is almost inevitably great, and this in itself incurs large legal and administrative expenses; a classic case of this being Plymouth's attempt in 1971 to obtain a private bill to construct a reservoir in the Dartmoor National Park at Swincombe. Protests against the proposal predictably came from innumerable amenity societies, as well as from Devon County Council, the Duchy of Cornwall and Devon River Authority. With such formidable opposition it is perhaps not surprising that the project was turned down after a 17-day public hearing before a parliamentary select committee. Plymouth alone spent £300,000 to promote the Bill, to which must be added the wasted engineers' survey fees and all the costs of the public inquiry. Secondly, it can also be argued that premature investment in vast surface storages may incur costs by not allowing advantage to be taken of such possible technological improvements as, for example, a cost breakthrough in the use of off-peak nuclear power for desalination.

Before embarking on expensive capacity development programmes of the traditional type, water managers should fully investigate the possibilities involved in three alternative strategies. Each of these will go some way to ensuring the optimal provision and utilisation of supply facilities, and will reduce the waste of resources now occurring in the industry. These alternatives are first, to improve the efficiency in use of existing supply capacity, second, to develop to their full potential forms of capacity which produce least environmental and social damage and third, to implement management programmes to control (and so to reduce) demand.

Swincombe on Dartmoor (*above*), focal point of perennial controversy over water supply in the South West. In 1970 Parliament rejected a Bill designed to dam it as a reservoir. But in 1975 farming interests (*below*) were still protesting that the alternative Devon reservoir sites—Roadford and Townleigh—had agricultural merits outweighing Swincombe's value as amenity. As part of the country's dwindling resource of remote wilderness Swincombe has been granted a reprieve for the present. But the question remains, is a reservoir needed at all?

(*Photos: Lady Sayer; Western Morning News*)

Some changes have already been made which should allow much greater effective use to be made of existing facilities. Greater emphasis has recently been placed on integrating the operation of reservoirs, so allowing transfers of supplies to meet varying local needs over time. A welcome feature in the Water Resources Board's national plan is its emphasis on integration and transferability of supply. Similarly, the recent reorganisation of the industry into ten multi-purpose regional authorities for the first time provides an administrative structure capable of ensuring an integration between the supply of water, the disposal of effluent and sewage and the reclamation of used water.

However, important though these changes in attitude and organisational structure are, there is considerable scope for further improvements in the use of existing capacity. A first priority is to take more positive action to reduce the large losses in potential supply which occur now through leakages in the distribution networks. Although it is never physically or economically feasible to eliminate all leakage, an active and efficient waste detection programme can produce a marked reduction in the level of loss. While some authorities have recently increased expenditure on waste prevention, it is clear that in England and Wales as a whole losses remain high. At a minimum they account for 21 per cent of unmetered supplies, a figure derived from the official returns made each year by every water supply authority to the Department of the Environment, but as few care to admit high levels of leakage these returns are known to be biased downwards. Authoritative sources claim that it is common for distribution losses to account for over 33 per cent of the total apparent water use in an area, and it would appear that in some residential localities up to 60 per cent of supply was being lost before reaching the households.[2] If indeed losses of 30 per cent of total supply are occurring on average in England and Wales, this is equivalent to having $4\frac{1}{2}$ reservoirs the size of the proposed Kielder scheme (Northumberland) built solely to provide for the leaks!

Given such wastage levels a more systematic and economically rational approach must be taken to the question of what level of expenditure on leak detection is appropriate. It is clearly not worth investing in new capacity if an effective increase in supply (or an apparent decline in demand) can be achieved at less cost by extending the waste control effort. If only a small proportion of the estimated cost of future capital works were devoted to research into leak detection techniques and to the implementation nationally of a waste minimisation programme, then the projected future needs for water could be significantly reduced, and the development of new capacity postponed. To get the most out of existing facilities, before embarking on new schemes, the expenditure on waste detection should increase until the cost of saving a further unit of water equals the cost of supplying extra

2. Giles, H. F., 'An assessment of the causes and extent of waste and undue consumption in distribution systems and on consumers' premises', Institution of Water Engineers: Symposium on Waste Control, 1973

water units. It has been calculated by an economist at the Water Resources Board[3] that the long-run cost of supplying water is at least 25p per 1,000 gallons (4,550 litres) rising to over 60p in some areas, and these figures are much deflated since they are at 1970 price levels and they omit any social or environmental costs of reservoir construction. No authorities are yet pursuing their waste control activities to anywhere near this long-run optimal level, thus leaving great scope for improvements. As late as 1960 a sizeable proportion of water undertakings had no waste detection service at all and even now it is true to say that waste control is the 'Cinderella of the distribution function'.[4] Some engineers even seem to feel that they are stigmatised as 'failures' if assigned to the detection of leaks rather than the development of new supplies. Before the 1974 reorganisation of the industry waste control practices in the various areas ranged from a *'laissez-faire* approach' where only reported leaks causing inconvenience were repaired to the sophisticated approach of using continuously monitored telemetering systems; it is to be hoped that the regional water authorities are now speedily rectifying the situation in the less waste conscious areas.

Further opportunities to increase the efficiency in use of existing supplies may also exist through ensuring that consumers use an appropriate quality of water. At present limited supplies of pure drinking water are being squandered on uses such as industrial processing, toilet flushing and garden watering, which could be adequately served from lower quality sources. It has been estimated that in most industrial societies only between 10–25 per cent of water is used for functions requiring high purity, and yet the overall quality of municipal supplies is dictated by this usage. The costs of providing such high quality water for all purposes are often much greater than generally realised. Not only are extra treatment costs incurred, but additional expenditure escalates if capacity has to be developed at great distances from the demand centres because nearby rivers cannot be economically treated to potable quality. This is very much the situation which has arisen in the East Midlands. Because the Trent cannot yet be used to provide drinking water, new reservoirs have to be constructed in the Peak National Park, at a high cost both in money and environmental damage.

There are basically two methods available for decreasing this form of waste. Firstly, separate piped systems of potable and non-potable supplies could be provided, and secondly, water re-use could be encouraged within factories and households. Neither of these two approaches are new, in fact both are to be found operating economically in other parts of the world. In Hong Kong, for example, sea water is provided in a separate system for toilet flushing in many government

3. Batchelor, R. A., Water Resources Board, Water Pricing, Study Technical Paper No. 2, typescript 'The economics of domestic metering', 1970

4. Giles, M. J., 'Waste control: a total systems approach', Institution of Water Engineers, South-Western Section, Bristol, 25 January 1973

built high-rise blocks. What is now needed is a systematic analysis of the costs and benefits involved in their implementation in Britain.

While piped non-potable supplies are already provided in bulk for a few large industrial consumers, the development of more widespread dual quality systems has been resisted on two main grounds, the potential health dangers, and the high cost of duplicating the distribution network. However the likelihood of any adverse effects on health is absolutely minimal as the non-potable water would be disinfected and occasional inadvertent use would create no problems. Recent work has also suggested that the extra distribution costs involved would not be great if dual supplies were developed in new towns, urban renewal areas, and new housing zones on the urban fringe. Although it is unlikely that complete redevelopment of the existing system in already heavily built-up areas will be economically feasible, a potential for dual supplies also exists where industrial users are clustered together. It has been estimated that provision of two water qualities for new towns only increases the distribution costs by 20 per cent. This cost differential is reduced further where population densities are high, particularly if reclaimed sewage is used as the non-drinking supply.[5] In these circumstances the expenditure on duplicate pipelines would be more than offset by the advantage of halting or at least delaying the construction of new reservoir capacity. It has also been argued that planned re-use of water is preferable to the present situation where re-use takes place by default. London's water may have already been used up to eight times, with the as yet unknown dangers to health of a build-up of minute quantities of contaminants.

Water re-use within factories and homes also offers considerable scope for reducing the need for further construction of supply capacity. Re-use techniques are already employed by some manufacturers. The fact that most industrial consumers are metered encourages them to install recycling equipment. As prices rise they are able to weigh up the relative costs involved in using a once-through water system of investing in re-use facilities. But in Britain, domestic consumers are given no encouragement to save as virtually all households are charged for water on the basis of the rateable value of their property. This charge remains fixed irrespective of the quantity of water taken. It is hardly surprising, therefore, that no progress has been made in the development of domestic re-use systems, where for example bath water could be stored for such purposes as toilet flushing or car washing. Experiments with such techniques are already in progress in a number of European countries and Sweden has started to install re-use systems. Unless domestic consumers are asked to pay for water on an economic per unit basis, or the authorities pursue an active policy of insisting that recycling equipment is fitted at least into new homes, good quality potable water will continue to be used wastefully for all household purposes.

5. Okun, D., National Academy of Sciences. Regional Workshop on Water Resources, 'Planning for Water Re-use', Singapore, 1972

In economic terms it may also be possible to get more out of existing resources by allocating the available supplies more efficiently between competing users, although this is likely to be a controversial issue. Theoretically, the key to an efficient allocation of available water is the unit price charged to consumers. The cost of supplying industrialists in bulk through one main pipeline is considerably less than that of supplying the same amount of water to many scattered households. To secure more efficient use of existing supplies each group of consumers should pay a price which reflects the costs they impose, although all consumers in the same group should pay the same price. These economically optimal pricing conditions are nowhere near being met. Domestic consumers are not metered and pay a flat rate; therefore they treat water as a cost-free resource, and will go on taking water so long as they have any use for it. On the other hand industrialists, who can be supplied more cheaply, are given a measured supply and pay approximately 20–40 pence per 1,000 gallons used. It should be possible, if each consumer pays a price that reflects the real cost of supply, to meet rising industrial demand by reducing domestic waste, without increasing the supply capacity.

The possibilities for considerably delaying the need to construct new capacity by making better use of available resources are good, particularly if present economic and demographic conditions continue to limit the rate of growth in water demands over time. The country's economic difficulties have meant that real consumer incomes are only increasing marginally, if at all, and this in turn affects people's ability to purchase more water-using consumer durables. Likewise poor industrial growth rates are keeping down manufacturers' demands on the municipal water systems. Another factor which may also have a significant limiting effect on future demands is the present extremely low birth rate. But since, in all probability demands for water will increase over time, a far bigger research effort should go into developing methods of supply which reduce the impact on the social and physical environment. One method is to institute stricter control over discharges of sewage and effluent. At present a number of our lowland rivers, of which the Trent is the most notorious, are so polluted by the waste discharged upstream that they cannot be used to supply water that is fit to drink. A major advantage of the recent administrative changes, which have created multi-purpose water authorities, is that one body is now responsible for sewage cleaning, river purity and water supply, and therefore is in a position to treat a river as a system, devising the optimal mix of uses. The Trent research programme represents the first major attempt to examine the physical, economic and social implications of improving effluent discharges to allow water to be taken from the river as an alternative to building new reservoirs. No firm decision on future policy has yet resulted from this work, partly due to the problem of determining what level of certain pollutants, present in microscopic concentrations, should be accepted in public supplies.

Although the research does have some major limitations, particularly in the economic analysis, it is to be hoped that the effort marks the direction for future work.

A second method of extending supplies, without causing marked environmental or social disruption is to restock underground water supplies during the winter months from the rivers. This practice, known as aquifer recharge, in effect uses natural underground storage areas to act as substitutes for reservoirs. Research into its potential has been carried out in Britain for the past five years, chiefly under the auspices of the old Water Resources Board, and the practice has already been used widely in other parts of the world. Recharge has two crucial advantages, first it saves on reservoir construction and second, the water undergoes considerable purification during its passage through the rocks thereby lowering treatment costs. So far recharge has only been used in Britain in a very limited way, primarily in the chalk west of London, but it is conservatively estimated that with its use groundwater could provide a quarter of the extra supplies likely to be needed by 2001. For this to occur much more on-site testing is required by the regional water authorities.

Finally, mention must be made of desalination. To date its use on any significant scale has been repeatedly rejected on economic grounds, as with present fuel costs desalted water is unlikely to be competitive with conventional supplies. However, an open mind should be kept on the subject since work at the Water Research Association found that some plants, located next to nuclear power plants and utilising excess electricity in summer, would possibly be viable if used to meet peak water demands in low flow periods. The potential for desalination may therefore increase markedly if the next nuclear power programme goes ahead. It is sometimes claimed that desalination plants are as environmentally objectionable as reservoirs, but this appears extremely debatable since they would be located next to existing power stations so causing little further degradation.

Although on a straight financial cost basis these three methods of supply may now be more expensive than traditional reservoir schemes, they have the crucial advantage of keeping our countryside land-use opportunities open. Once reservoirs are constructed the land can never be restored to its original condition. Valuable agricultural land, unique botanical communities and landscape are irretrievably lost, and these losses may gain great significance in the future if greater agricultural output is required or if public attitudes towards the environment change.

As has already been seen it is usually assumed that all water requirements have to be met, including those at peak periods. The level and rate of increase in water needs have been regarded as completely outside the control of the supply authorities. However, once attitudes in the industry change to allow a demand management policy to be employed, great influence can be exerted on consumer behaviour. A number of physical control techniques are available, for example, the use of flow restriction valves to cut the householders' capacity to impose excessive peak demands, or the installation of such water-saving equipment as sprinkler taps, showers or dual flush toilets. But, it is likely that the most effective measure is to use the price mechanism to provide financial incentives for individuals to restrict any wasteful or low value water usage. In order to use price in this way it is essential to meter domestic consumers and to introduce a unit charging system, whereby consumers pay for each 1,000 gallons taken.

The introduction of domestic metering has so far been rejected, although the technical feasibility is beyond question. Four main arguments have been put forward to justify its continued rejection. The first is that water is a basic necessity and any attempt to restrict consumption will adversely affect health and hygiene standards. Not only is there no evidence to support this contention in the many countries which now meter consumers, but also it ignores the fact that only a small and relatively static quantity of water serves a household's basic sanitation, drinking and cooking needs, the remainder goes for the ever increasing 'luxury' uses such as garden sprinkling, garbage disposal units or dishwashers. Moreover, any possible hardship can easily be averted by giving each household a basic allowance sufficient for all health and hygiene needs, against the payment of a small service charge. A second argument against metering is that water *should* be provided in abundance as a basic human right. Clearly this is a value judgement, but it should be borne in mind that this policy is a costly one, and favours the extravagant consumer at the expense of the economical, and of the environment. Directly contradictory to the first anti-metering argument is the third, which asserts that householders are completely unresponsive to price changes.

If this were true, British consumers would be completely atypical, since (as my own studies have shown)[6] domestic consumption in other countries has consistently fallen by between 20–50 per cent when meters are first introduced, and this represents a permanent lowering in the demand trend over time. Greatest falls in consumption appear to occur in areas where large quantities of water are used for garden watering. A similar picture emerges when attempts are made to compare consumptions in metered and unmetered cities, although varying climatic or socio-economic conditions make comparisons difficult. However, bearing these difficulties in mind the tables on p. 184 speak for themselves.

As it is difficult to extrapolate these results to Britain, particularly those from the United States where garden watering usage is much higher, it is crucial that analyses of consumer responsiveness to metering are begun here in earnest. Empirical studies are so far confined to

6. Rees, J. A., 'A Review of Evidence on the Effect of Prices on the Demand for Water Services', Department of the Environment Directorate General of Economics and Resources, June 1973

TABLE 1 *A cross-sectional study of water use in all US municipalities 1954 Consumption in UK gallons per head per day*

Settlement Population Size	Proportion of Water Production Metered			
	0–50%	50–95%	95–99%	Over 99%
5,000–9,999	152	103	102	99
10,000–24,999	157	107	100	106
25,000–49,999	174	109	102	107
50,000–100,000	162	114	102	100
Over 100,000	142	129	124	114
All Municipalities	145	122	117	109

From 'Factors influencing *per capita* consumption', by R. Porges, *Water and Sewage Works*, May 1957.

TABLE 2 *Consumption in 12 Major Dutch Towns*

	% of residences metered	Domestic Consumption *per capita* in UK g.p. day
Harlem	100	54
Leiden	100	54
Delft	100	53
Enschede	100	51
Den Haag	95	51
Hengelo	88	60
Nijmegen	83	61
Arnhem	61	62
Rotterdam	12·5	73
Amsterdam	0	77
Groningen	0	93
Zwolle	0	96

From *Economics of Water Supply*, Unpublished Ph.D Thesis, by J. J. Warford, University of Manchester.

the Malvern UDC area,[7] which has been fully metered since 1971, and a record small metering experiment in Fylde. In Malvern's case *per capita* consumption appears to be at least 20 per cent below that found elsewhere in the country and in Fylde, when pricing was introduced consumption fell by approximately 12 per cent even though participants in the experiment were guaranteed that they would not be asked to pay more than their usual flat rate charge.

The final argument against metering is the strongest, and is that metering costs are high and will not be compensated for by the savings to result from delaying the need to construct new capacity. Only by undertaking empirical research can the validity of this assertion be tested. From crude calculations I have made, based on the Malvern data, however, I believe that metering is already viable in such high water cost areas as Essex, Northamptonshire and Devon, particularly when installed in new housing areas, where consumptions tend to be higher and installation costs lower. It would appear that economic trends are moving rapidly in support of metering.

In areas where land, capital and water are all plentiful, it may be appropriate to allow water to be used liberally for all purposes, and to keep the use of waste detection or usage control measures to a minimum. However, in the United Kingdom such profligate use is clearly inappropriate. From a purely financial viewpoint, the country cannot afford to expend scarce investment funds on projects whose productivity is bound to be fairly low, particularly if it is posible to postpone expenditure by making better use of existing resources without causing any hardship to consumers. Similarly, in a country where pressures on the land are already considerable and must continue to grow, it is vital that environmental disruption from the expansion of water supply facilities is kept to a minimum. Certainly, it can be strongly argued that the need for many new reservoirs could be considerably delayed or avoided by adopting policies which increase the effective use of available resources, and which aim to control the demand for water. Water is no longer a cheap commodity, and by making consumers aware of this fact considerable premature losses in agricultural land and landscape values could be avoided.

7. Rees, J. A., 'Factors affecting metered water consumption: a study of Malvern U.D.C.', Social Science Research Council Report, 1971

12

The Prospect for Wildlife

BRUCE CAMPBELL

PERHAPS the first question to be asked in this chapter is: Have we a wildlife at all? These islands must be among the areas most highly modified by man's activities in the entire planet and, if we are confined to the strict limits of England, we exclude nearly all the most natural relict habitats still to be found on the oceanic islands and highest hilltops of Scotland and Wales. The rocky shores which so impressed the dying John of Gaunt may look wild enough, but the envious siege that they withstand is awash with flotsam of all kinds, bright plastic refuse prominent among it, and the waters of the moat defensive have been contaminated far out to sea by polychlorinated biphenyls and other polysyllabic scourings of the technological revolution.

Inland the landscape, from the summit of Scafell Pike to the deepest glades of the New Forest, has been arranged by man, his grazing animals and his engines so that it no longer resembles, except incidentally, the scenery through which the Roman legions and subsequent early invaders cursed their way in a variety of languages. It is true, however, that a majority of the species of plants and animals are, as far as we know, native: that is to say, they found their way to England at various times before and (mostly) after the Ice Ages, by foot, wing, wind or hooked to the fur of another invader.

Superimposed on or co-existing with the natives are hundreds of alien plants and good numbers of alien animals, many of them clinging close to the denser built-up areas but others straying far afield.

There can, in fact, be hardly a higher plant or animal that is not at some time in its life in contact with man, his animals or his works. And yet, if we half-close our eyes almost anywhere in the rural lowlands we realise the truth of the saying, by an author as yet unknown to me, that in England you are always approaching a forest but never reach it: the illusion of the ancient undisturbed carapace of woodland is still there.

A great deal of what has happened to England's wildlife has been accidental in the sense that man did not plan it. When his enclosures imposed the chequerboard pattern which is where we came in, he had no idea that by planting attenuated strips of woodland to divide his fields he was creating a habitat of maximum edge, with sunny and shady sides, ready to support a diversity of creatures expelled from the woodlands he had busily felled. Nor did he think that first his roads,

Conflicts between agriculture and wildlife conservation are anything but new. In the late 18th century this iron post was driven flush into the peat of the Fens. Today some 12 feet of the post is exposed. Drainage and consequent shrinkage have benefited agriculture—while sharply altering the patterns of wildlife the area sustains.

(Photo: NFU)

then his canals and railways would carry species, some of them introduced, for hundreds of miles as colonists. Nor, to take a specific instance, did he foresee that by piling up rubbish he would encourage the spread of mugwort and hence extend the range of the wormwood shark moth. The agency has not always been benign; when the Luftwaffe dropped its bombs on London, the crews had no idea the results would bring flowers of many kinds to bloom in the city centre and provide nesting places for the black redstart which has become, by transferring to power stations and other buildings, a permanent though scarce element in the metropolitan fauna.

The English naturalists, begot platonically by White out of Pennant and Daines Barrington, have traditionally been sturdily amateur. Two country squires, the classic eccentric Charles Waterton and the minor poet J. F. Dovaston, are the first recognised encouragers of bird life by putting out food and devising nesting places; and even though 'feeding the birds' had become firmly established at least among the more leisured classes by the last quarter of the nineteenth century, it is unlikely that many of the feeders realised that their activities contained the germ of what is now called conservation.

Even today, although nature reserves, bird sanctuaries, wildfowl refuges and mass garden feeding have come to stay, there is still some reluctance to consider actually managing a species for its own good, by improving its habitat after full study of its requirements or even by

187

Many disused railway lines, like this one at Rowland's Gill, Durham, have found new roles as footpaths and nature trails. Frequently untouched by agriculture or new development, they may provide rich habitats for flora and fauna. (*Photo: John Topham*)

withdrawing some individuals from the effects of predators, parasites or hard weather for release under more favourable conditions.

Considering the intense pressure of man and his technology upon all parts of the green and pleasant land, it is remarkable that England has, for a depauperate offshore island, such a tally of species (whether they are any longer truly wild or not) and that so few of them, compared to the extinctions on spicier and smaller islands elsewhere, have disappeared in recent historic times (some, of course, like the Celts, have been banished to Scotland and Wales). As the present century approached its last quarter, the Systematics Association held, in April 1973, a symposium at Leicester University.[1] The 450-page proceedings are full of treasure trove for the ecological planner who wants to find a base line for the next 50 years and who is not too frightened by Lord Avebury's warning to the Conservation Society in November 1973 that 'One of the most dangerous and expensive fallacies among policy-makers is that trends of the past are a reliable guide to the future.'

Bacteria, protozoa and a number of the invertebrate phyla were

1. *The Changing Flora and Fauna of Britain* (ed. D. L. Hawksworth), Academic Press

omitted from the symposium, but plants from the algae upwards, the better known invertebrates and all the vertebrate animal groups were covered and, as Kenneth Mellanby said in his summing up: 'The general impression . . . was one of optimism. . . . Nevertheless the dangers of pollution and human pressure were not minimised, and the need for the active conservation of endangered species and habitats was obvious.' History does not stand still and since those words were spoken the imminent energy crisis has put a question mark against some aspects of human pressure; but in general the processes that affect wildlife have not noticeably slowed up and the lessons of the symposium still hold good.

One reinforces the adage of the ill wind: in almost all groups of plants and animals there are some species which have adapted themselves to the man-modified environment—synanthropic is the jargon word—and thrive in it. Some of these are aliens we may feel we can do without, from the brown rat to the several kinds of cockroach, but what about the house cricket? It seems to have worked its way into our culture and out again, for it is probably now commoner on warm rubbish tips than in a hygienic bakery or by the electric glow of the modern hearth. But many synanthropes are natives. Among insects there is the peppered moth, classic example of industrial melanism, the process of selection by which the dark form of the moth, originally very much in a minority, has come to dominate the population in begrimed industrial areas, where the 'normal' light form is at a disadvantage against predators. We owe to Bernard Kettlewell this demonstration of evolution in action. Among plants there is the fireweed or rosebay willowherb, so rampant on waste ground that many people believe it must be a successful invader like the rosy balsam of the riverside. There are the degenerate suburban foxes that raid the garbage bins and, among birds, there are about 15 species, including three gulls, rooks, jackdaws, starlings, house sparrows and blackbirds, that will prosper as long as our civilisation has anything edible to discard.

In fact it could be argued that if man and all his works are still part of nature, we ought to let them rip until our wild life is reduced to a synanthropic community of a few dozen species, and then sit back for a million years or so and watch them re-evolve into a new diversity. In only a hundred years the populations of the house sparrow, which has over-run the USA, are beginning to show recognisable racial differences, so we might not have to wait all that long for the first new species.

Attractive as such a programme might be to the ivory-tower scientist (does he really exist?), who has plans to outlive Methuselah, it is unlikely to commend itself to most ecological biologists, let alone to a reasonably sympathetic public, conditioned for the past 25 years by television, if not by actual venturing into the field, to believe with William Beebe that 'when the last individual of a race of living things breathes no more, another heaven and another earth must pass before such a one can be again' (incidentally he wrote that in 1906).

What are the prospects of maintaining the still remarkable variety of creatures of which the Leicester symposium took stock, in the face of demands which we are told must be made on the land of England if it is to continue to support a large population in somewhat of the style to which the post-war years have accustomed us? What are the options before us?

We must first pull out the joker in the pack, nuclear disaster, which could, according to its scale and provenance, affect all or part of the country. In the extreme situation all higher species of plant and animal would disappear together with their potential observers. But enough research has been done in the USA to show that different species show different reactions when exposed to radiation hazards. It is known for example that 'plants which have low chromosome numbers and large nuclear volumes are most sensitive while polyploids and plants with high chromosome numbers and small nuclear volumes are highly resistant' (A. H. Sparrow and G. M. Woodwell), which indicates that some sort of wild life would emerge from all but the most devastating situations.

Quite apart from the military implications or the likelihood of leakages from peaceful nuclear installations, the disposal of radio-active waste is, as a recent report[2] pointed out with great force and clarity, the most difficult and long term (since it commits future generations for about as far ahead as *Homo sapiens* has existed in the past) of all pollution problems. We must assume, if our look towards 2026 is to be at all meaningful, that it will be solved at least for the next century.

The next possibility is complete economic collapse. If we are considering only the welfare of the greatest number of plant and animal species and not the comfort of the human population, this 'solution' holds great attractions. No amount of careful reserve management, no application of ecological expertise could equal in their beneficial effects the removal from the countryside of human pressures, agricultural, industrial and above all, recreational.

Some treasured habitats would suffer, pre-eminently the precious remnant of the close-cropped chalk and limestone grassland, pride of the southern counties and maintained principally by grazing sheep as a deliberate conservation measure. The introduced rabbit was, before myxomatosis, a good alternative. In the depression of the inter-war years the rabbit became a valued food item, energetically pursued by authorised persons and by poachers but able to stand up to them. The new factor is apparently endemic myxomatosis which would reduce its effectiveness as a grazer. So it might be goodbye to several orchids, to Chiltern gentians, candytuft and squinancywort, to Chalkhill, azure and little blue butterflies, except in small pockets.

Against such an admittedly grievous loss we should regain the wetlands as the ditches and drains blocked up and riparian vegetation

2. 'Energy and the Environment', report of a joint working party of the Committee for Environmental Conservation, the Royal Society of Arts and the Institute of Fuel

spread over the hard-won acres. At present our three best reed-bed nature reserves, Leighton Moss in Cumbria, Minsmere in East Anglia and Stodmarsh in Kent, are all the result of the natural reversion of once farmed land, so we know to what we can look forward elsewhere, to the recovery not only of spectacular marsh birds, but of frogs, toads, newts, dragonflies, perhaps even the glorious swallowtail butterfly.

On higher ground the botanical succession will begin its march by way of scrub to the eventual broad-leaved high forest, one of the habitats in which the Leicester symposium considered the country most deficient. The Oak Symposium, also held in 1973, showed the ecological importance of England's symbolic tree; the climax community of oak woodland is about the richest we possess.

Would a recession save the remaining heathlands? They constitute the habitat most at risk from agricultural development, afforestation, building and 'recreational pressures'; they are also the last resort of some of the rarest species of plants, invertebrates and vertebrate animals, notably the sand lizard, smooth snake and natterjack toad. I have a horrible feeling that fires would continue to ravage them and that volunteer trees would spread from the pine plantations unchecked. But at least they would be spared excessive trampling by the human animal on holiday, as would the beaches, often not far away, where the little terns and ringed plovers try to nest.

After this excursion into anti-social escapism let us swing the other way to suppose that present trends are able to continue, that England goes on losing 50,000 acres a year[3] to building development of all kinds and that this is coupled with 'high' farming: larger units, fewer hedgerows, increased chemistry, especially if the mouldboard plough at last gives way to minimum cultivations. A growing population continues to exploit every recreational resource, not only the seaside and the hills, but gravel pit lakes, reservoirs, riversides and, of course, a proliferating network of wider and wider roads.

Under these conditions nature conservation would have to retreat more and more into reserves, both those officially declared by government agencies and voluntary bodies and those *de facto* sanctuaries created by great estates primarily for sport, provided they are able to survive. Probably not many actual species would be lost altogether; indeed new species might even be found on the reserves, as Cetti's warbler has recently arrived in the south-eastern reedbeds; but total numbers would drop and the Common Birds Census of the British Trust for Ornithology would sadly and accurately record the decline. It would not be quite the world of Giles's famous Last Tree in England cartoon but it would be on the way and nature would really become something to be 'done' on special areas and not over the face of the countryside.

3. New annual loss of agricultural land for development of all kinds, excepting forestry and woodlands rose from 40,800 acres in 1966–71 to 62,800 acres in 1968–73, Hansard, 20 November 1974, col. 422

A clearing in the Grot
Wood Nature Reser
Suffolk — acquired a
managed since 1974 by t
Suffolk Trust for Natu
Conservation. A go
example of the growi
number of private reser
owned and administered
such voluntary trus
Groton Wood consists of t
adjacent but distinct parts
an ancient small-leaved li
wood (*in foreground*) and
later wood recolonised in t
middle ages from agric
tural land (*beyond clearing*)
(*Photo: Simon Warn*

The British genius strives almost automatically towards compromise,
so I make no apologies for putting forward my cherished expectations
for the future in the terms of one. Indeed, this is the way current trends
do seem to be running and, assuming the economy recovers some sort
of equilibrium in the next few years, the prospect for the coming half
century is by no means unattractive. Since farmland still occupies over
four-fifths of the English countryside, it is the vital arena in which the
battle, speaking purely metaphorically, will be won or lost, the battle
for a wildlife numerous not only in species but in individuals.

At the time of writing, 'New Agricultural Landscapes' (ccp 76, October

Kittiwakes and guillemots on the Farne Islands, Northumberland. Owned and managed as a nature reserve by the National Trust, the islands give security to tens of thousands of seals and seabirds—including a formidable colony of puffins.

(*Photo: Simon Warner*)

1974), the report of a study sponsored by the Countryside Commission of the changes which modern farming is making to the landscape of lowland England, is providing much discussion. It is both gratifying and astonishing to find what some of us have been bleating about at conferences for years surfacing as the first major conclusion of the consultants. 'The quality of farmed landscapes would be best improved by planting naturally unproductive areas such as steep slopes, damp patches, stream banks or soil boundaries. Similarly there could be planting of artificially unproductive areas such as farm boundaries, areas around farm buildings and roadside verges.' And the second is like unto it: 'New planting could be linked to existing valuable features to form a network of tree or shrub cover and wildlife habitat in the landscape; different from but no less attractive than the traditional landscape.' Added to these could be the excavation or creation by damming of small lakes as sporting resources. Whatever personal feelings about 'put and take' trout fishing and wildfowling may be, these new water bodies are just what is needed to redress the balance of lost wetlands. Dammed lakes are preferable because they lead to attractive marshes at the 'shallow end'; excavated lakes should all have one or more carefully planted-up islands. Thirty years ago, when American literature about ponds and woodlots on farms first reached me, I warmed to the idea; in December 1974, 130 enthusiasts met at a conference on artificial lakes organised by the Royal Agricultural Society of England and the Agricultural Development and Advisory Service.

The price of these new features is, of course, the disappearance of more and more hedges as arable fields become larger and larger. Writing as a naturalist rather than a landscape-lover, this is something I can face with relative equanimity. There will still be many districts where the dominant form of farming demands hedgerow cover, and if the move towards larger units itself falters and the small family farms come back into favour, miles of hedges may be reprieved.

At present the appearance of the southern farming landscape is at risk from quite another cause: Dutch elm disease. I venture no prognosis, except that farmers are unlikely to replace hedgerow elms by other species on any scale unless they are subsidised to do so and this presumably ties up with the conclusions of the Countryside Commission's consultants. And a footnote on the ill wind theme: the number of dying trees has certainly increased the lower fauna feeding on them and hence probably the numbers of woodpeckers, a most attractive group of birds.

What is vitally important for lowland England is that, in sum, the total amount of cover afforded by broad-leaved trees and shrubs should not be reduced any further and should, wherever possible, be increased. At present there is considerable financial encouragement to plant broad-leaved species and this must be maintained if the forest you never reach is to come from the shadows into reality. The work of the Wytham Wood survey, begun by Charles Elton and now continued by the Animal Ecology Research Group at Oxford University, shows that about one seventh—and, quite possibly after more research, one quarter—of the British fauna can be found on a few hundred acres of broad-leaved woodland, scrub and unimproved grassland. No more proof is required.

The previous paragraph implied my delight that the coniferisation of England's remaining hardwood forests is no longer policy. I also deplore the planting over of the remaining areas of heathland in the south. But I cannot weep tears over the bare hills of the north. Provided that large areas of both black (heathers) and white (grass-

A rich diversity of woodland habitats is found in this curious and distinctive Wealden landscape near Wadhurst, Sussex. The strips of wood bounding the fields are called shaws. They result from the clearing techniques of the first Wealden farmers. Perhaps the Countryside Commission's recent study 'New Agricultural Landscapes' can lead contemporary farmers to create similar small reserves in unproductive corners of farmland. *(Photo: Meridian Airmaps Ltd)*

dominated) moorland and of bogland remain, I see no objection to the march of the conifers as long as the type of mixed forest which the Forestry Commission so proudly exhibits at Grizedale in Cumbria is developed on a large scale. Across the Border mature coniferous forest has recently been shown to support a remarkably high population of birds of prey, proudly perching on top of a food pyramid of numbers which argues diversity of species.

In 50 years' time, then, we must hope that the relative acreages of open country and forest will have been worked out in a national plan.

The first steps should be taken now: there is ample expertise for the job, for we have had a government nature conservation agency since 1949. So we may look forward to a time when all the land-use studies, which began with Dudley Stamp's pioneer efforts in the 1930's (continued in greater detail in the Second Land Use Survey of Great Britain in the 1960s), have been made the basis of a planned countryside with agreed acreages of high farming, hill farming, broad-leaved and coniferous forest, moorland, heath and wetlands. In these main divisions lie the major wildlife habitats and in them the major populations of our common plants and animals will survive.

Strange that I should come so far without a mention of agricultural chemicals and their toxic effects; ten years ago I should have been fulminating right from the start. But the position does seem, as far as the most sensitive natural indicators show, to have been largely restored, the most dangerous formulations withdrawn, others used with restraint, and we must hope that this situation will continue, as one of reasonable compromise, in all habitats, even that of the suburban gardener, perhaps the worst sinner of all.

Dotted throughout the main divisions of the countryside will be the nature reserves, which I regard as essential in any future plans for wild life. But they will not be the ghettos of rarities which would be the case

Wistman's Wood on Dartmoor—a statutory National Nature Reserve. It is one of 142 such reserves in the UK administered by the Nature Conservancy Council. The 8½ acre wood consists principally of pedunculate oak, characteristic of other woodland on the granite of central Dartmoor. *(Photo: Simon Warner)*

if agricultural and urban development were let rip as envisaged earlier. On the basis of the present position, they should amount by 2026 to about half a million acres in England alone, owned, leased or managed under agreements by official and voluntary conservation bodies; and from them it should be possible for certain scarce plants and animals to spread out again into stabilised countryside. Under these conditions it seems certain that the number of known species will increase. One finding of the Leicester symposium, especially for the invertebrates and lower plants, was that the great increase in skilled interest since the war had led to the identification of many species that had no doubt been present but unremarked for thousands of years. Indeed this was one reason why speakers found it so hard to say whether declines had taken place. Careful conservation has also shown that higher animals, especially birds, can be encouraged to return or to increase.

On some reserves with adequate 'security', I would be in favour of reintroducing lost species, particularly butterflies (though there is good evidence that much of their fluctuations are climatic in origin) and a few mammals, beaver, wild boar, conceivably wolf, which could be a natural control if red deer became too numerous. This is an issue on which hackles rise, but I have already stated my view that the management of wildlife is now inevitable and this should certainly include restoration of our fauna.

We must hope that stability in the countryside is accompanied by a stabilisation of the human population (as seems increasingly probable) and that the amount of new land engulfed each year by concrete and bricks will be negligible in half a century's time. But towns need not be dead centres for wildlife: London, with its great parks and open waters, is a classic example of limited co-existence by man and nature and the efforts that other great cities are making will have borne fruit by 2026. Implicit in this is the modification of the park-keeper attitude and the establishment of 'wilderness areas', much as has been suggested for uncultivable corners of farms. Denis and Jennifer Owen have recently shown what a remarkably rich fauna exists in small suburban gardens.[4]

Cities are often indissolubly allied to their rivers and the clean-up of London has been accompanied by the clean-up of the Thames: the reappearance of the salmon, which occurred in October 1974, had symbolic significance beyond Britain, though the thousands of waterfowl which now visit the lower river in winter are far more spectacular. What has been done for the Thames will surely be achieved for the other major polluted river systems of England in the next 50 years, with beneficial results for all forms of wildlife. The canals also have a key role since they can carry new species over watersheds.

Particularly associated with the Thames valley is the gravel extraction industry, which probably has another 20 years of feverish activity

4. 'Suburban Gardens: England's Most Important Nature Reserve?' in *Environmental Conservation*, vol. 2 (1), 1975

to run. Then there will be a series of worked out pits, many of them deep and filled with water, extending into the Cotswold area, where a water park is already more than a planner's dream. Like the new reservoirs, these lakes are avidly competed for by recreational interests more or less compatible with wildlife. By 2026 the position should have sorted itself out and, besides the deep lakes popular with anglers, sailors and water-skiers, there must be enough shallow areas for wading birds (especially the little ringed plover whose colonisation of England has been bound up with the spread of gravel pits), amphibians, dragonflies and aquatic animals in general.

The roadside verge has received welcome attention, particularly from botanists, in recent years. In the next half century we shall see its importance realised as the shopfront of the countryside, the repository for numerous species of plants and invertebrates that may have been reduced or eliminated elsewhere by farming changes. Sensible cutting regimes are being accepted by highway authorities, the knowledge is there and by 2026 we may hope to see the verges of A40 over the Cotswolds once more blue with flowers of meadow cranesbill.

The roads will continue to carry the townsman of the future, whatever his vehicle, into the new landscapes of England and down to the sea where we began. Here may be the hardest nut to crack because international rather than domestic co-operation is involved and because of factors related to oil from the seabed and its carriage, the nature and effects of which are still hard to discern. But we have made progress in controlling the disposal of oil wastes at sea by international agreement and if we make similar advances against other causes of pollution in the next 50 years, the beaches of England, their marine life and the seabird colonies around the coasts may yet be saved. Many regard our seabirds, Britain's proudest wildlife possession, as symbols of the success of conservation like the salmon in the Thames and the ancient oaks of the New Forest. Certainly wildlife, through the period of history most unfavourable to it, has shown wonderful resilience to pressures of all kinds; the next half century will show whether twenty-first-century man can be its effective trustee.

13

The Voluntary Amenity Movement

ROY GREGORY

NORTH Oxfordshire, where the Cotswolds run down into the softer countryside south of Banbury, is not the most spectacularly beautiful corner of England. But the wooded hills, the reddish soil of a field under plough, the sunken country lanes and picture-book villages do give the landscape a certain homely and mellow tranquillity. A few feet beneath the pleasant folded ridges and meadows, however, lie thick bands of ironstone, an essential raw material in the production of iron and steel. And here, late in 1960, Richard Thomas and Baldwin, supported by the Iron and Steel Board, sought planning permission from the Minister of Housing and Local Government to extract ironstone over an area of some 4,700 acres—about seven and a half square miles—for use in their proposed new steel mill in South Wales. They were opposed by the county council and other local authorities, by a formidable North Oxfordshire Ironstone Protection Committee, a host of other local organisations and several national amenity societies. After a ten-day public local inquiry, in the course of which the opposition convinced the presiding Inspector not only that the proposed quarrying would have a calamitous effect on the district but also that the economic case for using Oxfordshire ironstone at all was decidedly weak, the Minister rejected the application.

It was a notable victory, for it showed that even the most powerful attacks on the environment could be beaten off, if the resistance movement was sufficiently determined and well organised. In this particular case, a prominent part in the struggle was played by the local planning authority. But defending the environment is not a task that can safely be left to the statutory guardians of amenity alone. They may not have the necessary staff or expertise. Amenity battles are often expensive, and local authorities are not always willing to spend public money on what can sometimes be represented as a minority interest. They may lack the sense of commitment and dedication that marks a body made up of those who feel themselves to be fighting for a cause and not simply doing to the best of their ability the jobs for which they are paid. On occasions, local authorities are themselves developers, with their own plans and schemes that threaten to damage the environment.

Fortunately, we do not have to rely exclusively on the efforts of statutory authorities. There now exist hundreds of voluntary organisations, new and old, large and small, permanent and ephemeral, that devote themselves to the improvement and protection of the environment. Whether it is the abatement of health hazards and nuisances, like noise and atmospheric and water pollution, the preservation of wildlife, the fate of buildings and other objects of architectural and historic interest, the provision of opportunities for recreation, the appearance of the coastline, or the protection of the countryside and its towns and villages, there are societies—local and national—to champion or defend the cause.

Many of the organisations that work on a nation-wide basis—the National Trust, the National Society for Clean Air, the Civic Trust, the Ramblers' Association, the Royal Society for the Protection of Birds and the Council for the Protection of Rural England, for example— are well known, by name and reputation at least, far beyond the world of environmentalists. The vast majority of amenity bodies, however, concern themselves with amenity matters only in their own locality, though some societies set up to watch over particularly attractive districts may draw their members from all over the country. And, in describing such societies as 'local' bodies, it should be remembered that their area of interest may range from a few streets to a whole county.

Since the end of the last war, and more especially in the last 15 years or so, there has been a rapid and remarkable growth in the number and vitality of local societies of this kind. In 1957, when the Civic Trust was founded, 213 such groups were registered with it; at the end of 1971 there were 763; and by 1974 the number had risen to something

Advertisements seen from the Portsmouth Road near Esher, Surrey, in 1933. The Council for the Protection of Rural England campaigned for the control of such advertisements from its inception in 1926—with ultimate success. (*Photo: CPRE*)

like 1,200. Indeed, in recent years almost every monthly newsletter issued by the Civic Trust has reported the registration of a dozen or more societies, associations, groups, committees or trusts bearing the name of this or that city, town, district, village or area of countryside. And, of course, by no means all such local bodies are registered with the Civic Trust. Admittedly, some local amenity societies are no more than ephemeral protest groups, hastily put together in face of a specific proposal—to build an airport or a motorway, for example, or to demolish one particular building or assemblage of buildings—which the group dislikes and is determined to resist. Bodies like this are often no more than loose alliances made up of all manner of pre-existing amenity and other organisations. Naturally, they tend to disband once their particular battle is clearly won or lost.[1] But occasionally the temporary 'action committee' does live on to become the nucleus of a flourishing permanent society that subsequently takes a continuing and well-rounded interest in anything and everything likely to affect the local environment.

Those already familiar with the aims and activities of amenity societies will need no telling that many of them devote a good deal of time and energy to the routine but practical and constructive work of 'improvement'. The CPRE, for example, has vigorously supported schemes to clear dereliction from the countryside and to encourage villages to maintain their good appearance. But the fact is that major changes in the quality of the environment are usually the product of somebody else's commercial and political decisions. And if voluntary bodies are to exercise any influence over these decisions, it is as pressure groups that they must enter the arena and compete with those who have different ideas about amenity and its importance. As with all pressure groups, in the last resort their only weapon is persuasion.

Chief among their targets must be the officials and politicians who make the recommendations and decisions that matter to the amenity society and its members or supporters. At the same time, the chances of persuading decision makers are clearly much better in a climate of opinion that smiles upon the amenity cause. Indeed, prevailing standards of acceptability—what the public seems likely to tolerate or reject in relation to the environment—may also serve to affect the proposals that developers, public and private, feel it prudent to bring forward. Victories can sometimes be won in the mind of prospective opponents without the need for an open battle. It is true that when it comes to influencing the public mood, nothing succeeds as well as an actual or predicted environmental disaster. But voluntary bodies

1. The North-west Essex and East Herts Preservation Association—an 'umbrella organisation' set up to oppose the siting of the third London airport at Stansted in Essex—consisted of no less than 70 different associations or affiliated bodies ranging from residents' associations and village anti-noise societies to cycling and cricket clubs, local hunts, parish councils, historical and archaeological societies and even church authorities.

Hindon, Wiltshire, before and after the undergrounding of electricity wires by the Southern Electricity Board. Amenity societies have been increasingly successful in exerting pressure on public authorities to safeguard amenity at local level.

(Photos: CPRE)

clearly do have a contribution to make. Simply by opposing individual schemes and projects damaging to the environment they generate controversy and publicity, and they alert and encourage others faced with similar threats elsewhere.

But valuable though the attendant publicity generated by opposition or by sustained campaigns may be, it is 'informed opinion' and the policy and decision makers themselves who are the main objects of the environmentalists' attention. Nowadays, access to the decision-making process is sometimes built into the law itself. The 1971 Town and Country Planning Act, for example, requires a local planning authority to provide (and to publicise) opportunities for members of the public to make representations about structure, local or action area plans—as indeed they must in relation to individual planning applications.

At the national level, too, official commissions and committees to inquire, advise and recommend may offer amenity bodies an important channel to the decision makers. For example, the National Trust, the Ramblers' Association, the Civic Trust and the CPRE nominate members to sit on the Department of the Environment's Advisory Committee on the Landscape Treatment of Trunk Roads, which not only monitors the work of the Department's landscaping experts, but is also consulted about the choice of motorway routes. And when their representatives or nominees do not actually sit on such advisory bodies, amenity bodies may still be able to submit evidence to them. To take but a single case, following the announcement in 1974 that the Royal Commission on Environmental Pollution was to conduct an inquiry into the overall organisation for radiological safety in the United Kingdom, the CPRE promptly responded with a document setting out its views on the siting of nuclear power stations.

Advice and consultation, however, do not always produce the desired effect. Sometimes it comes to a trial of strength between amenity bodies and their opponents. When it does, amenity societies tend to start with two advantages. First, they are part of an extensive and quickly activated 'amenity network'. Multiple and interlocking memberships and other personal and organisational links can often broaden and transform what starts as an essentially local issue or campaign into a controversy of national or even, very occasionally, international proportions. In any major environmental battle a voluntary amenity body will rarely, nowadays, have to fight alone. It will have plenty of potential friends and allies, not least in the House of Lords.[2] And secondly, the amenity movement is fortunate in that nowadays the press and television are often instinctively on its side. At the local level, editors do tend to sympathise with the aims of local societies, particularly resistance groups. On occasions, as in the case of the Abingdon gasholder for example, the press may even play a leading part in the battle. Nationally, too, a newspaper may help mobilise widespread but

2. Roy Gregory, *The Price of Amenity*, Macmillan, 1971

Mass walk to the summit of Latrigg, near Keswick, in 1973, organised by the Friends of the Lake District to publicise opposition to the A66 scheme through the Lake District National Park. Despite a disciplined campaign inside and outside Parliament and the opposition of the Countryside Commission, the scheme is going ahead.

(Photo: Geoffrey Berry)

latent anxiety about threats to the environment; the campaign waged by the *Sunday Times* against heavy lorries in towns is a case in point.[3]

How much success the amenity movement has achieved is not easy to measure. There is no comprehensive record of all the battles in which voluntary societies have taken part, or of the number of occasions on which they have been on the winning side. Sometimes, of course, amenity bodies have fought on opposite sides in the same conflict. Where they have fought in support of local planning authorities or other statutory bodies it is impossible to isolate and evaluate the contribution made by each to success, which is frequently reflected in the absence of what might have been. And of course there have been failures. The CPRE and other national and local amenity bodies were unable to prevent the Manchester Corporation from meeting part of their water needs from Ullswater and Windermere, the two largest lakes in the Lake District. The amenity interest also failed to persuade the Minister of Housing and Local Government to reject plans for the North Sea gas terminal on the coast at Bacton in Norfolk. On the other

3. Richard Kimber and J. J. Richardson, *Campaigning for the Environment*, Routledge & Kegan Paul, 1974

Few environmental intrusions exceed the offensiveness of the heavy lorry. This campaign for a by-pass at Ditchling, Sussex — led here by Vera Lynn — is typical of public reaction to the use of unsuitable village streets by increasingly large vehicles. In recent years, national amenity societies have campaigned for greater movement of freight by rail, as well as for the construction of by-passes and restrictions on heavy vehicles.

(Photo: Times Newspapers)

Longdale, Derbyshire, in the Peak District National Park. This was the site proposed in 1955 for a 200 mph motor-racing circuit in some of the Peak District's most beautiful countryside. A CPRE campaign defeated the proposal.   (*Photo: CPRE*)

hand, there have also been a great many important successes. For example, vigorous opposition from the CPRE and others deterred the Derbyshire County Council from proceeding with their extraordinary proposal to use roads in the Peak District for a motor-racing circuit. As a result of the efforts of the Shropshire branch of the CPRE, the Minister of Housing and Local Government upheld objections to the installation of a TV mast at the remote Stiperstones site. The Gloucestershire branch persuaded the Minister to refuse the CEGB's application for a 400 kV overhead power line across the river Severn. It was the CPRE that led the successful campaign against exploratory borings for natural gas in the North York Moors National Park. And the CPRE supported the local planning authorities' successful opposition to the building of a private enterprise new town in a stretch of open and attractive country-side at Catthorpe on the boundaries of Warwickshire, Northampton-shire and Leicestershire.

At the level of more general policy, too, the amenity movement has substantial achievements to its credit. Legislation putting an end to the closure of land in common use, and protecting rights of way in the countryside; measures making provision for the control of adver-tisements, and particularly roadside hoardings; legislation protecting ancient monuments; and pre-war moves in the direction of an effective system of town and country planning were all, in part, attributable to the efforts of voluntary amenity bodies. It was the establishment by the CPRE in 1935 of the Standing Committee on National Parks that paved the way for the 1949 National Parks and Access to the Countryside Act. More recently, the 'amenity section' included in the 1957 Electricity Act, the 1962 Pipelines Act, the 1962 Caravans Act and the 1963 Water Resources Act, together with measures such as the 1967 Civic Amenities Act, parts of the 1968 Town and Country Planning Act and the 1968 Countryside Act all owe a good deal to the work of the amenity movement. Nor are its achievements confined to legislative advances. In 1970 organisations such as the Civic Trust, the CPRE, the Georgian Group, the Victorian Society and the Society for the Protection of Ancient Buildings played a major part in persuading the Secretary of State for the Environment not to allow the increase in the maximum weight of goods vehicles sought by the hauliers and manufacturers.

But perhaps as important as anything is the shift in the climate of opinion that the amenity movement has helped bring about in recent years. There is no doubt that standards of propriety do change, and they do influence behaviour and decisions. In the early sixties, the then chairman of the CEGB told a Select Committee of the House of Commons that, so far as amenity was concerned, what would have been perfectly acceptable in the electricity supply industry 50 years earlier had become quite inconceivable. It simply did not enter the heads of his Board members, he said, to do some of the things that their predecessors had in the past considered merely routine. There are few politicians or public officials today who do not feel it prudent to pay at least lip-service to 'amenity' and its claims, a sure sign that it has entered the sacred circle of unarguably good causes.

But obviously, any appraisal of the amenity movement and its work must take into account more than the degree of success achieved by voluntary bodies in pursuit of their own particular objectives.

If there were an all-knowing umpire viewing the battle-field from a seat on Mount Olympus, he would doubtless say that many—perhaps most—of the victories won by amenity bodies have indeed been 'in the public interest'. But it is not likely that the divine umpire would always take this view, and there is no reason to think that the environmentalists are always right. What can be said, with more confidence, is that—successful or not—the efforts of amenity bodies probably do on balance improve the chances of getting the most appropriate decisions because, in both the public and private sectors, they do improve the quality of the decision making process.

Those who take, or advise upon decisions require, above all, reliable information. In the field of town and country planning, they need information about developers' projects and their possible consequences; they need information about the areas, sites, routes or buildings

The creation of national parks and nature reserves by the National Parks and Access to the Countryside Act 1949 was the culmination of a 20-year campaign which gradually won overwhelming support in Parliament. *Above*, a mass demonstration organised by the Ramblers' Association at Winnats Pass, Derbyshire, in the early 1930s. *Below*, at the summit of Cross Fell on the Pennine Way in May 1948, Hugh Dalton MP addresses a group of walkers including Barbara Castle MP (*seated behind him*), (Sir) Geoffrey de Freitas MP (*seated, in check coat*), Arthur Blenkinsop MP (*left hand raised*) and Ted (now Lord) Castle (*seated at top of cairn*). (*Photos: Tom Stephenson*)

affected by proposals for development or redevelopment; and they need evidence about the strength and direction of feeling in the locality concerned. In all of these respects, public participation can help bring to light more of what the decision makers need to know. True, amenity bodies may not always accurately reflect and represent public opinion in their area. That is a question discussed later in this chapter. But the fact remains that they are often made up of people with a considerable knowledge of—as well as affection for—the district in which they live or interest themselves. On the whole, it seems fair to say that amenity bodies do serve both to encourage public participation and also— because the organisation is usually better equipped to do battle than the individual—to make it more effective.[4]

The presence of amenity bodies—or at least the larger and more resourceful among them—at public local inquiries means that developers, private and public, are obliged not only to meet environmental objections to what they propose, but are required also to defend and justify the technical and economic rationale of the plans they are putting forward. To suggest that there is something wrong with what is proposed is not necessarily such an unpromising strategy as at first sight it may appear. The developer does not always command a monopoly of the relevant expertise, and there are often genuine differences of opinion among the experts. Amenity bodies may themselves be able to enlist the help of reputable specialists who are prepared to examine and take issue in public with the views of their fellow professionals. Nor, for that matter, does it always require a great deal of technical knowledge to bring out weaknesses, if they exist, in the developer's case. If claims or hints about employment opportunities, for example, are misleading or exaggerated they are sometimes quite easily shown to be so.

What is more, major projects frequently have long gestation periods. The merits of a scheme that was perfectly sound when first conceived may look rather more dubious, under close scrutiny, a year or two later. To change the metaphor, within large organisations there is often a reluctance to alter course after it has been set. Once taken, decisions tend to generate a momentum of their own, an inertia that propels them forward even though new information becomes available or circumstances change. When enough people are committed to a certain line of action there is also a tendency to treat fresh evidence selectively, emphasising what supports the conclusions already reached and playing down the significance of what does not. Because the forces of inertia and the temptations of selective perception are so strong, the role

4. Nor is the provision of information by amenity bodies confined to individual planning cases. The work of the Civic Trust in collecting evidence from local civic societies about the damage and nuisance caused by heavy lorries in villages and towns furnished the Department of the Environment with far more information than it could otherwise have amassed. See Richard Kimber and J. J. Richardson, *op. cit.*, and Tony Aldous, *Battle for the Environment* (Fontana), 1972.

played by voluntary societies in the adversarial inquiry process clearly has a good deal to be said for it. Their participation—when they can afford it—means that costly investment projects are subjected to the critical, and indeed hostile scrutiny of antagonists who, for reasons of their own, have a vital interest in unearthing, exposing and enlarging upon anything that could possibly be represented as flaw or weakness in the developer's calculus. If there are such flaws, no one is more likely to detect them than dedicated opponents assisted by experts of their own. And if dedicated opponents cannot find them, there must be a reasonably good chance that none exist.

For his part, the developer is well aware that his scheme may be opposed by amenity bodies, and that—if it is—the case for whatever he proposes may have to stand up to a rigorous and searching cross-examination. The knowledge that opposition inevitably means delay and additional costs provides a powerful incentive for the developer to incorporate amenity considerations into his thinking. If, however, opposition on amenity grounds proves unavoidable, the developer naturally wishes to win the contest of arguments; he therefore has every reason to take care that he leaves no opening for attacks from probing opponents, looking for faults which the developer himself might be prepared to gloss over. The mere existence of potential amenity objectors, known to be waiting in the wings, can scarcely fail to have some effect on the way in which major developers—as well as administrators and politicians—reach their decisions.

In all of these respects, voluntary bodies undoubtedly are a good thing. It is when we turn to the implications and consequences of what they advocate and achieve that it sometimes becomes more difficult to pass a wholly favourable judgement.

As a result of the successes achieved by the amenity movement, resources are directed towards environmental improvement and protection that would otherwise have been used for different purposes. How much is actually spent on amenity, or how much of it is attributable to the efforts of amenity bodies, or to what other purposes it would have been put we do not know. All that can be said is that amenity expenditure is almost certainly minute in relation to the total cost of the goods and services provided by developers, and that it is most unlikely that any other, better causes have suffered disastrously as a result of what is spent on the environment.

All the same, there may still be problems of equity. For example, if spending more on the environment raises the price of basic utilities like fuel, power and transport the effect is similar to that of a regressive tax; the poor are obliged to pay more for what everyone needs in order to preserve amenities from which they derive no more (and sometimes less) benefit than the rich.

Equally important, those who oppose industrial development and economic growth generally in the name of amenity can easily lay themselves open to the charge of class selfishness. There are critics—

including some by no means unsympathetic to the amenity cause—who suspect that much of what passes for an interest in environmental protection is no more than a desire on the part of the relatively well-to-do to preserve their own advantages, if necessary by 'kicking down the ladder behind them'.[5] That there is a 'class dimension' to the amenity movement is undeniable. It has attracted little working-class support, and in the countryside particularly it seems to be very much an upper and middle-class phenomenon. An examination of the CPRE's directory for 1970, for example, shows that among the branch chairmen and secretaries listed, there were an earl, a viscountess, a baronet, two knights, a vice-admiral, an air marshal, a commodore, a brigadier, a commander, two colonels, five lieutenant-colonels, five majors, two captains, two professors, one clergyman and a good many others with professional qualifications.

The amenity movement is not altogether unusual in this respect, for outside the trade union world most voluntary associations in Britain are either predominantly middle-class organisations or are dominated by their middle-class members. Nonetheless, the social bias of amenity bodies can have important implications, particularly when they take the field against industrial development.

In the first place, it is clear that whilst many major schemes and projects will indeed impair the amenities of everyone in the area con-cerned, some individuals will also gain from the higher rateable values and new opportunities for employment that often come with indus-trialisation. Though they frequently appropriate the name of their district, local societies and resistance groups do not necessarily speak for everyone in it. Even in those parts of the country threatened at various times by the proposed third London airport there were some—a min-ority admittedly—who welcomed the benefits an airport would bring, and were prepared to put up with its palpable disadvantages.[6] But because amenity groups are frequently made up of the most articulate and forceful members of the community, they usually speak louder and more convincingly than those for whom amenity comes somewhat lower in the scale of priorities. A victory for the environment is sometimes achieved at the expense of the relatively inarticulate and unorganised inhabitants of a district spared the horrors—and also the benefits—that go with industry and its trappings.

Secondly, it must be recognised that most local amenity bodies—understandably enough—are concerned to protect not the environ-ment but the environment of their own members and supporters. Occasionally, in face of some project that threatens them all they may

5. Anthony Crosland, *A Social Democratic Britain*, Fabian Tract 404, 1971

6. As Richard Kimber and J. J. Richardson, the authors of a study of the Wing Airport Resistance Association point out, once a majority view has been established, partly through the efforts of an energetic amenity society led by the most prestigious figures in the district, it may take 'a considerable degree of individualism and even courage' for people in the minority to make their views known.

Proposals for a third London airport led to sustained and sophisticated public debate and pressure over a period of eight years before the Labour Government finally dropped plans for Maplin in 1974. Here, parishioners of Takeley, Essex, sign a petition in 1967 against possible siting of the airport at Stansted in Essex.   (*Photo: Photocall*)

combine and argue that there is no need at all for the development in question which should therefore be abandoned entirely. But where schemes of national importance are concerned, local societies are naturally hesitant about adopting such an adventurous strategy. As at the original public local inquiry into the proposal to site the third London airport at Stansted, and at several motorway inquiries, the objectors may actually be told that it is *not* open to them to question the need for the development they oppose. Consequently, the resistance campaigns they wage can only be directed, for the most part, against the particular choice of site or route that will adversely affect the amenities of their own locality. By implication, or quite explicitly when (in the hope of improving their own chances of success) they propose alternative sites and routes, their object is to shift the obnoxious project from their own to someone else's territory.[7] As one observer wrote of the various organisations that constituted the anti-airport movement at the time of the Roskill Commission on the third London airport, there was always 'a shadow of potential rivalry hanging over them', for an element of divisiveness is inevitably present in environmental campaigning where one group's airport victory can mean an increased

7. See, for example, Susan J. Dolbey, 'The Politics of Manchester's Water Supply 1961–1967', and Roy Gregory, 'The Minister's Line; or, the M4 comes to Berkshire', in Richard Kimber and J. J. Richardson, *op. cit.*

burden of noise for another such group. Nothing better illustrates the point than the slogan on a banner carried at a demontration organised by the Wing Airport Resistance Association that read 'Don't Foul Bucks, Foulness'. Not surprisingly, the Action Committee against Foulness Airport and its successor organisations did not join in the widespread chorus of applause for WARA and its efforts. Nor should it be forgotten that, when it appeared that the Roskill Commission might not, after all, recommend the Foulness site, in order to save Cublington and themselves WARA was quite prepared to argue the case for inflicting an airport on the residents of another inland area, namely Thurleigh in Bedfordshire. As Anthony Crosland remarked in the House of Commons at the time, WARA was in danger of giving the impression that it did not 'care tuppence for anybody else's noise and environment'.

The real battle very often is not between developers and the guardians of amenity but between one group of citizens and another. In this struggle of each against all to preserve his own environment, different districts and the amenity groups that defend them may sometimes be evenly matched in terms of skills and resources. And then, with every conflicting interest adequately represented, the resulting clash of arguments may well help to achieve the outcome that best serves the public interest. But districts and amenity groups are not always evenly matched. Not every area has the kind of population that is able to generate and sustain an effective protection society. Although the home ground of the Wing Airport Resistance Association cannot be described as an overwhelmingly, or even predominantly, middle-class district, it was certainly not short of wealthy and influential people. And it is noticeable that, when the decision on the third London airport passed from the realm of objective inquiry into that of pressure group politics, it was Foulness that proved to be the eventual loser. This was the area which — of the four short-listed by the Roskill Commission — contained not only the smallest population, but also a population that was by far the poorest, least educated, and included the highest proportion of semi- and unskilled workers and state pensioners.[8] Because the social structure of different areas does vary considerably, the efforts of locally based amenity groups — through the medium of organisation — inevitably tend to magnify and accentuate the advantages in any case enjoyed by the better educated, the better off and the well connected when their interests come into conflict, as sometimes they will, with those of the less well endowed.

But there is not much point in blaming amenity bodies for this state of affairs. As long as there are conflicts of interest between localities and the individuals who live in them, those who can will naturally organise and seek to defend their own interests. It would be unreasonable to expect them not to do so. By their very nature, all pressure groups

8. See Commission on the Third London Airport, *Papers and Proceedings*, Vol. VIII, Part 2, Section 4, 1970

pursue sectional and private aims that may be contrary to what the public interest requires. Inevitably, there is always the danger that those who are incapable of organising themselves will, for that reason alone, suffer at the hands of those who are. But it is no use urging people to behave like disinterested angels or bemoaning the fact that they do not. The responsibility for identifying and protecting the public interest rests on public authorities. If pressure group influence becomes excessive (and this goes for amenity pressure groups as much as any others), or if the advantaged do well at the expense of the disadvantaged, censure must be laid not upon those who naturally look after themselves but at the door of the government for permitting them to succeed when they should not.

There may be no way in which public policy can implant in a poorly equipped area the native talent needed to organise and sustain an effective amenity society or resistance group. But, where the problem is mainly one of money, there may be an answer. Unfairness arising out of the unequal distribution of wealth might be somewhat diminished if there was provision for financial assistance to amenity bodies from public funds. The chances of any government making available public money to help private organisations oppose projects promoted from within the public sector — for this is a situation that would sometimes occur — may seem remote. But some form of state aid — akin, perhaps, to legal aid — would certainly encourage and enable more people to make their voices heard when the argument is about whose amenities are to be sacrificed.

Considerations of equity apart, such a scheme may even become essential if the merits of development proposals are to continue to be properly tested in combat at public inquiries. Large developers, public and private, are willing and able to spend whatever is necessary to present their case to best advantage. Amenity bodies are not so happily placed, and nowadays the legal and professional costs of major planning battles can be very costly indeed. As long ago as 1965 the cost to the amenity societies of opposing the Manchester Corporation's Ullswater and Windermere plans was over £11,000, of which the CPRE alone contributed about £3,500. Admittedly, that was the most expensive single case the CPRE has ever fought. But for an organisation with a total recurring income at that time of only £17,000 a year, it was a formidable sum. The advantages, in the public interest, of subjecting development schemes to a thorough scrutiny by dedicated opponents do not come into play if would-be objectors simply cannot afford to enter the lists. And unless some form of financial assistance is provided, that day may not be so far off.

Ordinary common-sense and experience suggest that the best time to influence decisions is before they are taken; it will almost always be very much more difficult and costly to get them reversed or altered afterwards. When public authorities, or, for that matter, private companies, are firmly committed to a particular line of action, they are much less likely to be deflected than when plans are still flexible and options still open. Only if amenity bodies know what is in the wind, and which way the wind is blowing, can they hope to bring influence to bear at a sufficiently early stage. And knowledge of that kind requires a constant look-out for tell-tale signs that something is afoot, and, if possible, contacts with those in a position to supply the 'advance intelligence' that will allow amenity bodies to go into action in good time. Friends and sympathisers in private industry, or on the 'inner circle' of Whitehall and Westminster, or its local equivalent, can be valuable assets in this respect. They will be equally useful later on, of course, if it proves impossible to head off, behind the scenes, development proposals and policies regarded by amenity societies as objectionable. All such considerations apart, it is certainly important that amenity bodies should take advantage of the opportunities they now have to participate in the plan-making process. If they let slip the chance of influencing the general framework for future development, it may prove very difficult for them subsequently to resist, piecemeal, objectionable schemes and projects in their own locality.

When it does come to an open fight—and it is important to fight only the right battles, for indiscriminate resistance to all change will almost certainly be counter-productive—amenity societies must be ready with relevant and objective evidence, reasoned arguments and, where possible, feasible and carefully considered alternative proposals. Unless they are lucky enough to find the appropriate expertise among their own members, the research, professional knowledge and legal representation required successfully to challenge major schemes put forward by large organisations may well be expensive. It helps, to say the least, to have members with money, or members willing and able to devote their time and energy to fund raising activities. A good deal of money contributed to an amenity society or resistance group in small amounts rather than in the form of one or two large sums, naturally helps to demonstrate that its efforts do indeed have the support of a substantial proportion of the local community. For whatever they undertake, amenity societies will clearly need members with the qualities of leadership and some administrative ability.[9] These are attributes that voluntary bodies either have, or do not have; if they do not, there is little that can be done about it. But this does not mean that there is nothing amenity bodies can do to increase their own effectiveness. For middle-class amenity societies to widen the basis of their social support is easier said than done. They are chiefly concerned with issues that most of the working class is not yet affluent enough to worry about, and few of their members have much experience of working-class problems. Nor is it realistic to expect people who have organised themselves to resist a specific project, or popularise a point of view, to become involved in wider issues on which they may be divided.

9. For practical suggestions designed to help local resistance groups, see Christopher Hall, *How to run a Pressure Group*, Dent, 1974

There may be other respects, however, in which they can broaden the scope of their interests without departing too far from their original *raison d'être* or the interests of their existing members. In the not so distant past 'preservation' attracted little popular sympathy or support. It was a term that conveyed the idea of negative, selfish and sometimes eccentric opposition to all and every change that might in any way alter the appearance of the countryside or interfere with the traditional life-style of the country gentleman. Certainly, it was a cause that had unfortunate connotations of privilege. Between the wars, it seems, some of the more enlightened leaders of amenity societies had already come to realise that they were being hampered by the 'preservationist image' of their membership, 'which', as one observer puts it, 'had come to be associated too closely with elderly colonels and afternoon tea and croquet on the vicarage lawn'.[10] As we have seen, this is an aura that has not been wholly dispelled.

Conservation, not preservation, is now the watchword. It has been defined as the 'careful management of a limited, valuable or natural resource so as to ensure maximum efficiency of use and continuity of supply', or the 'total management of rural areas for the fair and equal benefit of all groups which have a direct interest in their use'. In these senses it clearly marks an altogether more positive and flexible approach to environmental problems than preservation pure and simple. It implies a willingness to examine, without prejudice, the various alternative uses to which land—and water—can be put and a readiness not only to accept but also to help plan, direct and even press for such changes as seem to be beneficial and desirable. It also implies a recognition of the fact that sometimes the 'maximum efficiency of use' may require that unspoiled countryside should be devoted to recreational, agricultural or even industrial uses, for the very good reason that sometimes these *are* the best purposes for which land can be used.

Again, resistance groups formed solely to oppose some unwelcome development in their own immediate locality can hardly be expected to adopt such a high-minded attitude. To do so might require them to acquiesce in what they quite understandably abhor, and no one expects a man to co-operate in his own execution, whatever the wider public interest demands.

Amenity societies with a wider range of interests are in a different position, and rather more can reasonably be asked of them. The 'committed but rational' approach (required of national amenity bodies that hope to be consulted and taken seriously by the governmental agencies with which they deal) naturally will not always commend itself to local societies or branches whose wishes may have to be sacrificed in the interests of rationality. But an amenity movement made up solely of those with local axes to grind (worthy though the axes may be) would clearly exercise little or no influence on general

10. H. E. Bracey, *People and the Countryside*, Routledge & Kegan Paul, 1970, p. 216

policy. The very fact that local amenity societies are becoming so numerous and vociferous may well throw an added responsibility on to the national organisations. For they should be able both to understand and interpret the attitude of those directly affected by development schemes, and also be capable of taking a broad view of the best terms that can be secured for the amenity cause as a whole. This is bound, at times, to bring national bodies into conflict with their own local branches, but this is part of the learning process. Conservation calls for hard choices and difficult decisions about priorities. But if the voice of the amenity movement is to count (and this is particularly true in periods of economic stringency) it is the discriminating conservationist approach — seeking to guide and direct change rather than always to resist it — that must prevail.

Notes on the Contributors

TRISTRAM BERESFORD, CBE, farmer, past President Agricultural Economics Society; agricultural correspondent *Financial Times* 1951–65; author of *We Plough the Fields*.

VICTOR BONHAM-CARTER, author of *The Future of the English Countryside*; publisher of the Exmoor microstudies; one-time farmer.

BRUCE CAMPBELL, ornithologist, naturalist and broadcaster; trained as a forester; author of the *Oxford Book of Birds* and *Dictionary of Birds in Colour*.

ROY GREGORY, Reader in Politics, University of Reading; former Reading councillor; author of books and numerous articles on politics and administration, including *The Price of Amenity: Five Studies in Conservation and Government*.

ROBIN GROVE-WHITE, Assistant Secretary, Council for the Protection of Rural England; Member of Royal Society of Arts/CoEnCo/Institute of Fuel Working Party on *Energy and the Environment*.

IAN HARRIS, economist and transport planner; formerly with Colin Buchanan and Partners and the National Bus Company; now with an international firm of transportation and planning consultants.

LORD HENLEY, Chairman of the Council for the Protection of Rural England, landowner.

NIGEL LUCAS, Lecturer in Energy Policy, Imperial College, London.

MALCOLM MACEWEN, journalist and broadcaster; author of *Crisis in Architecture*; member of the Exmoor National Park Committee.

C. W. N. MILES, Professor of Estate Management, Reading University; Chairman of the Agricultural Wages Board for England and Wales; author of books on estate management.

ADRIAN PHILLIPS, planner; former Assistant Director of the Countryside Commission; now seconded to the United Nations Environment Programme, Nairobi; member of the Advisory Panel to George Dobry QC on development control.

COLIN PRICE, forester turned land use economist; Lecturer in Urban and Regional Economics, Oxford Polytechnic; D.Phil thesis at Oxford University (1975) on 'The Right Use of Land in National Parks'.

JUDITH REES, Lecturer in Economic Geography, London School of Economics since 1969; consultant to the Australian Government on the National Water Program; author of *Industrial Demands for Water*.

MARION SHOARD, zoologist turned land use planner; now Assistant Secretary of the Council for the Protection of Rural England.

GEOFFREY SINCLAIR, environmental consultant; chief surveyor the Second Land Use Survey 1963–72; has personally mapped the vegetation of nearly all the open landscape in England and Wales; author of *The Vegetation of Exmoor* and *Can Exmoor Survive?*

*

Opinions expressed by authors are not necessarily those of CPRE.

Index